Folk Groups
and
Folklore
Genres

Copyright © 1986
Utah State University Press
Logan, Utah 84322-7800
All rights reserved.

Second Printing, February 1987
Third Printing, December 1987

Library of Congress Cataloging in Publication Data

Folk groups and folklore genres.

    Bibliography: p. 1.
    Folklore. 2. Folklore—United States. I. Oring, Elliott.
GR66.F65   1986   398   86-15863
ISBN 0-87421-128-X

Folk Groups and Folklore Genres

An Introduction

Elliott Oring

UTAH STATE UNIVERSITY PRESS

LOGAN UTAH

For Renee F. Oring, Lawrence H. Levinson,
and other dedicated teachers

Table of Contents

Figures

Preface

The past thirty years have witnessed a tremendous growth in the number of folklore programs and courses to be found in North American universities. There are sixteen degree-granting programs (several offering the Ph.D); another eighty institutions offer minors or concentrations in folklore, and over five hundred colleges and universities offer courses in folklore of some kind. An increasing proportion of these courses is being taught by graduates of folklore programs who hold folklore degrees.

The proliferation of folklore courses, particularly introductory courses, has not been matched by any similar increase in the variety of introductory books available for use in these courses. The introductory books published over the past twenty years have their own particular strengths and weaknesses. But because they have been few in number and because they have been large and formally structured textbooks, they have not, for the most part, provided the kind of curricular flexibility that many folklore instructors seem to desire. *Folk Groups and Folklore Genres: An Introduction* is not a textbook, nor is it meant to directly compete with the folklore textbooks currently available. It is intended to provide an alternative to the textbook approach to introductory instruction.

Folk Groups and Folklore Genres is meant to be used in two ways. First, it is meant to be used in quarter- or semester-length introductory courses. The chapters should serve as core essays to be articulated with supplementary readings. The supplementary readings will depend to a great degree upon the major interpretive perspectives, folklore forms, and folk groups which an instructor wishes to emphasize. For example, although no chapter on foodways appears in this book, supplementary readings and discussion on foodways can be keyed to the chapter "Ethnic Groups and Ethnic Folklore," in which aspects of foodways are considered. Structural analysis might be appropriately introduced in conjunction with the chapter "Folk Narratives," content analysis explored in association with "Proverbs and Riddles," and psychoanalytic perspectives formally presented following the chapter "Children's Folklore." A consideration of the process of oral transmission and variation could be attached to the chapter "Ballads and Folksongs," fieldwork methodology articulated with the chapter "Occupational Folklore," and fieldwork techniques with "Documenting Folklore." Aesthetic considerations could be raised while exploring "Folk Objects," and family traditions highlighted in connection with the chapter "Religious Folklore." Each chapter makes use of different definitions, concepts, illustrations, and perspectives, so that a much broader range of the field of folklore is represented than might be suggested by the chapter titles alone. *Folk Groups and Folklore Genres* is intended to be used in conjunction with collections of theoretical and analytical essays, as well as in-depth descriptions of folk traditions in their sociocultural contexts. However, the precise articulation of the chapters of this book with other readings depends to a great extent on the interests and creativity of the individual instructor. The chapters of the book need not be assigned or read in any particular sequence, and there is no prescribed organization for an introductory course. It is hoped many instructors will find this openness and flexibility a valuable property of the book.

A second use of *Folk Groups and Folklore Genres* lies in those short courses that have emerged in intersessions, summer sessions, and extension programs at a variety of universities. Such brief and intensive programs do not usually permit the assignment of extensive collateral readings. In such courses, this book would serve as the sole reading assignment; lectures and discussions should probably range more narrowly around the specific topics, concepts, and perspectives addressed in the individual chapters.

As the subtitle indicates, *Folk Groups and Folklore Genres* is meant to be introductory; a student needs no previous exposure to either the materials or theoretical perspectives of folklore in order to benefit from reading this volume. Yet the notion of introductory should not be confused with notions of programmatic or simplistic. The study of folklore is not straightforward nor is it reducible to a set of formulas or recipes.

Folklorists are eclectic in their approach. The variety of talents and skills that folklorists require to observe and describe folklore forms and processes is matched only by the range of conceptual systems they use in their attempts to render these forms and processes intelligible and sensible. The authors of these chapters have attempted to introduce concepts and perspectives which they have found productive or effective in their efforts to describe, analyze, and understand folklore. The chapters are filled with many original examples, and much of the interpretation reflects the efforts of the authors themselves to come to some kind of understanding of the materials which they present. Consequently, the essays are conceptually varied and rich, but this variety and richness may not necessarily be recognized by a student who comes fresh to the subject. While students can gain much from reading this book on their own, its full value will be realized only in the context of an organized course taught by a trained instructor.

Although this is not a book on American folklore, there is a decided emphasis on examples and illustrations drawn from contemporary American culture. It should be recognized that many of the basic concepts could be easily exemplified with groups, forms, processes, and events drawn from other societies, cultures, geographical areas, or historical periods. There is a real value in the encounter of those exotic systems of behavior and belief which have been described by both anthropologists and folklorists. Even so, the American emphasis is deliberate. The value of the discussion in each chapter will be greatly amplified when it can be related to the knowledge and experience of the student. In a certain respect, folklore courses differ from most other introductory courses offered in the university. Students of folklore have a wealth of personal experience directly bearing upon the subject matter under study. We all participate in folk groups and folklore processes. In some measure, our sense of these experiences must serve as a basis for the evaluation of the concepts and perspectives which are proposed to explain them. The concepts and perspectives presented in these essays are not for memorization and rote reproduction. They are supposed to engage the student's attention, promote reflection, and provoke critical response.

This process is more likely to occur when the requisite cultural resources are available, hence the proliferation of examples drawn from the contemporary American scene.

In the effort to keep this book short and affordable, the editor and authors have made certain choices in organization and presentation. The book makes no attempt to be comprehensive. The chapter titles represent only a few of the groups and genres studied by folklorists. Undoubtedly, there are additional chapters that one could wish for. The chapters on genres primarily focus upon oral forms, although custom and belief are well represented in the chapters on folk groups. Furthermore, the authors have all emphasized those concepts and perspectives which they believe to be useful in introducing students to the analysis of folklore. Except for Chapter 1, "On the Concepts of Folklore," no effort has been expended in tracing the historical development of the folklore scholarship concerning the groups and genres under discussion. Theoretical perspectives are introduced only as part of the effort to analyze and interpret particular forms or behaviors. They constitute part of the interpretive background and are not highlighted or featured independently. References to these theoretical perspectives can often be found in the notes to each chapter.

Authors have not included complete bibliographies of their subjects. However, each author has included a "Further Readings" section so that the student can find other useful related material. It is expected that the excellent bibliographical essays which have appeared in some of the introductory folklore textbooks (cited in the "Further Readings" section) will also be consulted.

Many contribute to a project such as this, and not all their names appear in the Table of Contents. Of course, all the authors are to be thanked, not only for their fine essays, but for their graciousness in submitting to a rigid schedule of manuscript submission and revision. Mahadev L. Apte, Robert A. Georges, and Michael Owen Jones all read portions of the manuscript and offered valuable criticisms. Barbara Walker of the Fife Folklore Archives encouraged this project from its inception, and Linda Speth and Nikki Naiser of the Utah State University Press proved enthusiastic editors and professional publishers. They are owed many thanks. Finally, Benjamin Fass, Norman Klein, and Taffe Semenza all agreed to proof any galleys which I could get them to read, while Norman Lavin thoughtfully demonstrated how this project might have been a great deal more difficult than it was.

Further Readings

The most helpful introductions to folklore are Barre Toelken, *The Dynamics of Folklore* (Boston: Houghton Mifflin Co., 1979); Jan Harold Brunvand, *The Study of American Folklore: An Introduction*, 2d ed. (New York: W. W. Norton & Co., Inc., 1978); and Richard M. Dorson, ed., *Folklore and Folklife: An Introduction* (Chicago: The University of Chicago Press, 1972). Each of these introductions differs in focus, organization, and style. All, however, provide a useful bibliography following each chapter.

There are several published collections of folklore essays which are designed for introductory instruction. Alan Dundes, ed., *The Study of Folklore* (Englewood Cliffs, N.J.: Prentice-Hall, Inc., 1965) includes excellent explanatory headnotes to each selection. Jan Harold Brunvand, ed., *Readings in American Folklore* (New York: W. W. Norton & Co., Inc., 1979) was designed to be used with his textbook cited above. Rosan A. Jordan and Susan Kalčik have edited a collection of original essays on women's folklore in *Women's Folklore, Women's Culture* (Philadelphia: University of Pennsylvania Press, 1985). Collections of regional essays have been compiled by W. K. McNeil, *The Charm is Broken: Readings in Arkansas and Missouri Folklore* (Little Rock, Ark.: August House, 1984), and Linda Dégh, *Indiana Folklore: A Reader* (Bloomington, Ind.: Indiana University Press, 1980). Richard M. Dorson has presented folklore texts from different American regions in *Buying the Wind: Regional Folklore in the United States* (Chicago: The University of Chicago Press, 1964), and Alan Dundes has also compiled a reader devoted exclusively to Afro-American folklore: see *Mother Wit from the Laughing Barrel: Readings in the Interpretation of Afro-American Folklore* (Englewood Cliffs, N.J.: Prentice-Hall, Inc.,

1973). Also interesting and useful are Dundes's collections of his own essays, *Analytic Essays in Folklore* (The Hague: Mouton, 1975) and *Interpreting Folklore* (Bloomington, Ind.: Indiana University Press, 1980), although the former volume is too expensive for classroom use whereas the essays in the latter rely almost exclusively upon a psychoanalytic approach.

Students are encouraged to seek out articles in the numerous folklore journals which have been published. Among the best known and most worthwhile of the English-language journals are: *Journal of American Folklore* (1888), *Folk-Lore* (1890), *Southern Folklore Quarterly* (1937), *Western Folklore* (1947) [originally *California Folklore Quarterly* (1942)], *Keystone Folklore Quarterly* (1956), *Kentucky Folklore Record* (1955), *Fabula* (1957), *Journal of Folklore Research* (1983) [originally *Journal of the Folklore Institute* (1964), originally *Midwest Folklore* (1951), originally *Hoosier Folklore Society Bulletin* (1942)], *Folklore Forum* (1968), *Indiana Folklore* (1968), and *New York Folklore* (1975) [originally *New York Folklore Quarterly* (1942)].

For a listing of folklore programs and course offerings in North American universities, see Ronald L. Baker, "Folklore and Folklife Studies in American and Canadian Colleges and Universities," *Journal of American Folklore* 99(1986): 50-74.

Chapter 1
On the Concepts
of Folklore

Elliott Oring

Although the word "folklore" is regularly employed in our everyday speech, its precise definition presents a problem. The term is clearly a compound made up of "folk," implying some group of people, who have something called "lore." In his prefatory essay to *The Study of Folklore*, the eminent folklorist Alan Dundes attempts to simplify the issue for the introductory student: "'Folk' can refer to *any group of people whatsoever* who share at least one common factor."[1] The common factor creates a sense of collective identity, so that any population with such a sense could be regarded as a "folk," according to Dundes. This sense of identity can be based upon such salient social factors as ethnicity, occupation, kinship, religious belief, sex, age, or on an almost limitless number of other factors, such as health (e.g., people suffering from heart disease), spatial proximity (e.g., people in the same room), or personal habit (e.g., cigar smokers). Theoretically, the number and kinds of folk groups are limited only by the number and kinds of elements which can serve as the basis for group identities. Since Dundes argues that "folk" can refer to *any* group based on *any* factor (rather than a specific group formed on the basis of select factors), it would seem that the term "folk" does not contribute significantly to the definition of "folklore" as a whole (other than suggesting that it characterizes human rather than nonhuman populations). Consequently, the semantic weight of his definition must rest upon the notion of "lore."

1

Dundes attempts to define "lore" as an itemized list of genres. Even though the list is lengthy, he considers it only a sampling of folklore forms:

> Myths, legends, folktales, jokes, proverbs, riddles, chants, charms, blessings, curses, oaths, insults, retorts, taunts, teases, toasts, tongue-twisters, and greeting and leave-taking formulas (e.g., See you later, alligator). It also includes folk costume, folk dance, folk drama (and mime), folk art, folk belief (or superstition), folk medicine, folk instrumental music (e.g., fiddle tunes), folksongs (e.g., lullabies, ballads), folk speech (e.g., slang), folk similies (e.g., as blind as a bat), folk metaphors (e.g., to paint the town red), and names (e.g., nicknames and place names). Folk poetry ranges from oral epics to autograph-book verse, epitaphs, latrinalia (writings on the walls of public bathrooms), limericks, ball-bouncing rhymes, jump-rope rhymes, finger and toe rhymes, dandling rhymes (to bounce the children on the knee), counting-out rhymes (to determine who will be "it" in games), and nursery rhymes. The list of folklore forms also contains games; gestures; symbols; prayers (e.g., graces); practical jokes; folk etymologies; food recipes; quilt and embroidery designs; house, barn and fence types; street vendors' cries; and even the traditional conventional sounds used to summon animals or to give them commands. There are such minor forms as mnemonic devices (e.g., the name Roy G. Biv to remember the colors of the spectrum in order), envelope sealers (e.g., SWAK — Sealed With A Kiss), and the traditional comments made after body emissions (e.g., after burps or sneezes). There are such major forms as festivals and special day (or holiday) customs (e.g., Christmas, Halloween, and birthday).[2]

This list is exceedingly useful in providing the novice with a sense of what folklorists document and study. Included are forms that the beginning student undoubtedly expects to find (e.g., myths, legends, folktales, folksongs, and superstitions), as well as some that perhaps appear as something of a surprise (e.g., fence types, envelope sealers, latrinalia, epitaphs, and practical jokes). In any event, it is important to recognize that this list in no way *defines* "lore." For a list to do so, the items included must be clearly defined (which they are not) and the list must be *complete* (which it is not). Dundes himself acknowledges that the terms are not well defined and that his list is not comprehensive. Even if one could define each genre on the list, an incomplete list would still remain unacceptable as a definition. How would we go about deciding whether something not on the list were "lore" or not? For example, is a barn decoration or a football cheer a kind of lore? Barn types and quilt designs are mentioned, but not barn decorations. Taunts, rhymes, and games are mentioned, but a football cheer only accompanies a game, and if it were neither a taunt nor in poetic form, how would we decide?

Perhaps the list is meant only to provide examples of lore, and only a common denominator for the numerous items need be identified to formulate an adequate definition. Then it should be relatively easy to decide whether any particular form (including barn decorations and football cheers) is or is not "lore." In theory, this approach could work; however, it is no easy matter to identify this common factor. Not only must this denominator adequately characterize all the items on the list, but it should not characterize any significant items omitted from the list. For example, it might be argued that all the items on the list are products of human invention and creativity. But so, too, are law, agriculture, marriage, and the parliamentary system. If "products of human invention" is indeed the informing principle of the list, we should certainly expect these items to be given precedence over tongue twisters and practical jokes. So it is not sufficient to find merely a common denominator; it is necessary to find a common denominator which is peculiar to the items on this list and which does not require the admission of glaring omissions or oversights.

Readers are encouraged to search for a principle in Dundes's list, but it is unlikely that they will find one that meets both qualifications for an adequate definition. Either the proposed principle will not characterize all items on the list, or if it does, it will force us to acknowledge glaring omissions. Of course, the possibility always exists that a principle fulfills both conditions but is otherwise trivial. For example, we might define "lore" as those forms of human expression that Alan Dundes so identifies. Such a definition includes everything on the list and probably omits nothing major. (If it did, Dundes probably would have included it.) But this definition is altogether unhelpful because it lacks intersubjectivity.

3

"Folklore is what Alan Dundes studies" is a definition to which not even Alan Dundes would subscribe.

The enumeration of forms not only frustrates the successful definition of lore in its own right, but also raises questions about Dundes's previous characterization of "folk" as well. If "folk" really implies "any group of people whatsoever," why should this term be needed as a modifier for some items on the list? Why do the terms *folk*tale, *folk*song, *folk* art, *folk* drama, *folk* speech, and *folk* dance appear while other items on the list — legends, curses, jump-rope rhymes, and mnemonic devices — escape such qualification? Why not simply enumerate tale, song, art, drama, speech, and dance? After all, these forms of expression regularly occur within the context of groups and consequently should not need the modifier "folk." Suspicion should be immediately aroused that not all song, art, or drama expressed in the context of groups is really folklore. In other words, perhaps Dundes really regards folksong or folk dance as song and dance which is characteristic of some special kind of group, rather than just any group, as he first leads us to believe. Otherwise, the unqualified terms "song" and "dance" should have been sufficient for his list.

It would be convenient if the problems that we have identified could be ascribed to the definition of Dundes alone, and be dismissed in favor of the definitions of other authorities. However, Dundes's definition is hardly idiosyncratic; it characterizes (or has conditioned) the perspective of a good number of contemporary folklorists. Rather than dismiss Dundes's formulation, much can be learned from it. If we seek to discover why no single principle seems to emerge from his lengthy list, and if we address the reasons for the reintroduction of the term "folk" after Dundes generalizes it almost to the point of meaninglessness, we may emerge with a greater appreciation, if not a better definition, of folklore. The answers to these questions are not self-evident, however. The problems are more historical than logical. To approach a solution at all, we must attempt to gain a sense of the development of the concept of folklore over time.

A serious study of forms that today are labeled "folklore" took place in Germany at the turn of the eighteenth century. A romantic and nationalistic spirit dominated the times. Romantics bemoaned the rise of civilization which exalted the artifical and intellectual at the expense of the natural and spiritual. They felt that, divorced from nature, man was nothing, his efforts empty and meaningless. Art and poetry could never result from the mere intellectual manipulation and imitation of forms. Poetry was not a deliberate act but an involuntary reaction to the natural and historical environment, a product of feeling and the sensation of a total and natural reality. If civilized man had been cut off from these sensations, more primitive peoples had not. The romantics collected *Volkslieder* (folksongs) in the belief that they were essential for reinvigorating national literatures and saving these literatures from sterile intellectualism. The creation and perpetuation of folksongs was thought to be a function of a group which had not severed its connections with nature. The folk were once thought to comprise the nation as a whole, but with the development of urban civilization they survived only as an unlettered, uneducated, and marginal stratum of society — the peasantry.[3]

Nationalistic impulses directed the effort to describe and recapture the traditions of the primitive nation. For brothers Wilhelm and Jacob Grimm, the publication of *Kinder- und Hausmärchen* [Children and Household Tales (1812-15)], *Deutsche Sagen* [German Legends (1816-18)], and *Deutsche Mythologie* [German Mythology (1835)][4] was an effort to document the poetic and spiritual character of the Germanic people. The Grimms were concerned with the reconstruction of the ancient Teutonic mythology which had been destroyed by the incursion of Greek, Roman, and Christian civilization. The materials used for this reconstruction were the tales, games, sayings, names, and idiomatic phrases still to be found among the peasantry.[5]

These early scholarly and artistic interests betray a particular set of assumptions about the materials which we have since labeled "folklore." First, the unlettered peasants, uncorrupted by civilization, were the remnants and spiritual heirs of a native heathen nation. Second, their distinctive tales, songs, speech forms, and customs reflected the past, they were the fragments of the philosophy and way of life of an ancient people. Third, the material and spiritual life of these ancient peoples could be

5

reconstructed through the judicious analysis and comparison of contemporary peasant tales and customs. What seems crucial for our purposes is the recognition that the serious scholarly and scientific study of these kinds of materials was based upon a belief that peasants were the remnant of that ancient people who once lived upon the land, and that peasant tales, songs, sayings, and customs echoed the life and spirit of these ancestral folk.

The work of the Grimms proved enormously influential. In England, a long tradition of antiquarian scholarship existed, focusing upon anything old: old buildings, old legal documents, old artifacts, old tales, old songs, old customs.[6] These latter forms were often labeled "popular antiquities" to designate their preservation among the people, i.e., the peasantry and other common classes.[7] In 1846 William John Thoms proposed that these popular antiquities be described by the term "Folk-Lore." He modeled his suggested program for the study of folklore directly upon the work of the Grimms. Thus the term "folklore" came into being to designate materials believed to survive primarily among the rural peasantry and to reflect life in the distant past.[8] Although the term "folklore" would be redefined and qualified many times over, these associations would never be eradicated entirely.

In the latter part of the nineteenth century, English folklore research was further influenced by the development of cultural anthropology and the evolutionary perspective of Edward B. Tylor and his disciples. Tylor felt that the history of mankind reflected a development from simple "savage" stages through "barbarism" to "civilization." ("Savage" and "barbarian" did not quite have the same pejorative connotations as they do today.) The proof of this evolutionary progression was demonstrated by *survivals*, "those processes, customs and opinions, and so forth, which have been carried on by force of habit into a new state of society different from that in which they had their original home."[9] Survivals did not quite "make sense" in more advanced stages of society and thus betrayed their savage origins. For example, a Scottish legend told how Saint Columba buried Saint Cran beneath the foundation of his monastery in order to propitiate the spirits of the soil who were demolishing at night what was built by day. Tylor demonstrated that this legend was rooted in the practice of foundation sacrifice, a practice widespread among primitive peoples, but which survived in Europe only in legends.[10]

Although such survivals abounded in peasant society, they could also be found in industrial urban society; Tylor articulated, for example, the relationship between primitive incantations to keep the soul from leaving the body and contemporary sneezing formulas, (e.g., God bless you!).[11] Tylor's evolutionism provided a new and more encompassing theoretical framework for the kind of folklore studies initiated by the Grimms. The study of folklore came to be defined as a historical science concerned with "the comparison and identification of the survivals of archaic beliefs and customs in the traditions of modern ages."[12] Unlike the Grimms, Tylor's researches were neither romantic nor nationalistic in their orientation. Instead, they were concerned with the history and development of humankind as a whole, not just one particular nation or race. The mythological beliefs and attitudes of the primitive past were regarded as something to escape, not something to cherish. Folklore was not a relic of the national spirit, but rather a relic of systems of primitive thought and belief. In fact, the evolutionists envisioned their science as a "reformer's science," promoting greater rationality, morality, and societal progress through the identification and elimination of remnants of these mistaken beliefs.[13]

It is important to emphasize that the identity between folklore forms and the past was not a matter of fact but established by definition. Though survivals of past custom and belief may be embedded in the various genres of lore, not every song, custom, riddle, or tale existing in peasant society necessarily needs to be a primitive survival. Not every peasant tale containing a supernatural motif requires linkage with primitive principles of animism and magic. When W. J. Thoms coined the term "folklore," he had in mind the "manners, customs, observances, superstitions, ballads, and proverbs, etc."[14] which would throw light upon the British past. But proverbs, customs, and belief as expressive forms — as genres — are not de facto carryovers from the primitive past. We can imagine examples of such genres as completely contemporary and novel creations with no privileged connections to the ancient past. But nineteenth-century folklorists did not entertain this perspective. Folklore had been *defined* as a survival and therefore, the study of folklore necessitated the description and analysis of these primitive connections. Questions concerning the relation of these forms to the people from whom they were collected — the peasants who continued to tell and express them — were almost irrelevant since these forms had been defined as relics with no meaningful relations to the present.

When the American Folklore Society was organized in the United States in 1888, its mission, as its founders saw it, was to continue the work of their British colleagues. William Wells Newell, the first editor of the *Journal of American Folklore*, instructed folklorists to collect the fast-vanishing remains of folklore in America: the relics of English folklore, the lore of French Canada and Mexico (i.e., that brought by the other colonizers of the American continent), the lore of the Negroes, and the lore of the Indian tribes.[15] In fact, the category of Indian folklore was something of an anomaly, since many of these societies were still judged to be in a stage of savagery. As folklore was defined as a survival *from* that stage into more advanced stages, Indians could not have folklore in the technical sense. "Mythology" was the term utilized to characterize the *living* systems of tales and beliefs of primitive peoples, whereas "folklore" was reserved for the survival of these systems in civilized societies. The American Folklore Society dedicated itself to the study of both. Only unwieldiness saved the Society's journal from the title, *The Journal of American Folklore and Mythology*.[16]

Only a few years later, however, the distinction between folklore and mythology began to evaporate when Newell redefined folklore as "oral tradition and belief handed down from generation to generation without the use of writing."[17] This redefinition was not meant to be revolutionary. Not accompanied by any proclamations of change in kinds of materials to be studied or the methods of inquiry, it was probably promoted to obviate the need for a distinction between "folklore" and "mythology." Nevertheless, the adoption of this definition had important ramifications. Whereas previous conceptualizations of folklore assumed it to be *ancient* or *primitive*, this new definition required only that it be *traditional*, handed from generation to generation. In other words, folklore was related to the past but not necessarily a dark, distant past. Furthermore, this new definition was predicated on a type of communicative channel — oral transmission. It did not require the existence of some particular "folk" who must do the transmitting; nor did it delimit a specific kind of "lore" — that is, a special kind of information to be transmitted. "Lore" in Newell's definition is simply reduced to *anything* which is transmitted over time without the use of writing. Furthermore, whereas previous conceptualizations regarded folklore as only a remnant of something that had once been whole and alive, the definition "oral tradition" does not presuppose such a perspective. An oral tradition could be dying out, but it could also be growing and thriving; the existential condition of folklore is not predetermined by this definition. Of course, the ready adoption of "oral tradition" by folklorists did not cause them to turn away from the tales, songs, or superstitions which they had been studying. It did not immediately change the opinion that these kinds of oral expressions were dying out. It did not substantially alter their view of folklore as a historical science. They simply directed their attention to the "tradition" aspect of the definition — the information and belief that comes down from the past — rather than to the "oral" aspect per se.[18] Nor did they immediately divert their attentions from those quaint, unlettered country peoples from whom they believed such traditions could yet be harvested in abundance. But the definition also contained within it the seeds for change — change in the kinds of forms that could be regarded as folklore as well as the kinds of questions that could be asked about them.

For example, although both the romantic-nationalists and the evolutionists collected and studied legends, neither paid any attention to jokes. In their conceptualization, jokes were simply not folklore. Jokes were considered neither to reflect the spirit of the ancient folk-nation nor to indicate the survival of primitive belief and thought. Consequently, they fell outside the purview of folklore. But in terms of a definition of folklore as "oral tradition," jokes could be studied (and the joke form eventually gained prominence as an object of American folklore research).

9

Even with genres that had been studied under the older conceptualizations, new questions could now be asked. For example, folksong had been examined only as a reflection of primitive poetry, belief, and ethos. However, if folksong is redefined as a song which participates in, and is shaped by, the oral process over time, then other aspects of the conception of folksong require reformulation. If a folksong is conceived to be any song transmitted orally from generation to generation, questions about creation, transmission, and transformation become crucial: How is it composed? Who sings it? How is it transmitted? How and why does it vary through time and across space? The process of change thus emerges as a central concern. In each generation aspects of the song are transformed while others remain stable. The song is essentially re-composed in each generation.[19] If a song is to continue, a generation must find something in it worth continuing while altering aspects which are no longer consonant with its own values and beliefs. If this perspective is persistently advanced, a song cannot be adequately conceptualized as the reflection of some ancient past. At any point in its history, the song is the distillation of generations of cumulative modification. If it can be said to reflect any group at all, perhaps it can only reflect the group in which it is currently sung — that group which has (for conscious or unconscious reasons) maintained and transformed elements from the past in the creation of a meaningful, contemporary expression.[20]

Perhaps the reformulation of the concept of folklore was inevitable in the United States. With no peasant society to regard as the physical and spiritual embodiment of the ancestral folk — indeed, with no native ancestral population (the Indian tribes were native but not ancestors) — folklore study in the United States could never be anything more than the study of Indian mythology or the collection of Old World folklore in America. The notion of a genuine American folklore would never be possible under the older European conceptualizations. Perhaps that is why the conceptual shift from "survival" and "relic" to "oral tradition" found such ready acceptance among folklorists in the United States. American born and bred oral traditions existed, but native American survivals were far less likely to be found.

If the concept of a peasantry was somewhat problematic for folklorists in the United States, it nevertheless remained seminal in Europe. As various nations in Europe sought or achieved cultural and political independence, the peasantry as an ideological concept increased in importance. The peasantry remained, after all, the physical embodiment of the people and way of life tied to the land. Peasants were regarded as the symbol of a genuine national culture. Consequently, a tradition of peasant ethnography arose which was devoted to the study of the whole of peasant life. Peasant material, economic, social, and spiritual culture were to be documented. Thus their houses, barns, fences, and crafts as well as their tales, dances, songs, and calendar customs were extensively described and studied. In Germany, this inquiry was known as *Volkskunde*, in Sweden as *folklivsforskning*, and in English as *folklife*. Clearly, in the conceptualization of folklife, "folk" is central.[21]

American folklorists, on the other hand, were more inclined to predicate their notions of folklore on the concept of a "lore" (in reality a process) and less on the concept of a "folk," although the concept of folk was not entirely abandoned. The initial directive to study specific groups — Indians, Negroes, French-Canadians, and Mexican-Americans — was being faithfully fulfilled. American folklorists did not seem to recognize the existence of oral traditions beyond the boundaries of traditional types of unlettered or illiterate societies. They gave little thought to the specific characteristics of such groups, however, and rarely addressed the relations of such groups to the larger societies in which they were found.

American anthropologists working with peasants in Mexico and Latin America did regard the idea of a "folk society" as a useful construct. Robert Redfield argued that the "folk society" is distinguished by specific characteristics. It is isolated and has little communication with outsiders, although there is intense communication among the members themselves. The society members are to a great extent physically, behaviorally, and ideologically similar, with little change from one generation to the next. Economically independent, the members produce what they consume and consume what they produce. They use few secondary tools (tools to make other tools) and they have no rapid

11

machine manufacture. There is an absence of books. People communicate and pass on knowledge by word of mouth. There is little critical or abstract thinking and no attempt to systematize knowledge; rather, magical, anthropomorphic, and symbolic thought and expression are standardly employed. Traditional values are regarded as sacred. People behave in personal and familial ways, even toward inanimate objects. Members of folk societies express social relationships and ritual obligations through economic exchange. There is a simple division of labor, and commercial exchange at a money price is unknown.[22]

Redfield did not believe any society existed which fully embodied all these traits. It was an ideal type meant to contrast with the modern city.[23] Some societies approximated this folk ideal more closely than others. Overall, primitive societies resembled it to a greater degree than peasant societies. Peasant societies, in Redfield's estimation, were "part-societies" with "part-cultures." Despite the fact that they reflected many of the traits of the folk society, they were profoundly influenced by the civilizations of which they were a part. The "Great Tradition," the tradition cultivated and recorded in the academies, temples, and other great urban institutions — the tradition of the reflective few — flows into and out of the "Little Tradition" of the unreflective and illiterate many. Peasant societies and cultures are the products of this interaction. Despite continuities between primitive and peasant societies, peasant societies remain incomplete and have to be studied with reference to the Great Tradition of the urban centers with which they are in contact.[24]

Redfield chose "folk" to designate his ideal type of society because he felt that it was this society that possessed folklore and folksongs. He regarded folklore and folksongs as the touchstones of the homogeneous society, distinctive from the popular song and literature generated by specialists in the city. For Redfield, folklore encountered in the urban environment never occurred in robust form; it was always diminishing, always a vestige.[25] It was a survival — not of some ancient folk, but of that homogeneous group whose expression it once had been.

Because Redfield predicates his definition of "folk" upon a set of objective criteria rather than a single kind of society, we are free to examine the "folkness" of any particular group. Redfield's "folk" is a *relative* term. A society is more or less folk to the extent that it more or less approximates the characteristics of the ideal type. Primitives are generally more folk than peasants, who in turn are generally more folk than modern city dwellers. But the nineteenth and twentieth centuries had witnessed tremendous upheavals in the structure of traditional society, so that even this characterization was insufficient. Urbanized states had conquered tribal peoples, assimilating them or relegating them to aboriginal enclaves. Entire communities had been transplanted through voluntary and involuntary migration. City people formed pioneer settlements in the wilderness. The peasants in one culture had become the urban dwellers of another. Individuals had isolated themselves in comparatively homogeneous occupational communities (e.g., cowboys, sailors, and lumbermen).[26] By the time folklorists came to formally ask the question, "Is there a folk in the city?" the answer was already a foregone conclusion.[27] Relative to the guardians of the formal, written, and reflective Great Tradition of the modern urban center, there were innumerable folk.

Redfield's formal expansion of the concept of "folk" from a strict European peasant model to a quality of society, measured according to specific criteria, in a sense paralleled the American folklorists' expansion of "lore" founded upon the notion of "oral tradition." But these expansions were to condition yet other changes. Technically speaking, if the folklorist studied "oral tradition" — anything transmitted through unwritten channels — no distinction whatsoever between the fields of folklore and anthropology could be made, at least in respect to the study of primitive societies. Since *all* of culture was unwritten tradition among technologically primitive peoples, the concept of folklore was, in effect, indistinguishable from the concept of culture. This conceptual congruence not only irked some anthropologists, but posed problems for many folklorists who never did believe the term "folklore" characterized the whole of culture. (Students of folklife, of course, did regard the entire culture of what they considered to be a folk group as their proper field of study.) Consequently a new definition of folklore was proposed —

13

"verbal art" — that is, the aesthetic use of spoken words.[28] Suggested by an anthropologist, this definition assured that folklore could never comprise the whole of culture. (After all, what people can subsist on verbal art alone?) In technologically primitive as well as industrial urban societies, folklore would be destined to delimit only some portion of the culture.

"Verbal art" is an important and novel definition because it makes no reference at all to the past — neither the ancient past nor pasts of more recent vintage. This definition reflects the current anthropological preoccupation with the cultural present as well as the effort to explain social and cultural forms in terms of the larger social and cultural systems in which these forms play some part. To the extent that this definition embodies a conception of folklore in an immediate and contemporary field of thought and action (i.e., its social and cultural context),[29] it accurately reflects the perspective of the great majority of contemporary folklorists.

The definition of folklore as "verbal art" is important for another reason. It requires no assumptions about the kinds of groups in which folklore is to be found. While the importance of folklore may be magnified in completely oral cultures, folklore can and should emerge whenever and wherever spoken language serves as an important medium for communication — that is, among *all* groups in *all* societies. This definition characterizes folklore as an expression common to all individuals and groups rather than peculiar to some of them. If *they* have folklore then so do *we*. The term can no longer be used merely to characterize (whether affectionately or pejoratively) the behavior of others. In this sense, we are all "folk," and to the extent that we are all folk, the term becomes empty of meaning. This, of course, is precisely Dundes's perspective.

Although the definition of folklore as "verbal art" does reflect the current orientation toward folklore as part and parcel of the societies and cultures in which it is found, and even though it resolves the folklore-equals-culture problem which "oral tradition" posed, this "solution" has not been embraced wholeheartedly by folklorists. The definition, in fact, succeeds too well in narrowing the field. If this definition were to be enthusiastically adopted, folklorists would have to abandon their long-held interest in materials that either were not artistic (e.g., belief, medicine, custom), or not formulated in words (e.g., dance, music, craft). At present, most folklorists remain reluctant to do so.

This brief review is not intended to serve as a history of the emergence and development of folklore studies. It is intended, however, to illustrate concepts that have informed the characterization of folklore in the past and which continue to do so in the present. At the very least, an understanding of the problematic aspects of Dundes's definition should become apparent. One difficulty was that Dundes's list of forms failed to reflect any single underlying principle. The reason should now be clear. Dundes has listed a great variety of folklore forms, but these forms can be considered "folklore" only if several definitions are employed simultaneously. For example, such forms as myths, legends, tales, riddles, proverbs, jokes, and tongue twisters can easily be subsumed under a conception of folklore as "verbal art." But medicine, dance, festival, custom, drama, art, symbols, gestures, music, recipes, etymologies, and belief cannot, although they can be considered folklore under the definition "unwritten tradition." Epitaphs, latrinalia, limericks, envelope sealers, and autograph-book verse, however, are written forms. They might be characterized as folklore because they are expressive forms that stand apart from the "Great Tradition," apart from the formal, "official" institutions cultivated and sanctioned at the centers of position and power. House, barn, and fence types, as well as quilt and embroidery designs, are probably included because they have been given serious attention by "folklife" scholars who have emphasized studying the material aspects of the culture of some designated rural "folk." Of course, many of these forms can be conceptualized as folklore under more than one of these definitions. However, none of these definitions can be used to characterize adequately all the forms on the list. What Dundes has given us, therefore, is not a definition of folklore but a characterization of those forms, both old and new, that have fascinated folklore scholars over the past two hundred years.

The other difficulty with Dundes's list was the reintroduction of the term "folk" to qualify such diverse forms as tale, song, art, costume, dance, music, medicine, drama, belief, metaphor, and etymology. This difficulty results from a peculiar dilemma that Dundes and most other contemporary folklorists face. On the one hand, they believe that folklore is a universal category, characteristic of all human groups rather than just some (hence the enormously expanded definition of folk as "any group of people whatsoever"). On the other hand, they do not regard folklore as simply art, music, dance, medicine, or custom whenever or wherever found. Like the earliest of the romantics, they feel that folklore is distinctive from the traditions of fine art, "classical" music and dance, haute couture, and scientific medicine cultivated by elite, urban society. Not that they regard folklore as aesthetically or spiritually superior (although some folklorists may), but they do not view it as emanating from the elite and their centers of political, cultural, and commercial power, or from institutions of media communication. In their view, folklore cannot be legislated, scripted, published, packaged, or marketed and still be folklore.

In some sense, for something to be folklore in an urban society, it must be touched and transformed by common experience — ordinary humans living their everyday lives. As the romantics heard in peasant songs and tales the echoes of an ancestral folk, and the antiquarians attended to the manners and customs of the common classes, many contemporary folklorists still seem to see in folklore the reflection of an intangible, ordinary man. In other words, folklore is often regarded as a mode of expression which emphasizes the human and personal as opposed to the formal and institutional. That is why the term "folk" came to modify tale, art, music, song, dance, and the like in Dundes's list. Since these forms are also created and communicated within the formal institutions of the privileged elite, a means had to be found to distinguish those forms that live primarily in the common, informal communication channels of ordinary people.[30]

Contemporary folklorists do document folklore in the context of the statuses and functions of elite institutions, but this folklore is invariably described as the stuff that fills the gaps and spaces between prescribed official duties and responsibilities. Very few folklorists would regard the forms and reports generated and transmitted by Washington bureaucrats as folklore. However, the jokes about the bureaucracy that they circulate, the xeroxed cartoons and letters posted on the bulletin board, the locally generated slang used to describe the work and personnel, the office parties, and the stories the bureaucrats tell to one another at the local bar would be considered folklore by many.

Dundes's list was never fully meant to serve as a definition of folklore at all. It was more of an attempt to identify for the introductory student those forms that have traditionally interested the folklorist. But it is important to be able to identify the concepts which have directed this interest because these concepts fundamentally motivate, even if they do not adequately define, folklore research. It is important to recognize that the difficulties encountered in Dundes's definition are not idiosyncratic; they reflect larger issues in the conceptual base of the field as a whole.

For those who find brief definitions helpful, there is no dearth of contemporary formulations: "Materials . . . that circulate traditionally among members of any group in different versions, whether in oral form or by means of customary example" (1968);[31] "The hidden submerged culture lying behind the shadow of official civilization" (1968);[32] "Artistic communication in small groups" (1971);[33] "Communicative processes [and] forms . . . which evidence continuities and consistencies in human thought and behavior through time or space" (1983).[34] All these definitions have been proposed by prominent folklorists in an effort to delimit their field of study. A student, however, will benefit more from the effort to identify the concepts that underlie these definitions and from the attempt to characterize their novel implications, than from memorizing the definitions, recording them in a notebook, and accepting them uncritically.

At this point, a definition is not really necessary. The field is still being mapped and any hard and fast definition is likely to prove partial, idiosyncratic, or inconsistent. What is necessary is an orientation, however, and this orientation should be based upon those concepts that seem to regularly inform the perspective of folklorists in their research. As we have seen, folklorists seem to pursue reflections of the *communal* (a

17

group or collective), the *common* (the everyday rather than extraordinary), the *informal* (in relation to the formal and institutional), the *marginal* (in relation to the centers of power and privilege), the *personal* (communication face-to-face) the *traditional* (stable over time), the *aesthetic* (artistic expressions), and the *ideological* (expressions of belief and systems of knowledge). Usually, folklorists approach the study of forms, behaviors, and events with two or more of these concepts in mind. The advantage of an orientation over a definition is that it is productive rather than restrictive. It allows one to think of folklore less as a collection of things than as a perspective from which almost any number of forms, behaviors, and events may be examined.

The search for new definitions of folklore should and will go on of course. Each new definition will undoubtedly reflect new or refined concepts, introduce new perspectives, and probably create new problems. In this respect, however, the study of folklore is not unique. Art, literature, music, history, culture, philosophy, and mathematics are equally difficult to conceptualize within a single and precise definition.[35] Each of these domains is founded upon implicit and problematic concepts. The tension that such problems produce, however, may be dynamic and creative. The failure to successfully corral a field within a single, neat, handy, and mutually agreeable definition does not suggest that a field lacks value. Actually, it may indicate a special vitality and excitement. This does not mean that we do not need some working definitions with which to approach inquiry, or that we should cease our attempts to formulate comprehensive theoretical definitions. But we need not desire them or cherish them too greatly. Definition is only a regaining of equilibrium and composure from the stimulation and exhilaration of research and discovery — an intellectual "catching of the breath," so to speak. Until we participate in research and experience that discovery, we should not need to catch our breath too often.

Notes

1. Alan Dundes, "What is Folklore?" in *The Study of Folklore*, ed. Alan Dundes (Englewood Cliffs, N.J.: Prentice-Hall, Inc., 1965), 2.

2. Ibid., 3.

3. Robert T. Clark, Jr., *Herder: His Life and Thought* (Berkeley, Cal.: University of California Press, 1969), 147, 253.

4. For available English translations of the Grimms' works, see Grimm Brothers, *German Folk Tales*, trans. by Francis P. Magoun and Alexander H. Krappe (Carbondale, Ill.: Southern Illinois University Press, 1960); *The German Legends of the Brothers Grimm*, ed. and trans. by Donald Ward, 2 vols. (Philadelphia: Institute for the Study of Human Issues, 1981); Jacob Grimm, *Teutonic Mythology*, 4 vols., trans. from the 4th ed. with Notes and Appendix by James Stallybrass (New York: Dover Publications, 1966).

5. Ibid., 5-6, 11.

6. For a discussion of antiquarian perspectives see Francis A de Caro, "Concepts of the Past in Folkloristics," *Western Folklore* 35 (1976): 3-22.

7. For example, see John Brand, *Observations on the Popular Antiquities of Great Britain*, 2 vols., arranged, revised, and enlarged by Sir Henry Ellis (London: Bell and Daldy, 1873). The work by Brand first appeared in 1777.

8. Ambrose Merton [W. J. Thoms], *The Athenaeum* 982(1846): 862-63.

9. Edward Burnett Tylor, *Primitive Culture*, 2 vols. (London: John Murray, 1871), 1:16.

10. Ibid., 104-8.

11. Ibid., 97-108.

12. George Laurence Gomme, ed., *The Handbook of Folklore* (London: The Folk-Lore Society, 1890), 3.

13. Tylor, 2:539.

14. Thoms, 862.

15. "On the Field and Work of a Journal of American Folk-Lore," *Journal of American Folklore* 1(1888): 3-7.

16. "Folk-Lore and Mythology," Ibid., 163.

19

17.   W. W. Newell, "The Study of Folk-Lore," *Transactions of the New York Academy of Sciences* 9(1890): 134-36. The term *oral tradition* had already been used by John Brand in 1777 but not as a defining principle. See John Brand, 1:xi.

18.   Ralph Steele Boggs, "Folklore: Materials, Science, Art," *Folklore Americas* 3(1943): 1; Stith Thompson, "Folklore at Midcentury," *Midwest Folklore* 1(1951): 11.

19.   See Gordon Hall Gerould, *The Ballad of Tradition* (New York: Oxford University Press, 1932), 163-71.

20.   John Greenway, "Folk Songs as Socio-Historical Documents," *Western Folklore* 19(1960): 1-9.

21.   See Åke Hultkranz, *General Ethnological Concepts*, International Dictionary of Regional European Ethnology and Folklore, vol. 1 (Copenhagen: Rosenkilde and Bagger, 1960), s.v. "Volkskunde," "Folklivsforskning."

22.   Robert Redfield, *Human Nature and the Study of Human Society: The Papers of Robert Redfield*, 2 vols., ed. Margaret Park Redfield (Chicago: The University of Chicago Press, 1962), 1: 234-47.

23.   Ibid., 231-32.

24.   Robert Redfield, *The Little Community and Peasant Society and Culture* (Chicago: Phoenix Books, 1960), 40-42.

25.   Robert Redfield, *Tepoztlan, A Mexican Village: A Study of Folk Life* (Chicago: The University of Chicago Press, 1930), 1-2.

26.   Redfield, *Human Nature*, 253.

27.   Richard M. Dorson, "Is There a Folk in the City?" *Journal of American Folklore* 83(1970): 185-222.

28.   See William R. Bascom, "Folklore and Anthropology," *Journal of American Folklore* 66(1953): 283-90; William R. Bascom, "Verbal Art," *Journal of American Folklore* 68(1955): 242-52.

29.   William R. Bascom, "Four Functions of Folklore," *Journal of American Folklore* 67(1954): 334, 336.

30.   The concepts of "common" and "ordinary" are explicit in the title of the 1725 work by Henry Bourne, *Antiquitates vulgares, or the Antiquities of the Common People*, upon which John Brand's work was based; these concepts remain

explicit throughout the writings of William J. Thoms and William Wells Newell as well.

31. Jan Harold Brunvand, *The Study of American Folklore: An Introduction* (New York: W. W. Norton & Co., Inc., 1968), 5.

32. Richard M. Dorson, *Folklore Forum* 1(1968): 37.

33. Dan Ben-Amos, "Toward a Definition of Folklore in Context," *Journal of American Folklore* 84(1971): 13.

34. Robert A. Georges, "Folklore," in *Sound Archives: A Guide to Their Establishment and Development*, ed. David Lance, International Association of Sound Archives, Special Publication 4(1983): 135.

35. For example, see Phillip J. Davis and Reuben Hersh, *The Mathematical Experience* (Boston: Houghton Mifflin Co., 1981), 6-8.

Further Readings

An overview of the development of folklore scholarship in Europe is provided by Giuseppe Cocchiara, *The History of Folklore in Europe*, translated by John N. McDaniels (Philadelphia: Institute for the Study of Human Issues, 1981). The development in Britain is amply documented in Richard M. Dorson, *The British Folklorists: A History* (Chicago: The University of Chicago Press, 1968). Alan Dundes gives some sense of American trends in the "The American Concept of Folklore," *Journal of the Folklore Institute* 3(1966): 226-49, but also in this journal see Michael J. Bell, "William Wells Newell and the Foundation of American Folklore Scholarship," 10(1973): 7-21 and Regna Darnell, "American Anthropology and the Development of Folklore Scholarship, 1890-1920," 10(1973): 23-40. Gene Bluestein outlines the development of the romantic interest in folksong in "Herder's Folksong Ideology," *Southern Folklore Quarterly* 26(1962): 137-44. How this and other early folklore perspectives shaped later research can be glimpsed in Ellen J. Stekert, "Tylor's Theory of Survivals and National Romanticism: Their Influence on Early American Folksong Collectors," 32(1968): 209-36 in the same journal. Alan Dundes extends the European nationalistic involvement with folk materials into the American domain in "Nationalistic Inferiority Complexes and the Fabrication of Fakelore: A Reconsideration of Ossian, the Kinder- und Hausmärchen, the Kalevala, and Paul Bunyan," Journal of Folklore Research 22(1985): 5-18. The Midwestern Journal of Language and Lore 3(1977) includes several essays devoted to past conceptualizations of folklore, and the journal The Folklore Historian (1984) is entirely devoted to the history of the discipline.

For examples of folklife studies and their emphasis on the material culture of rural societies, see Don Yoder, ed., American Folklife (Austin, Tex.: University of Texas Press, 1976) and Geraint Jenkins, ed., Studies in Folklife: Essays in Honour of Iowerth C. Peate (London: Routledge and Kegan Paul, 1969), as well as the Welsh journals Gwerin: A Half-Yearly Journal of Folklife (1956) and Folklife: A Journal of Ethnological Studies (1963). A recent American journal is Folklife Annual (1985).

Åke Hultkrantz has compiled a useful dictionary of folkloric and ethnological terms and concepts in General Ethnological Concepts, International Dictionary of Regional European Ethnology and Folklore, vol. 1 (Copenhagen: Rosenkilde and Bagger, 1960). Many of the essays in Toward New Perspectives in Folklore, edited by Americo Parédes and Richard Bauman (Austin, Tex.: University of Texas Press, 1971) [Journal of American Folklore 84(1971): iii-171] critically examine basic folklore concepts and definitions. For useful overviews of the theoretical perspectives brought to the analysis of folklore materials, see Richard M. Dorson, "Current Folklore Theories," Current Anthropology 4(1963): 93-112; J. L. Fischer, "The Sociopsychological Analysis of Folktales," Current Anthropology 4(1963): 235-95; and Thomas A. Burns, "Folkloristics: A Conception of Theory," Western Folklore 36(1977): 109-34.

Chapter 2
Ethnic Groups
and Ethnic Folklore

Elliott Oring

Ethnicity seems an omnipresent force in contemporary American society. When people are hungry, a host of restaurants offer "ethnic cuisines" which compete for their attention and capital. They read in the newspapers of numerous ethnic events, festivals, and other entertainments which vie for their attendance during leisurely weekend afternoons. They decorate their homes and offices with "ethnic" objects and enjoy exchanging ethnic jokes with neighbors and friends. When they apply for jobs, they may be requested to fill out ethnic identification forms which require that they locate themselves in one of several predefined ethnic categories. The pervasiveness of the ethnic idea might lead us to assume that both the term and the concept are ancient. This assumption, however, is only partially true.

The term "ethnic" indeed derives from ancient Greek words — "ethnos" and "ethnikos" — the first meaning "nation" and the second having the sense of "heathen" or "Gentile." This latter notion of "heathen" or "pagan" (derived from the New Testament Greek usage) dominated the sense of the English term "ethnic" well into the nineteenth century. The term was generally applied to peoples who were neither Jewish nor Christian; in other words, not of God's chosen. In the mid-nineteenth century, the term came to characterize groupings conceptualized on the basis of race or nationality, and only in the twentieth century did it become common to characterize as "ethnic" groupings that were culturally distinguishable from a larger social system of which they formed some part.[1]

This minor historical digression is not entirely without significance. First, it illustrates that "ethnic" derives from a term employed to designate groups *other* than one's own, and that this designation was to some degree pejorative. Second, it suggests that current notions of "ethnic group" and "ethnicity" address a different categorization of humankind than that which preoccupied western thinkers before the nineteenth century, when human groups were mainly conceptualized in terms of their ideological proximity to Christian doctrines. During the nineteenth and twentieth centuries, sociocultural changes in western society precipitated changes in the categorization of human populations. In other words, although derived from an ancient root, "ethnic" is a term with relatively contemporary meaning.

Any consideration of ethnic folklore must begin with some understanding of what is meant by an "ethnic group." As currently conceptualized, members of an ethnic group, it is claimed, share and identify with a historically derived cultural tradition or style, which may be composed of both explicit behavioral features as well as implicit ideas, values, and attitudes. Furthermore, membership in an ethnic group is acquired primarily by descent. Finally, an ethnic group is conceived as part of a larger social system rather than independent and self-sufficient. "Ethnic identity," we might add, is the intellectual and emotional sense that an individual has of his relationship to the behaviors, ideas, and values of an ethnic group. And by "ethnicity," we simply mean any speech, thought, or action based upon this sense of identity.[2] At first, these definitions may seem somewhat dense and may require careful rereading. Nevertheless, they can help to both distinguish ethnic groups from and relate ethnic groups to other kinds of folk groupings.

First, let us examine the notion that ethnic groups are based upon the *claim* of a shared common cultural tradition or style. This notion of claim is important. The perception or recognition of groupness is exactly that — a perception. Groups, indeed all categories, result from perceiving some similarity within a broader population of individual elements. Groups exist only if they are recognized and some claim is made for their existence (if only by the members themselves). Some groups are merely *statistical* in nature.[3] That is, a population may be recognized as sharing some common characteristic, for example, wearing a size nine shoe or suffering from athlete's foot. Although we may agree there is some common characteristic that defines each group, we do not generally accord them much importance. Nevertheless, we can readily appreciate how important such groups might be to a shoe manufacturer or pharmaceutical salesman whose livelihood depends on the identification and description of just such statistical groupings. This example should also alert us to the fact that the perception of groups is usually *motivated*; that is, such perceptions stem from the particular interests of particular parties. Groups that seem "significant" in the unfolding of our everyday lives generally are more widely recognized, and they are recognized by both those within the group defined as well as by those without. Such groups are generally based upon characteristics that create a *consciousness of kind*. This consciousness produces a new dynamic which not only allows for the definition of a population category, but also conditions the possibility of activity by the group based upon this consciousness. Folklorists call such groups "folk groups." Other social scientists call them by other names. In any event, the existence of such groups is still based upon a claim. They do not exist until someone claims that they exist. And like the example given earlier, these claims, whether they are made by those within the group or those without, are also motivated.

Ethnic groups, like other folk groups, can exist only after a claim has been made for their existence. The social significance of such groups will depend upon the degree to which the claim for their existence is widely recognized both by those within and those outside the group. Sometimes no community of agreement on the existence of certain ethnic categories occurs. Undoubtedly, most people have heard of "Gypsies" and realize that Gypsies can be found in North America. The category of "Gypsy," however, is, for the most part, only recognized by those who are outside the designated grouping. Outsiders apply the term to what they perceive as a common cultural tradition and style of life. Individuals who fall within the designation recognize several different ethnic identities — primarily Ŗom, Ludari, and Romničel. They have no sense of solidarity with one another, no community of interests, and their interaction with one another is not greatly different from their respective interactions with *"gaže,"* the other groups that comprise American society. Indeed, although all these groups generally practice endogamy and avoid marriage outside the group, research indicates that Ŗom, Ludari, and Romničel more frequently intermarry with *gaže* than with each other.[4] Thus an ethnic category which is broadly recognized in American society has little congruence with the ethnic classifications of the peoples so classified.

A more complex but interesting example of differences in ethnic classification is portrayed by the Lumbee Indians of Robeson County, North Carolina. Descended from early frontier farmers, they seem to be of Euro-American and Indian ancestry. Scotch and English homesteaders found them already on the land in the early eighteenth century. They became enclaves of subsistence farmers segregated from these later settlers and were disenfranchised along with the blacks and Indians in the nineteenth century. After the Civil War, as North Carolina was attempting to create a school system for their youth, the Lumbee found that only black schools were open to their children since no other provisions had been made for "people of color" who were not black. Refusing to be classified as blacks, they worked to obtain an Indian school for their children. Their representative in the state assembly argued that they were descendants of Walter Raleigh's colony established at Roanoke Island in 1587. He claimed that when the colony was abandoned, its surviving members had taken refuge with the Indians of Croatan, intermarried with them, and moved inland as the frontier developed. Despite the lack of any documentary evidence to support this claim, in 1885 the state legislature designated this group as the "Croatan Indians" and gave them separate schools. This designation did not diminish the discrimination they encountered in the surrounding community, however, so in 1911 they petitioned the legislature to be known as "the Indians of Robeson County." The legislature more than obliged by "restoring" to them their ancient name "the Cherokee," although there was no empirical basis for such a designation. Under this name they petitioned the Bureau of Indian Affairs to recognize them as "the Siouan Tribes of the Lumber River." The Bureau of Indian Affairs could find no justification for this claim and refused. In 1953, the North Carolina legislature recognized the name Lumbee Indians for this group, accepting the designation of what was supposed to be the original Indian name of the Lumber River. Because the Lumbee constitute one-third of the populations of Robeson County, they have considerable political clout in the legislature and have secured rights to land and education. The Lumbee do not speak any Indian language nor do they have any identifiable Indian customs. They do not even "look" Indian. What they do have is a shared sense of descent from early settlers in the region who were neither immigrants nor slaves, i.e., descent from peoples who were the precursors of the two-caste system later established throughout the South. This consciousness of difference has led some Lumbee to become active in Pan-Indian affairs as they continue to assert their Indian identity in relation to the blacks and whites of Robeson County.[5]

Even when a group's existence may be recognized in theory, it may not be acknowledged within certain prescribed spheres of interaction. For example, the federal bureaucracy and its members would recognize and have recognized the existence of Jews as an ethnic group. However, within the sphere of ethnic identification for bureaucratic purposes, this category carries no recognition. When one Jewish university professor was filling in the ethnic identification form administered by the Affirmative Action office of his university, he checked the box labeled "Other" and wrote in the blank line "Jewish." The form made no explicit provision for a Jewish ethnic identification, and he refused to check "Caucasian" because he did not recognize it as an ethnic group nor did he identify with Caucasians as a group. Later he discovered that the university reclassified him as Caucasian since it did not recognize a Jewish ethnic category. He went to the Affirmative Action office and petitioned for a change. Since Jewish would not be recognized, however, he checked "Other Spanish" on the premise that his Jewish ancestors were among the Jews expelled from Spain in 1492 by King Ferdinand and Queen Isabella

27

and who are generally known today as *Sephardim* [Jews of Spanish descent]. This individual was by no means certain of his Sephardic ancestry but he preferred Other Spanish as his bureaucratic ethnic identity to Caucasian. On the other hand, the Affirmative Action officer was also displeased with the professor's change of categories and felt it to be "outside the spirit and intent of Affirmative Action." The officer, however could not do anything about it since the policy of that university held that ethnic identification was a matter of self-definition rather than ascription by others.

These examples not only demonstrate that ethnic statuses may not be agreed upon, but they also introduce the idea that the existence of an ethnic group and the sense of ethnic identity is *situational*. Rather than being something constant and immutable, the recognition of a group or the sense of an identity may vary with situation and circumstance. When Sigmund Freud was in Paris in 1886 to study with Jean Martin Charcot, the famous professor of Pathological Anatomy at the University of Paris, he attended a party at Charcot's house. During a conversation, when a French guest predicted a ferocious war between France and Germany, Freud promptly explained that he was a Jew, adhering neither to Germany nor Austria.[6] Freud, born in Moravia (a part of present-day Czechoslovakia) and raised in Vienna, was a citizen of the Austro-Hungarian Empire. Yet it is also known that on many occasions, Freud considered himself thoroughly German, both linguistically and culturally, and was attached to the idea of a greater Germany. Yet when it came to the moment of identifying himself at a party in Paris to a Frenchman who was in the midst of predicting a great conflict between the French and Germans, Freud opted to activate his Jewish identity in order to distance himself from any potential identification with either party in the predicted conflict. This situational alteration of identities is possible because ethnic groups and ethnic identities are based upon the claims of people rather than being phenomena out there in the real world awaiting discovery by the keen observer.

Let us examine more closely the notion that ethnic groups are predicated upon the sharing of a common cultural tradition or style. This characteristic, first of all, distinguishes ethnic groups from groups based purely upon physical characteristics, for example, those who share a similar blood type or disposition to contract a particular disease. In the nineteenth century, the term "ethnic" was used to characterize racial groupings, but in the twentieth century the term "race" had become too restricted and problematic to usefully conceptualize the multitude of groupings characteristic of a modern society. Of course, physical characteristics may become the chief markers of ethnic identification — as they do with differences of skin color — but they are not in themselves sufficient to define an ethnic group. We shall distinguish what might be called racial groups from ethnic groups, with racial groups being statistical groups defined solely on the basis of physical or physiological characteristics.

The notion that an ethnic group's cultural tradition or style should be "historically derived," and that membership is regarded as primarily recruited by descent, helps to distinguish ethnic groups from other subcultural groups which are less predicated upon a sense of history. Members of occupational groupings may share elements of culture but they are, for the most part, conditioned primarily by their sense of the present, the demands of their present tasks. To the extent that new members are regularly recruited from outside the occupation, and no pervasive feeling of identity occurs with the body of past members of the occupation of their culture, the bases for ethnic grouping are absent. As a university professor, I acknowledge that there is a definite academic subculture. But to the extent that neither I, nor many of my colleagues, claim descent from or identity with the group or culture of university professors who have existed since the Middle Ages, my occupational affiliation seems distinct from an ethnic identification. However, in situations in which occupational culture is rich, recruitment is primarily restricted to the offspring of holders of that occupation, and identity with the occupational past is strong, it might be said that an occupational group approaches being an ethnic group. Thus ethnic status might perhaps be claimed for the guilds of medieval Europe or the occupational caste groups of India.

29

While an ethnic group is generally much broader than a kinship group, and thus not predicated upon face-to-face relations, membership is nevertheless regarded as *primarily* determined by descent rather than marriage or voluntary affiliation (although membership may indeed be achieved by both these means). On the other hand, ethnic groups are generally conceived to be units within a broader organization of social relations. This means that they are to be distinguished from the citizens of a nation and form subgroupings within or across national boundaries. Like nation-states, ethnic groups may invoke a sense of community. Unlike nation-states, however, ethnic groups may lack the political machinery to implement their will unhindered by forces outside the community. On this point we should perhaps be cautious in that there may be little to distinguish behaviors predicated upon ethnic memberships from those based upon citizenship in nation-states. Jews, who constitute one of the more enduring identity groupings, are generally recognized as an ethnic group in virtually all the nation-states in which they are found. In Israel, however, the primary ethnic categories (called *edot*) refer to the ancestral origins and traditions of its citizenry. Thus Israeli Jews are grouped as Yemenite, Kurdish, Russian, Bukharian, Iraqi, and so forth. This point is made quite clear by an Israeli joke:

> An old Romanian Jew after thirty-five years in Israel tells his friend that he is returning to Romania. His friend can't believe his ears. "After all these years you are going to go back to Romania? There is nothing for you there. No family. No friends. What are you going back there for?" The man says, "At least in Romania I can die as a Jew. Here in Israel I will die as a Romanian."

The paradox, of course, is that in Israel, "the Jewish State," one's Jewish identity is the most generally assumed and therefore the least relevant for purposes of identification. All in all, the relationship of national and ethnic identities is a complex one. To a certain extent, their distinction is purely situational. One may be a Jew in the United States and an American abroad. Indeed, the idea of the modern nation-state and the contemporary notion of the ethnic group emerge together and are products

nationalism

of the same set of forces and circumstances. They are, in some degree, opposite sides of the same coin.

An ethnic group may or may not be distinguishable from a religious group, however. Religion may comprise the central core of the tradition or style which creates the sense of ethnic identification. To exclude a religious tradition as a central or defining determinant of ethnicity would be to eliminate the ethnic status of numerous groups which are not only considered "ethnic," but which in many respects provide the very models for contemporary notions of an ethnic group. We should remember that the earliest denotations of the term "ethnic" in English referred to a group's religious constitution (or we should say, to the lack of a Jewish or Christian religious constitution), and we should be hesitant to distinguish too decisively between religious and ethnic groupings.

Enough consideration has been given to the concept of "ethnic group." Not that the definitions which have been offered are, by any means, the last word on the subject or can be regarded as entirely valid. Scholars and scientists also base definitions upon perceptions, and as we have seen, perceptions may not be agreed upon or they may change. Nevertheless, the common sense of ethnic group, ethnic identity, and ethnicity which we have outlined should greatly facilitate communication.

Let us turn to other questions: Where do ethnic groups come from? What factors lead to their recognition and importance? We might initially answer these questions by referring to three social forces, *nationalism*, *colonialism*, and *immigration*, which are to some extent interrelated. Colonialism is based upon the perception of one nation being ruled and exploited by another. Immigration is conceptualized as coming to one nation from another. And nationalism is often born from anti-colonial feelings.

By far, immigration is considered the most important force in the creation of ethnic groups and identities in the United States today. Most of the ethnic groups we currently recognize are composed of immigrants from abroad and their descendants. We recognize Polish-Americans, Swedish-Americans, Italian-Americans, Greek-Americans, Mexican-Americans, Latin-Americans, and a host of others. Since a certain cultural

31

and linguistic primacy is generally accorded to the seventeenth century, English-speaking colonizers of the Eastern seaboard, we have no category of English-Americans.

Given that the majority of our most widely recognized American "ethnic groups" consist of immigrants and their descendants, we should be careful not to confuse immigrant and ethnic. Not all ethnic groups have an immigrant base, nor are the descendants of all immigrants de facto members of an ethnic group. This second point is perhaps well recognized. There are numerous American citizens who claim no ethnic identity beyond that of being American, even though they may clearly be identifiable as the descendants of immigrants. What is perhaps less recognized, however, is that ethnic groups are not merely residual immigrant groups, but *any* group with a sense of a common cultural tradition. There is no prescription, however, on how old this tradition must be. Although many people would probably base ethnic identification upon an ancient rather than a modern cultural tradition, our definition of ethnic group admits identifications with traditions of any age, including recent ones. Hence we may recognize ethnic groups that have arisen in the United States which do not ultimately depend upon Old World traditions carried across the Atlantic or Pacific oceans. Africans, who were forcibly separated from their families and homelands by slave raiders and traders, arrived on the shores of this country as atomized individuals with no social bonds, common languages, or common cultural traditions. They constituted a social category, of course, a category of slaves, a pariah caste of laborers with whom most social contact was deemed polluting and defiling. The chief symbol of their caste was the color of their skin. But the caste was not as yet an ethnic group. Their common experiences, however, both in slavery times and after freedom, led them to develop and identify with a tradition of symbols, behaviors, and values. An ethnic group of black-Americans was born, and it was native born.[7]

The Mormons illustrate another example of a homegrown ethnic group whose cultural tradition and style did not directly derive from Old World traditions. Beginning as a religious sect in the early nineteenth century, their attempts to establish a new Zion, coupled with the persecution of the communities in which they resided, led them to become a near-nation on the North American continent. Their identity rests upon a common religion, a conception of a common homeland, common institutions, and a sense of history distinct and separate from all other groups in the nation.[8] If the Mormons do not qualify as an ethnic group, according to our previous definition, it would be difficult to argue that any group should be accorded ethnic status.

One other major force in the creation of ethnic groups in the United States is colonialism. Numerous Native American groups, in one way or another, came under the domination of the United States government. These aboriginal groupings were originally self-sufficient societies and cultures prior to their conquest by Euro-American settlers fulfilling their "manifest destinies." Given the history of the American government's relations with these groups — ranging from treatment as sovereign nations to lawless hostiles to be contained or eliminated — it was ensured, for good or for ill, that many would retain a sense of their distinctiveness and separation from the dominant society. They too are to be numbered among America's ethnic groups.

All these examples have been cited in order to show that our definitions can lead us to consider a very broad range of ethnic groups in America with diverse origins. They are not necessarily based upon residual Old World identities nor are they forged by the same set of forces and circumstances. In fact, we may sometimes wonder whether we are always discussing comparable groupings and whether the differences between such groups overshadow their similarities. We should constantly keep in mind that our definitions of ethnic groups and ethnicity are tentative constructs which we should be ready to abandon when we find they lead us to misconceptions and misunderstandings.

How does folklore relate to all of this? What is "ethnic folklore"? In a nutshell, we shall designate as "ethnic folklore" folklore which plays a part in the definition of ethnic groups, which comments upon or governs the interactions between different ethnic groups, which contributes to the sense of an ethnic identity, or which constitutes and contributes to any ethnically based action. In this brief overview there is little point in attempting to identify and document how each of the numerous genres or forms of folklore plays a part in ethnic identification and ethnically based action. Probably more will be gained by illustrating how one type of folklore participates at various levels in the processes of ethnic classification, identification, and action.

It should be obvious that as ethnic groups are recognized on the basis of a particular cultural tradition or style, folklore can and does contribute to this tradition or style and hence may provide the central symbols of ethnic definition. Hence the definition of and identification with ethnic groups are often based on folklore. Being a Navajo, for example, involves knowing the traditional myths, legends, games, and tales. A Navajo not only knows the stories themselves, but also understands and appreciates the stories, is aware of the appropriate situations to tell particular stories, and is familiar with the kinds of behaviors appropriate to participation in a storytelling event. To no small extent, to participate in and identify with an ethnic group is to know and to be able to use its folklore.[9]

Let us consider another example — traditional foodways — in some depth. Foodways are only just beginning to receive the attention they deserve from folklorists and other social scientists. Eating is one of the earliest interactive behaviors of a newborn, persisting as a situation for intimate human interaction throughout life. Eating affects us biologically and physiologically as well as socially and ideologically. Consequently, we are likely to bring a great fund of emotion to the behavior of eating. It is necessary only to call attention to the feelings that are often engendered by the foodways of others to succinctly illustrate this point. Not only would each of us find many food traditions in various parts of the world unappetizing, we would regard some of them as downright revolting. On the other hand, we can all think of foods which are not only appetizing, but emotionally satisfying — one might even say consoling. Here I might cite the cases of numerous Americans who lived abroad for great lengths of time. Although they may have learned to appreciate the local food traditions, on certain occasions they develop tremendous cravings for familiar foods from home, and they may travel hundreds of miles or go to great expense to obtain a meal of hamburgers and fries. With this kind of emotional attachment to food and eating, it is not surprising that foodways serve as highly charged markers of ethnic identity both for those within a group and for those without.

It is unlikely that anyone who feels some stirrings of identification with an ethnic group cannot think of some dish, recipe, or kind of meal that they particularly associate with their group. One individual, whose father's parents came to the United States from Romania, knows nothing of Romanian language, Romanian history, or Romanian culture, nor does he identify himself as a Romanian-American. Nevertheless, he continues to prepare one Romanian food dish. It is the sole artifact in his cultural repertoire that he consciously associates with Romania. I cite this example not to argue so much for its ethnic significance, but to illustrate that food traditions are likely to be tenacious and survive when other aspects of culture are transformed or disappear.

Often, ethnic food traditions are based upon systems of symbols and behaviors that involve complex patterns of preparation, display, and consumption. Foods identified by members of an ethnic group may be thought of as more aesthetic, more wholesome, or indeed, more "foodlike," than non-ethnically identified foods. Even the mention of such foods can evoke feelings of pleasant interaction, security, and a sense of family and community. Take, for example, the Jewish dish *cholent*. It involves long but not overly complex preparation. It is generally made with meat, usually beef, although it can be meatless. Ingredients include large quantities of potatoes and lima beans. The meat is cut into cubes, rubbed with salt, pepper, and garlic, and browned in a pan or dutch oven. The meat is put in a large, heavy pot which may be lined with bones to keep the ingredients from adhering to the bottom of the pot. The potatoes are peeled, and the beans, which have been presoaked overnight, are added with several onions which have also been browned. Barley may also be added along with a bay leaf and other seasonings. Boiling water is added to cover the ingredients in the pot. The whole pot is then brought to a boil on top of the stove. When it boils, the pot is covered and placed in a preheated oven at 400 degrees for one-half hour. The oven temperature is then lowered to 250 degrees and allowed to cook for about

15-20 hours — that is, well into the next day. It should not be stirred. If it begins to dry out, hot water must be added to keep it moist. When it is removed from the oven, it is ready to eat, requiring only liberal applications of salt.

Cholent seems to have originated in eastern Europe, and the recipe I have given is traditional, although, like all good examples of folklore, there are numerous variants. Basically a stew, the long time that a *cholent* spends in the oven gives the potatoes and beans a somewhat unusual appearance, flavor, and texture when compared with other forms of stew. What is not apparent from the recipe for this dish, however, is its symbolic significance. *Cholent* is primarily thought of as a Sabbath dish, eaten at luncheon after return from the synagogue. The Jewish Sabbath is traditionally a day of rest on which no work is permitted. What is meant by "work," however, does not accord with our contemporary notions of work. It is forbidden, for example, for observant Jews to light a fire or to do any cooking on the Sabbath. Yet it is also traditional on the Sabbath to eat well, for the Sabbath is a day to be celebrated, not simply to be observed. According to Jewish Law, food which has been cooked before the Sabbath may be kept warm; it may be removed from the oven and consumed, although the oven flame may not be extinguished. This makes *cholent* an ideal Sabbath dish since it can be kept in the oven for long periods of time without danger. Thus, what initially appears to be nothing more than a somewhat unusual stew recipe is really more closely integrated into a ritual context. Note that *cholent* is not a ritual dish per se, but the fact that it is so suitable for the Sabbath accords it ritual significance. Thus *cholent* is not merely a "Jewish dish," but can signify the Sabbath, the Law, as well as the Jewish family and community.

This point is made especially clear in a cookbook published by a Jewish women's organization. Under the recipe for *cholent*, the compilers of the book include the following anecdote:

> An interesting story is related in the Talmud about the special taste of cholent. A certain Roman Emperor used to visit frequently with Rabbi Yehuda Hanasi ("The Prince"), the leader of the Jews at that time. The

Rabbi and the Emperor would converse for long hours on Torah and other important matters.

Occasionally, the Emperor would visit on *Shabbos* [Sabbath] Day and would be particularly enamoured of the cholent. He begged Rabbi Yehuda Hanasi for the recipe. But when the Rabbi gave it to him, he told him it wouldn't taste the same since its preparation involved the use of a certain spice that was available only to Jews. The Emperor returned to his palace to give the recipe to his great chefs.

A few days later he returned and admitted that the Rabbi had been right. "What is this special spice you have?" he asked. Rabbi Yehuda Hanasi smiled and answered, "it is called *Shabbos.*"[10]

This little tale captures the idea that *cholent* and celebrating the Sabbath are inextricably united. It is interesting to note that the cookbook has been somewhat liberal in its use of Talmudic sources. The Talmud [Sabbath 119A] tells the story of the Emperor Hadrian and Rabbi Joshua ben Hanania. No mention is made of *cholent*. The Emperor merely inquires of Rabbi Joshua why Sabbath dishes have such a fragrant scent. The rabbi responds that they put in a certain spice called the Sabbath. When the Emperor requests some of the spice, the rabbi informs him that it is effective only for those who observe the Sabbath. The change of the Talmudic source to the tale elaborated in the cookbook reveals how *cholent* has come to symbolize the entire category of Sabbath food.

Cholent is regularly prepared by many observant Jewish families in the United States today. But it may also be prepared by nonobservant Jews as a dish relished for its taste as well as its nostalgic associations to European Jewish life and culture. Indeed, the dish may mark their ethnicity as they interact with members of other ethnic groups. Used as one symbol of their Jewish identity for others, it may be prepared for friends at home or brought to pot luck dinners that call for a variety of ethnic cuisines or specialty foods. In other words, ethnic foodways — and even more generally, ethnic folklore — may not only serve symbolic purposes for those within the group, they may be deliberately manipulated as symbols of ethnic identity for those outside the group. Ultimately, ethnic folklore may be employed to create and enhance relationships with those outside the group as well as among the members themselves.

Another example may serve to illustrate the power of food as a symbol of in-group identification. One Italian-American family gathers together every Christmas Eve to celebrate, and one food always prepared is *baccala*, a dried and salted codfish served in a tomato sauce. One aunt in the family always prepared it, and when she died, the task of preparing it was assumed by another aunt. What is particularly interesting about this food custom is that almost no one in the family likes *baccala*. Nevertheless, everyone in the family, except for the children, eats some of it. My informant, who really detests the dish, also did not eat any of it when he was young; but as someone who strongly identifies himself as an Italian-American, and now with several children of his own, he feels compelled at least to eat a portion at each Christmas Eve gathering.

While foodways may serve as powerful identity symbols for those within the group, and as means of creating and solidifying relations with those outside the group, they may also serve as the bases for negative stereotypes. Indeed, these stereotypes are in themselves folklore and may be properly considered within the topic of ethnic folklore. A number of derisive terms have been regularly employed to label different ethnic or national groups. On occasion the French have been called "Frogs"; the British — "Limeys"; the Germans — "Krauts"; the Mexicans — "Beaners." All these labels derive from what others perceive to be some distinctive element in their menu. Here a conception of an ethnic group's cultural tradition may be used to emphasize differences between groups and to express the hostile emotions attending those differences. Recently, as large numbers of immigrants from southeast Asia and the Pacific Islands settled in American communities, rumors began to circulate that people's cats and dogs were disappearing. In this case, a bizarre food choice is used to categorize a group of people and to imply that they cannot be considered "proper" American citizens.[11]

The previous examples should serve to show that ethnic folklore may be used to create a sense of community within groups, as well as to define and delimit boundaries between groups. A good example of using folklore to emphasize boundary definitions comes from the work of a folklorist in Carbon County, Utah. This folklorist focused upon Italian-Americans and attempted to illustrate how foodways, and stories about foodways, were used to emphasize and to comment upon the distinctiveness of the Italian and Mormon communities. One Italian-American informant recalled in a personal narrative how her mother's offer of a plate of *frazzini*, a pretzel-shaped bread prepared with anise seed, was refused by a group of visiting Mormon women. The mother later learned, according to her daughter's story, that the anise seed had reminded the visitors of rat droppings. The narrative was told with a sense of outrage and moral indignation that a traditional offer of hospitality was refused. Another Italian-American informant commented that Mormons thought she did not know how to cook because she was unable to give them the precise measurements for the ingredients of some dish. She claimed that the Mormons have to have a recipe for everything, and that the recipe needs to be expressed in exact amounts. Following her account, she grabbed the salt shaker, sprinkled some salt in her hand, and told the folklorist, "That is how much salt I use to make *scalledi!*"[12]

Because spaghetti is widely recognized as a particularly Italian food, to the extent that Italians were occasionally called "spaghetti benders" in Carbon County, many stories circulate about the inability of some Mormons to properly prepare it. One individual elaborated on how his Mormon foreman put the spaghetti in the water and set them on the stove to boil together. The story gleefully recounted how the spaghetti naturally turned to mush, with the teller commenting that his foreman didn't know how to cook spaghetti the Italian way — a dente — so that your teeth stick in the pasta when you bite into it. This personal narrative climaxed with, "And then he turns around and puts catsup on spaghetti. Can you believe that? Catsup on spaghetti?" All this the informant recounted amidst squeals of laughter and gasps for air. The informant then went on to give the recipe for spaghetti from his home town in Italy. Goat intestines are wrapped around *finoccio* — fennel stalks — and simmered in a tomato sauce so that the sauce acquires a licorice taste from the fennel and a sweet accent from the intestines. Stories about food use and misuse

39

can express and exemplify broader and more profound aspects of social and cultural difference.[13]

We have looked at ethnic foodways as symbols of identity, as creators of community, and as markers of group difference. I would suggest that there is another important role that folklore regularly plays in the ethnic process. This is the *self-reflective* role that allows the dynamic of the ethnic group and aspects of ethnic identity to be reflected back to its members. It is a form of self-exploration and self-contemplation. An example is the following song about *cholent* sung to the tune of "California Dreamin'."

> All the beans are brown and it's Friday
> I was so eager to cook for the *Shabbos* [Sabbath] day
> I forgot the water shouldn't smell this way
> Cholent was a-burnin' on a winter's day.
>
> Stepped into my *shul* [Yiddish: synagogue] had to walk away
> I came running home and I began to pray
> I was so ashamed having company
> For cholent was a-burnin' and the heat was on me.
>
> Cholent *bren* [Yiddish: burnt] is a *nechtigetag*
> [Yiddish: literally, "like yesterday";
> colloquially, "of no account"] when
> You forget the water and then
> It's the *Shabbos* [Sabbath] meal *in drerd*
> [Yiddish: literally, "in the earth"; colloquially, "gone to hell"]
>
> All the beans are black and it's Saturday
> Cholent had been burnin' and it had burnt away
> I forgot the water shouldn't smell this way
> My cholent had been burnin' spoiled my *Shabbos* day
> Oh what can I say
> Other than "Oy *vay*" [Yiddish: "Woe!"; "Oh my!"][14]

A song about the burning of *cholent* sung to a 1960s Mamas and Papas' tune is most certainly a different form of expression than the preparation of the dish itself. Why should such a song be composed? What is its significance?

First, it is necessary to recognize this song as a parody of the well-known "California Dreamin'." Furthermore, we should note that this song inverts several of the symbols and themes of the original. "California Dreamin'" is about too much *cold* whereas our song text concerns the result of too much *heat*. "California Dreamin'" concerns *leaving home* whereas the parody is concerned with company *coming to the house*. Also, the *shul* [synagogue] stands in opposition to the *church*, which figures prominently in the original song, and Yiddish intrusions in the parody contrast with the completely English original. These thematic and symbolic inversions heighten the sense of incongruity and the sense of its comic intention. In other words, "Cholent Was a-Burnin'" rests upon more than the borrowing of a popular tune, meter, and assorted bits of phraseology.

Overall, the text of this song, which concerns the failure to properly prepare a traditional Sabbath meal, stands in high contrast to the content of "California Dreamin'." Los Angeles, California, the particular object of the original song's yearning, holds a place in American symbology as an avant-garde, "laid-back," fun-oriented, sunny paradise. In fact, all these attributes conflict rather markedly with the images and values of orthodox Judaism symbolized by the *cholent*. Orthodox Judaism is often conceived as an Old World, traditional, conservative, restrictive, and even anxious way of life. Traditional Judaism, associated with a history of persecution and suffering, is not easily reconcilable with the hedonistic philosophy which, in the popular imagination, has come to be associated with the California lifestyle.

"Cholent Was a-Burnin'" communicates the sense of conflict and discordance experienced by members of the modern, American, orthodox community — by those individuals who are faithful to Jewish law and custom, yet at the same time are fully competent participants in mainstream American culture. (Even to understand the text of this song, one must have some competence in both cultures.) In this sense, the song can be regarded as a self-reflective expression of identity, a symbolic statement about the ideological incompatibility of the two worlds in which many observant American Jews live. "Cholent Was a-Burnin'" is

41

not great poetry nor is it a brilliant piece of humor. It is, however, a humorous, poetic expression which manages to communicate a serious message about a group's conceptualization of its own identity.

We have glimpsed some of the ways in which folklore can participate in ethnic processes. It may be at the core of ethnic identity, or it may serve as a symbol of that identity. Folklore may be used to create ties between members of different groups or to define boundaries and erect barriers between them. It may even serve as a means of reflection upon the process of ethnic identification itself. Yet we have by no means exhausted the subject. The understanding of folklore's place in the processes of ethnicity and ethnic identification demands a close study of folklore unfolding in a large variety of ethnic groups and social contexts. Such studies will undoubtedly deepen as well as broaden the sense of folklore's contribution to ethnic identification and action, as well as the sense of what folklore can mean and how it can function in a larger universe of relationships and groups.

Notes

1. *Oxford English Dictionary*, corrected reissue, s.v. "ethnic."

2. Anya Peterson Royce, *Ethnic Identity: Strategies of Diversity* (Bloomington, Ind.: Indiana University Press, 1982), 20-28.

3. On the distinction between statistical, societal, social, and associational groups, see Robert Bierstedt, *The Social Order*, 2d ed. (New York: McGraw-Hill, Inc., 1957), 293-301.

4. Matt T. Salo, "Gypsy Ethnicity: Implications of Native Categories and Interaction for Ethnic Classification," *Ethnicity* 6(1979): 88-92.

5. Alice B. Kehoe, *North American Indians: A Comprehensive Account* (Englewood Cliffs, N.J.: Prentice-Hall, Inc., 1981), 201-3.

6. Sigmund Freud, *The Letters of Sigmund Freud*, ed. Ernst L. Freud, trans. Tania and James Stern (New York: Basic Books Inc., 1975), 203.

7. R. A. Schermerhorn, "Ethnicity in the Perspective of the Sociology of Knowledge," *Ethnicity* 1(1974): 5.

8.   Thomas F. O'Dea, *The Mormons* (Chicago: The University of Chicago Press, 1957), 115-17.

9.   See Barre Toelken, *The Dynamics of Folklore* (Boston: Houghton Mifflin Co., 1979), 93-103.

10.   *The Spice and Spirit of Kosher-Jewish Cooking* (n.p.: Lubavitch Women's Organization — Junior Division, 1977), 121.

11.   Susan Kalčik, "Ethnic Foodways in America: Symbol and Performance of Identity," in *Ethnic and Regional Foodways in the United States: The Performance of Group Identity*, ed. Linda Keller Brown and Kay Mussell, (Knoxville, Tenn.: The University of Tennessee Press, 1984), 37.

12.   Richard Raspa, "Exotic Foods Among Italian-Americans in Mormon Utah: Food as Nostalgic Enactment of Identity," in Brown and Mussell, 188.

13.   Ibid., 190-91.

14.   *Rechnitzer Rejects: Volume III* (Perfect Impressions, 450 Seventh Avenue, New York, N.Y. 10001), HP29568.

Further Readings

An excellent overview of ethnic group and ethnic identity concepts may be found in Anya Peterson Royce, *Ethnic Identity: Strategies for Diversity* (Bloomington, Ind.: Indiana University Press, 1982). *Ethnicity*, a journal entirely devoted to the investigation and discussion of ethnic issues, was founded in 1974. A comprehensive and readable survey of the role of folklore in the definition of identity can be found in Alan Dundes, "Defining Identity through Folklore," in *Identity: Personal and Socio-Cultural: A Symposium*, edited by Anita Jacobson-Widding, Uppsala Studies in Cultural Anthropology 5 (Uppsala: Acta Universitatis Upsaliensis, 1983), 235-61. William Hugh Jansen's "The Esoteric-Exoteric Factor in Folklore," *Fabula: Journal of Folktale Studies* 2(1959): 205-11 [reprinted in Alan Dundes, *The Study of Folklore* (Englewood Cliffs, N.J.: Prentice-Hall, Inc., 1965), 43-51], also provides a helpful introduction to the differential perceptions of group membership and identity.

43

Four case studies of ethnic groups and their lore along with a comprehensive essay on the development of folklore-ethnicity research can be found in Larry Danielson, ed., *Studies in Folklore and Ethnicity* (Los Angeles: California Folklore Society, 1978) [*Western Folklore* 36(January 1977)]. A number of folklore dissertations published by Arno Press deal with Swedish-American, Greek-American, Romanian-American, Latvian-American, Jewish-American, and Ukranian-American folklore. For an in-depth study of the use of folklore in interethnic conflict, see Gladys-Marie Fry, *Night Riders in Black Folk History* (Knoxville, Tenn.: University of Tennessee Press, 1975). For a collection of essays on the place of food in ethnic and regional cultures, see Linda Keller Brown and Kay Mussell, eds., *Ethnic and Regional Foodways in the United States: The Performance of Group Identity* (Knoxville, Tenn.: University of Tennessee Press, 1984). An excellent overview of issues in foodways research can be found in Michael Owen Jones, Bruce Giuliano, and Roberta Krell, eds., *Foodways and Eating Habits: Directions for Research* (Los Angeles: California Folklore Society, 1983) [*Western Folklore* 40(January 1981)]. Robert A. Georges provides an overview of the models governing immigrant-ethnic folklore research in the United States in "Research Perspectives in Ethnic Folklore Studies," *Folklore and Mythology Studies* 7(1983): 1-23. (If not available in university libraries, a copy can be ordered from the Folklore and Mythology Program, University of California, Los Angeles, California 90024.) For a European perspective, see Linda Dégh, "The Study of Ethnicity in Modern European Ethnology," *Journal of the Folklore Institute* 12(1975), 113-29. A comprehensive bibliography of ethnic folklore studies in the English language can be found in Robert A. Georges and Stephen Stern, *American and Canadian Immigrant and Ethnic Folklore: An Annotated Bibliography* (New York: Garland Publishing, 1982).

Chapter 3
Religious Folklore

Larry Danielson

Religious folklore is folklore that has to do with religion. This definition is direct and simple, but raises several difficult questions. For instance, what distinguishes religious folklore from institutionalized religious practice and belief? What types of behaviors make up this kind of folk tradition? Is religious folklore to be found outside of religious services, in contexts other than worship settings? Can the same folk tradition be religious in one context and nonreligious in another? How do we go about studying the possible meanings of a religious folk tradition for its participants? Can we analyze the folklore of our own religion without impugning the integrity of our religious belief and personal religious experience? These questions will be explored in the following pages, but I will restrict the discussion to the folk traditions of certain Christian groups in the United States because of my familiarity with them and because of their accessibility to American folklore students.

Religion, like politics and sex, is a topic that most of us introduce cautiously into conversation, alert to the possibility of conflict or offense when we exchange opinions about it with people we don't know very well.[1] Therefore it seems appropriate to describe my own religious associations in order to provide some context for the suggestions about religious folklore, my own and that of others, which follow.

I was raised a Lutheran and have remained active in a liberal Lutheran denomination most of my adult life. A few years ago I chaired my

45

congregation's worship and music committee, seeing to various matters concerning Sunday and holiday church services, musical events in the church, and sanctuary decor. This responsibility alerted me to the wealth of folk tradition practiced within the Lutheran church and its significance to many congregation members.

A particular experience as worship and music deacon illustrates the presence of folk tradition within the organized church. One year the worship and music committee, in consultation with our pastor, instituted a worship service to take place on January 6, the festival of Epiphany, which commemorates the manifestation of Christ to the world and focuses on the magis' gifts to the infant Jesus as described in the Gospel of Matthew. Epiphany is a very old Christian celebration, antedating Christmas, but it has not been very important as a religious festival in the Lutheran church.[2] In our local revival of the celebration, we incorporated the lighting of incense into the service because Matthew notes that one of the wisemen's gifts was frankincense. The service took place as planned, until I was to light the altar candles from the sanctuary lamp, a candle that burns continuously in the area of the church altar. In the process I inadvertently snuffed out the sanctuary candle, and a woman in the small group present commented in a stage whisper, "We know what happens to people who put out the eternal light!"

This minor incident illustrates the influence of two religious folk traditions which are not immediately obvious from the preceding account. First, a residual attitude, learned by many older Lutherans in childhood, was covertly expressed by a few congregation members during and after the service. They were disturbed by the use of incense in the church because of its association with Roman Catholic worship, but were probably unaware that the most recent Lutheran liturgical manual suggests its use in certain services.[3] Although doctrinal and behavioral conflict between Lutherans and Roman Catholics has diminished significantly in the past generation due to ecumenical dialogues between the two groups, anti-Catholic biases persist among some older, conservative Lutherans. These members privately complain about the Catholicization of the Lutheran worship service. In particular, they resent several liturgical suggestions in the revision of the worship liturgy in 1978; for example, worshippers may make the sign of the cross at certain points in the service.

Interpreting the woman's remark is more complicated. Known for her ready wit and occasional iconoclastic statements, she publicly mocked a commonplace attitude in Lutheran culture concerning the sanctity of the altar area. Most Lutherans perceive this space as sacred, and they regard playful behavior around the altar or the careless treatment of worship objects, for instance communion vessels, as inappropriate.[4] Learned from early childhood, the folk attitude persists and dramatically affects behavior in this arena of the sacred (usually delineated by a communion rail which encloses the altar area). The sanctuary lamp, found in many Lutheran churches, is popularly called the eternal light and suggests the presence of the sacred. Officially, the candle and its holder have no special properties in and of themselves.[5] Nevertheless, concerns about keeping the candle constantly lit and discomfort if the candle goes out, especially in the course of a worship service, are common. Official Lutheran doctrine and liturgical directives have nothing to say about the treatment of the object.[6] The remark, "We know what happens to people who put out the eternal light," deliberately satirizes traditional attitudes about altar area behavior in the Lutheran sanctuary, as well as the folk belief about the possible consequences for those who do not carry out with care their responsibilities in the sacred space.

This anecdote illustrates folk attitude and folk belief occasioned in a worship service context. More importantly, it indicates the necessity of understanding the larger religious context in which the traditions are enacted. Anti-Catholic bias, the connotation of incense in the Lutheran sanctuary, and the import of the woman's statement (undoubtedly considered by some members present to be an inappropriate use of humor in a worship service) are all necessary to understand the behaviors in the scene described. The behaviors themselves are invisible to most outsiders as religious folk traditions and would seldom be conceptualized as religious folklore by insiders.

Recognizing and understanding these visible and invisible factors in the event require either participation within the religious group or extensive study of the group's religious life. A primary concern in the description and interpretation of religious folk tradition, then, is familiarity with the religious community in question and an understanding of the conventional beliefs and behavior followed by its lay members as well as those prescribed by its official leadership and literature. Without such contextual information, it is difficult, if not impossible, to separate religious folk tradition from ecclesiastical tradition, a central task in the study of religious folklore.

Christian groups, of course, vary dramatically in official religious doctrine, organization, leadership traits, and worship behavior.[7] Churches like the Roman Catholic, Episcopal, and Lutheran are characterized by a complex administrative organization, a professionally trained clergy, an elaborate literature made up of official interpretations of holy writ, and a systematized complex of dogma and doctrine. Their worship services usually are formal and highly structured, following liturgical patterns associated with the seasons of the church year which form a kind of sacred calendar: Advent, Christmas, Epiphany, Lent, Holy Week, Easter, and Pentecost.

At the opposite extreme are religious groups in which oral tradition and customary example play much more important roles. These churches, often unaffiliated with a national or international organization, tend to be led by lay ministers who have been prepared for their religious vocation by personal spiritual experience rather than a formal religious education. Dogma and doctrine have not been synthesized over a long period of time into complex codes prescribed by nonlocal religious officials. Their worship services tend to be informal in that they do not follow a predictable liturgy printed in a service book and do not emphasize the seasons of the liturgical year.

Between these two extremes lie many religious groups and denominations, such as Methodist and Presbyterian churches. Other churches in the United States, for instance the Unitarian-Universalist, the Seventh-Day Adventist, and the Church of Christ, Scientist, present special problems in their placement on the spectrum suggested here.

The presence of folk tradition within specific religious contexts is more easily observed in some instances than in others. An excellent historical illustration of a Christian-American folk religion is the pre-Civil War slave church.[8] Because so many black-American slaves were purposely kept illiterate by their masters, oral tradition played a crucial role in creating and maintaining religious worship practices in slave culture. African elements, the observation of white church services, and innovations in worship behavior created a distinctive form of religious life, well documented in the personal-experience narratives collected from former slaves.[9] The spiritual, anthem, and ring-shout,[10] baptismal rituals, lengthy and vigorous sermons based on oral versions of Biblical texts, call and response exchanges between worshippers and preacher, and ecstatic trance were all components of slave church worship. Sometimes these services were held in secret because Christian practices were prohibited by some masters. Sometimes they were held in the white church after the white service had concluded. When slaves were allowed to worship with the white congregation (though spatially separated from their spiritual brethren), the elements of folk tradition were not as important. The legacy of these worship practices continues in many black-American churches today, although the roles of print and the professionalization of ministers and musicians have become more important in congregational life.

A related illustration of a coherent religious system indebted to oral tradition and customary example can be found in Pentecostal Holiness congregations which emphasize the handling of serpents as a public act of faith. The services of these independent groups, often led by charismatic personalities, seem to be very informal, but they follow a traditional pattern of hymn-singing, exhortation, testimonial, the handling of snakes, the occasional ingestion of toxic substances, glossolalia (speaking in tongues), and the ecstatic dance of believers filled with the Holy Ghost.[11] Behavioral example plays a major role in structuring these worship services. No service book or hymnal is used to indicate when hymns are to be sung, when testimonials are appropriate and how they are to be presented, when the caged snakes are brought into the church, or how they are to be handled. Nevertheless, the pattern of religious behavior is quite predictable from service to service, as is the highly formalized Roman Catholic service of the mass, which relies on a printed text.

In contrast, religious folk beliefs and rituals practiced in liturgical churches are not immediately apparent because they are not obviously incorporated by congregation members into the formal worship service. Instead, they are utilized by the faithful in private or are unobtrusively enacted in the course of the service. Some of these traditions may, in fact, contradict official church doctrine and dismay local church leadership when their practice is disclosed.

Some Roman Catholic students and friends have recounted to me their anxieties about their first communion, during which, according to the Roman Catholic doctrine of transubstantiation, the communion wafer is transformed into the body of Christ. They had been warned by their elders, sometimes by their parochial school teachers, that if they chewed the communion wafer, their mouths would fill with blood. Most Catholic priests categorize such a belief as troublesome superstition. A folklorist, however, finds it a good example of religious folk belief, not countenanced by the church and maintained through the means of oral tradition.

Another religious folk tradition, attested to by many of my Roman Catholic students, involves burying a statue of St. Joseph in order to ensure the sale of a home. The statue, borrowed or purchased, is usually buried upside down on the property offered for sale. It is not unusual for students to affirm that the ritual is effective and to include in their description of the tradition a family story about the successful sale of a home when the ritual was followed. No official dogma countenances this act; it is, in fact, discouraged or silently tolerated by most priests and church leaders today.

These two religious folk traditions, associated by their practitioners with important elements in their church life — the Eucharist and the recognition of certain figures from the New Testament and church history as sanctified and capable of interceding with God on the behalf of humankind — play no role in prescribed public worship. For some Roman Catholics, however, these traditions serve as means of dealing with critical situations, even though they may be regarded as superstitious behavior by equally devout Roman Catholics.

A more commonplace religious folk tradition found in many American families is the practice of family prayer, often at children's bedtime or before a meal. Here we have a ritual act of verbal expression, often formularized, which is actively encouraged by church leaders and validated by scriptural sources. In many cases, however, such prayers and proper prayer behaviors are transmitted from parent to child orally or by customary example. The religious act involves much more than the recitation of text. Denominational, ethnic, and familial variation are significant in accounting for the diverse forms of this widespread religious folk tradition.

The performance rules affecting family table prayers are numerous, as suggested by the following questions which can be asked concerning a specific family's observance of the tradition: Is the prayer a traditional text that varies little from occasion to occasion? If it changes from time to time, do the variations follow any particular pattern? Are some topics considered inappropriate, for example requests for personal gain ("Please, God, give me a bicycle for my birthday.") or humorous petitions ("And keep the kids quiet during dinner.")? Does the prayer have limitations in length? Is it ever sung? Does it take place before or after the meal, or both? What constitutes a meal deserving of table prayer? (A pastor recalled to me, half in jest, that in her childhood home if the food on the plate was worth more than thirty-five cents, it deserved a prayer of thanks.) Does it take place daily or only on special occasions? Does one person pray aloud, or is the act a collective one? What physical gestures are involved in the act, for example folded hands, crossed arms, or the holding of one another's hands about the table? What is the parental response when children race through the prayer in a thoughtless manner? What language is used in the prayer? (Non-English-language prayers are sometimes recited in ethnic American families and may function simultaneously as a religious act and as an expression of ethnic identification.) Is a prayer used when nonreligious guests are present? A careful ethnography of family prayer behavior which describes its performance, inquires about its origins in the family, and explores family members' attitudes toward the ritual can provide valuable insight into the life of a religious folk tradition familiar to many of us, but which has yet to be thoughtfully described and interpreted. Prayer is a good example of religious folklore practiced outside the context of the worship service and actively maintained in many American homes, regardless of denominational affiliation.

Some religious folk traditions may be so familiar as religious acts that it is startling to consider the behaviors as folklore. Or it may seem so unusual that it appears to belong to an alien religious world. Such traditions, the commonplace and the exotic, can be categorized according to conventional folklore genres: folk narrative (e.g., a community story about the miraculous restoration of sight to a blind worshipper);[12] folk music (deliberately singing in unison during worship service hymns); folk belief (the Blessed Mother weeps if one puts shoes on the table); folk ritual (lighting Advent candles at home during the Advent season); folk medicine (drinking seven kinds of tea on Ascension day in order to escape contagious diseases for the rest of the year); folk art (constructing nativity scenes in the home each Christmas season); folk cookery (incising a cross on homemade bread to be used for communion); folk dress (wearing black on Good Friday or not wearing clothing fastened with buttons); and folk demeanor (encouraging the preacher with affirmations of agreement during worship). As is often the case in genre categorization, some traditions involve more than one kind of behavior. For example, a conversion testimonial is not only a narrative performance, but is also reliant on a religious belief shared by the group, and a construction of a backyard grotto which celebrates the Virgin Mary indicates belief in her importance in the family's religious life.

Another complication suggested by this list of religious folk traditions is the interrelationship between folk elements and nonfolk elements. Unless we are dealing with a relatively isolated society in which the mass media and mass-produced goods are not available, folk traditions interact vigorously with their urbanized cultural contexts. Contemporary Americans may purchase aerosol cans of perfumed spray in certain religious supply stores to sanctify dangerous locations, order religious statuary from catalogs, follow radio and television programs that broadcast personal conversion stories to millions of listeners, subscribe to religious periodicals which suggest ideas for family devotions, and print stories and poetry that may find their way into a family's oral tradition. The use of purchased, mass-produced materials and the electronic media in religious acts should not preclude their definition as folklore. The Charlie Brown Christmas Special, one of the few explicitly religious programs on American network television during the Christmas season, could, for example, be incorporated into a family Christmas folk tradition. The family may view the program every year, finding it significant because of its religious content, and other customs may accrue to the event. In such a case, the television cartoon is not folklore, but the customary act of viewing it by the family becomes a religious folk tradition.

Thus far I have argued that religious folklore can be found in a variety of religious groups; that it can be observed within official worship services and outside the church; that it can contradict or complement official doctrine; that it can comprise a variety of interrelated genres; and that it can make use of nonfolk sources and materials. Keeping in mind these suggestions, it is important to locate and describe religious folk tradition in order to document its continued practice in an age often characterized as a secular one. It is equally important to study the life of specific religious folk traditions in order to learn something about the religious sentiments and ideology of an individual or group and to consider the intent and consequences of the traditional behavior in question. Religious folklore is a lens through which religious experience as well as nonreligious experience can be investigated. The following discussion of three examples of religious folk tradition suggests the value of such studies.

The traditional Polish-American Christmas Eve celebration, called *wigilia*, illustrates seasonal religious folk rituals observed within the home, related to, but separated from official worship in the Roman Catholic church.[13] Christmas Eve dinner is served on a tablecloth spread over a covering of hay or straw, a symbol of Christ's birth in a stable. The meal consists of thirteen kinds of food, a reference to Christ and the twelve apostles, and no meats or animal fats are used in its preparation because of the ancient proscription concerning the meatless fast before taking communion. In some families the bread eaten during the meal has been signed with the cross before placing it in the oven to bake, a ritual that accompanies all bread baking in very tradition-oriented Polish-American families. Some place a lighted candle in a window on Christmas Eve as a sign to homeless travelers, like Mary and Joseph, that they are welcome in the home.

The most important ritual act in the *wigilia* is the breaking of the *oplatek*, a wafer about the size of a four- by six-inch card, usually imprinted with a nativity scene. Writes a third-generation Polish-American:

> The ones we use are obtained from Polish missionaries. They also can be purchased through various Polish Catholic churches or societies for a small donation . . . . My mother puts two of them together with honey and goes to each member of the family and the guests to break bread with them. She wishes each person health, wealth, and happiness in the coming year. In the case of a child, they are wished good grades and many Christmas presents. This breaking of [the] *oplatek* often leads to tears as my parents reminisce about their own parents and childhood; sometimes they reflect on the loss of a dear one, but there is laughter, too, usually with the children.[14]

Another account describes a variation in the ritual:

> Whatever is left of the wafer is placed on the straw centerpiece on the table to signify Jesus in his bed of straw in the manger. A special Christmas grace is recited and a wine toast to the holidays starts off the *wigilia*. Each person is given one bowl, spoon, and fork. The different foods are placed one at a time on the straw and wafer in the center of the table. Everyone dips into this community serving bowl. When the bowl is empty, it is lifted to see if any wafer has stuck to the bottom of the dish. If it has stuck, this means that there will be an abundance of this food for the next year. This is done with each dish of traditional Polish food.[15]

After the dinner, the family exchanges Christmas gifts, may sing

Christmas carols, and attends midnight mass, preferably in their predominantly Polish-American parish.

These descriptions of *wigilia* rituals indicate that certain foods, the decoration of the table, and the lighting of the candle in the window are regarded as religious symbols and that the sharing of the *oplatek* is the primary ritual that defines the celebration. Many Polish-American families also send wafers to family members who cannot return home for the holidays.

Interpreting the meanings of the event for its participants requires much more information, however, because there is a wide range of response to the sharing of the *oplatek*. The child anxious to get on with the meal to the more important matter of Christmas gifts, the family member who has suffered a crisis in religious faith and has left the church, and the devout Roman Catholic would respond differently to the same ritual. For the child, it may be only a necessary step leading to the gift exchange. For the lapsed believer, it may be important, nevertheless, because it provides a means to indicate continued membership in the family unit, in spite of religious differences. In addition, for this individual the *oplatek* ritual may affirm ethnic affiliation. For the committed Roman Catholic, the religious symbols and the sharing of the wafer are Christmas Eve traditions crucial to the celebration of a sacred event.

This exploration of the *wigilia* suggests the difficulty of interpreting the meaning of symbolic acts in human behavior. For example, in order to impute a religious meaning to the thirteen kinds of food served in the meal, we must be aware of their referents, Christ and the twelve apostles. Similarly, the lighting of the candle in the window may or may not be perceived as a sign to the world that Mary and Joseph are welcome in the family's home. The belief concerning the prognostic meaning of the wafer stuck to the bottom of the food dish may be taken seriously or as a curious amusement, an interesting survival from the peasant past. The ritual sharing of the wafer is reminiscent of the Eucharist: both center upon a special bread imprinted with religious motifs, which is broken and shared, accompanied by a special blessing. The parallels between the Eucharist and the sharing of the *oplatek* must be obvious to good Catholics, although the former is an official sacrament of the church and the latter a holiday tradition of religious import, a vernacular "communion" in a secular setting. In addition, for Polish-Americans in daily contact with a non-Polish-American world, the ritual becomes an ethnic-religious experience, a distinctive affirmation that the family is not only Christian, but also Polish-American and Roman Catholic.

Religious affiliation often involves ethnic identity. Church members may categorize themselves as Italian-Catholics, Swedish-Lutherans, or Scotch-Presbyterians, for example. For others, their denomination has no ethnic significance. The Polish-American *wigilia* is a religious tradition which can be used to express one's ethnic identification because of its old-country origins and the ways in which it distinguishes the Polish-American Christmas Eve from non-Polish-American holiday observances.

In contrast is another Christmas tradition practiced within the family, a custom having no ethnic antecedents, but with provocative analogues in a variety of sources. A family in central Illinois customarily displays a manger scene, or crèche, each Christmas.[16] It consists of the usual figures, most importantly Mary, Joseph, and the infant Jesus, who lies in a manger, as well as various angels and animals, including a small, pink pig about the same color and size as the Christ child figurine. Although the crèche is set up a week and a half before Christmas each year, the Christ child is not placed in the manger until December 24. Before the birth date, to the dismay of the mother of the house, the pig appears from time to time in the empty manger, placed there by her mischievous children. As adults, they have continued this seasonal prank when they return home for Christmas. The placement of the infant Jesus figurine in the manger on Christmas Eve does not put an end to the game. As long as the crèche remains in the family living room, the Christ child risks replacement by the pink pig, and the figure of the infant Jesus may be relocated to lie on the stable roof, hang on a star at the front of the stable, or be hidden in the miniature forest that stands to the right of the manger scene. Comments the person who initiated the prank in his childhood,

Every time a person passes the hutch cupboard he changes the positions.

It almost comes down to a contest — who can put the Christ child in the most humorous position. My father ignores the whole thing, but my mother gets very perturbed . . . . At every chance someone puts the pig in the manger. Mom gets mad. But no one ever steals the Christ child and no one ever steals the pig . . . . All the kids take it as a big joke, but it's a continuing joke, something that happens every year. It could've been anything, but the pig's the most humorous of the major animals . . . .[17]

This family Christmas tradition seems to be isolated and idiosyncratic, traditional because it has been practiced in the family some fifteen years. At first glance, it has no aged pedigree or any remarkable religious import. Further scrutiny, however, indicates that it relates in an important way to religious experience. Furthermore, it parallels a very old motif found in western folk literature. It is a prank played in life as well as in literature, independently reinvented in a moment of mischief in central Illinois.

The student who described this family tradition in a fieldwork assignment has noted a number of analogues to the custom appearing in folklore literature, most of them related to a medieval source, the story of Mak in *The Second Shepherds' Play*.[18] This fifteenth-century mystery play culminates in the adoration of the Christ child by the shepherds, but begins with a comic episode. In it, Mak steals a sheep and his wife hides the animal in a cradle. She pretends to have just given birth to the creature when the other shepherds arrive, and Mak appropriately sings a lullaby to his new "child." The context of this comic incident is religious, a dramatic treatment of the mystery of Christ's birth. The central act in the scene is the fraudulent placement of the animal in the cradle. Similarly, the family tradition in twentieth-century Illinois takes place in a religious context — the nativity scene set up for a Christian holiday — and the family's mischief involves the placement of an animal in the manger. The custom is a prank, meant to upset the mother of the household, who is disturbed by the exchange and regards it as a sacrilegious act. It is interesting, however, that she does not permanently remove the offending pig from the nativity scene, but instead tolerates the family's profane play. Even though the tradition does not express religious belief, it is

57

practiced because the family shares a sense of the separation of the sacred and the profane, regarded quite seriously by the mother and acknowledged by the children, who no longer consider themselves to be religious.

The writer who described and interpreted this seasonal custom is married to the person who instituted it as a child. Her discussions with her husband and her observation of the tradition in action provided her with information helpful in understanding its possible functions. She writes:

> Although I don't feel that the children's current lack of religion is what motivates them to continue with the switch (in other words, I don't feel that this is a sublimated conflict over belief), it certainly leaves them in a frame of mind conducive to the game. In addition, I think there is still a strong element of the child's delight in getting the goat of the parents by attacking, in a humorous way, that which he knows is important to the parents. In this case, that target is religion.[19]

The writer then goes on to suggest an explanation for the behavior, relating the Illinois family tradition to the comic incident in the medieval mystery play:

> This custom can also be seen as a traditional family way of breaking the barriers between proper and improper behavior without fear of any serious retaliation. This idea of boundary crossing might also explain the appeal of the central image: the animal in the cradle or bed, as it is seen in the [mystery play and folk narrative] annotations. Those who carry out the switch, children (or "adults" re-enacting a childhood ritual) and thieves, are already in some sense either immune to boundaries or willing to cross them, and the result of the switch presents us with an ironic image that even we as "boundary abiding" folks can see the humor in.[20]

It is also noteworthy that the tradition can be practiced only during Christmas, a holiday season when playful behavior is tolerated, even sanctioned in our society. It is very difficult to imagine the same family practicing similar mischief with a Bible or a painting of Christ throughout the year.

In addition to providing an illustration of pranksterism empowered by a collective sense of religious domain, the tradition raises questions concerning relationships between the forms it has taken as a family custom and as a folk literature motif. There appears to be no genetic relation between versions of Aarne-Thompson tale type 1525M, *Mak and the Sheep*, and the dramatization of the motif in the Illinois family's holiday play. The writer concludes, "There would seem to be something very powerful and appealing in the image of the animal in the cradle that would cause it to arise, seemingly spontaneously, in so many places, times, and situations."[21] My daughter, when she was seven, initiated such an exchange in our own nativity scene. Even now, almost a decade later, a Christmas elf is surreptitiously placed in the manger scene, a token violation of sacred space by the secular.

It is tempting to consider these related incidents as independent inventions which have become traditionalized over time. The many narrative versions of Aarne-Thompson 1525M, *Mak and the Sheep*,[22] may be indebted to medieval literary sources, which in turn may be based on earlier oral tradition. Other enactments, like the Illinois holiday custom, may be initiated because the human imagination is stimulated to probe the boundaries which separate one kind of order from another. The categories of animal and human are violated in the literary analogues and the categories of the sacred and the profane by a youngster in twentieth-century Illinois.[23] His transgression of the boundary is satisfying to other family members and tolerated by the parents, at least for the duration of the Christmas season, and a family tradition which relies on a profound religious distinction is born.

I will conclude this examination of religious folklore as I began it, with a personal consideration of folk tradition in the Lutheran worship service. Worship style and aesthetic preference may or may not be related to official doctrine, but they are usually learned through customary example in informal ways. Lutheran worship style, formal and predictable, is an important trait often referred to by Lutherans and former Lutherans in discussions of Sunday services. It seems to play a significant role for the group in differentiating Lutheran from non-Lutheran religious experience. When an alternative worship format is used in a traditional Lutheran congregation, for example, an improvised service using folksong or gospel music, members' responses are positive only if the change is an occasional one and a return to the regular worship service format is guaranteed. I once chaired a worship and music committee meeting in which the pastor suggested an alternative service each Sunday, one that would not rely on the traditional liturgy and would incorporate popular music forms. A committee member responded, "That's a good idea, but we'd still have two 'real' services, wouldn't we?" Most Lutherans hold to a rigidly defined concept of what constitutes a worship service, and continued deviation from that model, though still within the boundaries of Christian worship, is regarded as a threat to the congregational sense of Lutheran community.

When a revised service book is introduced into the national body of Lutheran congregations, variation and change initiated by liturgical and musical specialists within the church can cause problems in local congregations. The 1978 revision of the liturgy, prepared by a North American Inter-Lutheran Commission on Worship, included a ritual known as "the passing of the peace," during which worshippers are asked to greet one another before the sacrament of communion with the words "Peace be with you."[24] Almost a decade later, popular response to this innovation is mixed. Many people still feel uncomfortable during the exchange (although it is a tradition that has antecedents in the early church), and either resist participating in it, or, more likely, do so in a quick, perfunctory manner. One of my acquaintances so resents the ritual that if he is seated with family or good friends he purposefully transgresses its intent and substitutes the words "Have a banana" for "Peace be with you."

Church decor focuses Lutheran attitude toward religious art and its theological implications. The empty cross is much more common than the crucifix in Lutheran sanctuaries, reflecting the conventional position of church leaders in the past that Lutheran doctrine emphasizes the resurrected Christ instead of the crucified Christ, as in the Roman Catholic church. This distinction, now on the wane as Lutheran and

Roman Catholic leaders engage in ecumenical dialogue, is still articulated, however, by lay Lutherans. The use of the crucifix in worship processions in my own congregation prompted several calls from concerned members when I chaired the worship and music committee. Imagine the lay response in a northern Illinois Lutheran church when its leaders chose to display a contemporary depiction of the crucified Christ above the altar: the sculpture of a nude torso, the lower portion of its arms and legs dismembered.

A Lutheran congregation in California now faces a related question of church decor. Because the congregation is attempting to make welcome neighborhood Hispanic-Americans who have close associations with Roman Catholicism, the church council has decided to include a representation of the Virgin Mary in the sanctuary. In spite of insistence that using such a figure does not sanction acceptance of the Roman Catholic concept of the Virgin Mary as "Mediatrix of all Graces, Co-redemptorix of man, and Queen of Heaven,"[25] the innovation is controversial, even for Lutherans far removed from the congregation. When I described it to several midwestern Lutheran relatives, who grew up in the church in the 1940s and 1950s, their response was one of surprise and dismay. Traditional aesthetic norms are often associated with religious belief; they can be important factors in a congregation's resistance to change.

These details of worship style and attitude toward worship behavior, it seems to me, indicate an ambivalence about the liturgical format of the Lutheran service. On the one hand, reverent demeanor and formalized behavior are valued as appropriate, but on the other hand, some forms of ceremonialism, for example the use of incense in worship and bowing to the altar each time it is approached, are regarded as extreme, ostentatious, and by some, as dangerously close to Roman Catholic worship practices (at least those commonly followed in Catholic congregations before Vatican II). Some Lutheran pastors, sensitive to this distinction and resistant to elaborate liturgical rituals suggested by the Inter-Lutheran Commission on Worship in 1978, use the term "chancel prancers" to describe their peers who are more

61

enthusiastic about high church ceremonialism. Most Lutherans sense this ambivalence and are aware of the spectrum of liturgical aesthetics within the national body of congregations, but stalwartly resist innovations feared to affect the liturgical core of the Lutheran worship service. Those very anxious about variation in the service call their pastor and worship and music deacon or voice their opinions at annual congregational meetings. Others complain in private and nostalgically contemplate the worship service traditions familiar to them from childhood. And some, like the woman who mockingly admonished, "We know what happens to people who put out the eternal light!" and the man who murmurs, "Have a banana" in the midst of a worship service, use humor to satirize certain traditional attitudes and to criticize liturgical innovation.

Garrison Keillor, who has created the town of Lake Wobegon, Minnesota, out of his own personal experience and sensitive observation of community folkways in the upper Midwest, has commented insightfully on his childhood response to Roman Catholic ritual as a member of the Sanctified Brethren. His guilty attraction to it is, in some ways, rather Lutheran:

> My affections were not pure. They were tainted with a sneaking admiration of Catholics — Catholic Christmas, Easter, the Living Rosary, and the Blessing of the Animals, all magnificent — especially the Feast Day of St. Francis, which they did right out in the open, a feast for the eyes . . . .
> "Christians," my uncle Al used to say, "do not go in for show."[26]

At the Lake Wobegon Memorial Day observance he again envies the Catholics for their procession from their church, Our Lady of Perpetual Responsibility. It is elaborate and brilliant, but he must join the municipal Lutheran procession made up of "nothing but a bugler, two flags, the Sons of Knute, and a big crowd. 'Christians don't go in for show,' my father says, explaining the difference."[27] We might revise this statement to relate it to Lutheran attitudes toward liturgical worship: Lutherans believe that they do not go in for show (which may surprise nonliturgical

Protestants), but they insist that their services follow a predictable liturgy with little room for informality and the idiosyncratic expression of emotion.

My discussion of aesthetic norms in the worship service and sanctuary and the congregational reactions when they are not followed does not represent all Lutherans, past and present-day. These illustrations of traditional concerns about the manner of worship and sanctuary decor, however, apply to many Lutherans, especially those raised in rural midwestern congregations in which the tensions between liturgical worship practices and high church ceremonialism as well as anti-Catholic biases are matters of historical record. Today, ecumenical efforts by Lutheran leaders and the encouragement of alternative worship forms are prominent at the national level of denominational organization. A folk aesthetic persists, however, informed by decades of worship experience and related to doctrinal emphases absorbed in childhood. Such traditions comprise an important category of religious folklore that may be found in various forms in a congregation's worship life, no matter what the denomination.

This examination of religious folk tradition has concentrated on Christian groups in North America because of their familiarity and accessibility to folklore students. The same questions and suggestions can be used in exploring religious folk traditions in non-Christian and nonwestern contexts — for example, Native American religious communities, orthodox Jewish congregations, or utopian communitarian settlements founded on religious principles. The subject matter is diverse, its various genres multifunctional, and its relation to nonfolk traditions and nonfolk institutions complex. A summary generalization of even more importance is that, whether an insider or an outsider, a believer or a nonbeliever, religious folk tradition must be investigated from the inside out and the point of view of its participants must be addressed. In order to understand the meanings of religious folk tradition, we must understand the religious belief and experience of its practitioners. In the process, we are allowed privileged insights into some of the most fundamental concerns of humankind.

63

Notes

1.   A recent Gallup poll states that 55% of the respondents believe that religion is very important in their lives, 71% are church members, and 42% attend church in a typical week. The *Los Angeles Times* Syndicate, reprinted in "Religion: A Constant in Our Lives," *Champaign-Urbana News-Gazette* (Illinois), 16 January 1986, p. A5.

2.   *New Catholic Encyclopedia*, 1967 ed., s.v. "Epiphany, Feast of," by C. Smith, and *Encyclopedia of the Lutheran Church*, 1965 ed., s.v. "Worship, Seasons of," by Edgar S. Brown, Jr.

3.   Philip H. Pfatteicher and Carlos R. Messerli, *Manual on the Liturgy: Lutheran Book of Worship* (Minneapolis: Augsburg Publishing House, 1979), 279-80, 282, 327.

4.   Helpful discussions of the distinction between the sacred and the profane, important in many religious traditions, appear in Mircea Eliade, *The Sacred and the Profane: The Nature of Religion*, trans. Willard R. Trask (New York: Harcourt, Brace, & World, 1959) and Roger Caillois, *Man and the Sacred*, trans. Meyer Barash (Glencoe, Ill.: The Free Press, 1959).

5.   The advertisements for sanctuary lamps in a recent Lutheran supply catalog make no reference to noteworthy religious attributes of the object. See *Ecclesiastical Arts: 1983-1985* (Minneapolis: Augsburg Publishing House, 1985), 15.

6.   Pfatteicher and Messerli, *Manual on the Liturgy*, and *Encyclopedia of the Lutheran Church*, s.v. "Lights," by Edward T. Horn III.

7.   Michael Argyle in the *International Encyclopedia of the Social Sciences*, 1968 ed., s.v. "Religious Observances," suggests a more detailed categorization of religious observance types.

8.   Melville J. Herskovits, chap. VII, "The Contemporary Scene: Africanisms in Religious Life," in *The Myth of the Negro Past* (Boston: Beacon Press, 1958), 207-60, and E. Franklin Frazier, chap. 1, "The Religion of the Slaves," in *The Negro Church in America* (New York: Schocken Books, 1964), 1-19.

9.   See, e.g., B.A. Botkin, *Lay My Burden Down: A Folk History of Slavery* (Chicago: The University of Chicago Press, 1945); Norman R. Yetman, *Life*

Under the "Peculiar Institution": Selections from the Slave Narrative Collection (New York: Holt, Rinehart, & Winston, Inc., 1970); and Charles Joyner, chap. 5, "Come by Here, Lord," in *Down by the Riverside; A South Carolina Slave Community* (Urbana, Ill.: University of Illinois Press, 1984), 141-71.

10.   Harold Courlander, *Negro Folk Music, U.S.A.* (New York: Columbia University Press, 1970), 34-79, 194-200.

11.   Weston La Barre, *They Shall Take Up Serpents* (Minneapolis, Minn.: University of Minnesota Press, 1962) and Steven M. Kane, "Ritual Possession in a Southern Appalachian Religious Sect," *Journal of American Folklore* 87(1974): 293-302, arrive at different conclusions in their discussions of Pentecostal snake handling.

12.   This and the following illustrations are drawn from informal interviews, personal experience, and ethnographic literature concerning religious tradition.

13.   The ethnographic details in this discussion are drawn from the following student papers in my personal files: Susanne Macander, "Polish-American Holiday Customs and Their Probable Origins" (1973), Julie Mallak, "Polish Folk Traditions" (1976), and Stephanie Meyer, "Polish Christmas Traditions in the Lesiecki Family" (1983).

14.   Mallak, 34.

15.   Ibid., 36.

16.   My description and analysis of this family tradition is indebted to an excellent student paper by Leslie Wainger, "The Pig in the Manger" (1977), in my personal files.

17.   Wainger, 5-6.

18.   *The Norton Anthology of English Literature*, ed. M.H. Abrams et al., 2 vols. (New York: W.W. Norton & Co., 1979), 1: 344-66.

19.   Wainger, 7-8.

20.   Ibid., 8.

21.   Ibid., 12.

22.   American versions of Aarne-Thompson 1525M can be found in "Analogues to the Mak Story," *Journal of American Folklore* 47(1934): 378-81; "Another Analogue to the Mak Story," *Southern Folklore Quarterly* 3(1937): 5-6;

and Richard M. Dorson, *American Negro Folktales* (Greenwich, Conn.: Fawcett Publications, 1967), 137-39.

23.   Mary Douglas, throughout *Purity and Danger: An Analysis of Concepts of Pollution and Taboo* (New York: Frederick A. Praeger, 1966), discusses cultural categories and their importance.

24.   *Lutheran Book of Worship*, prepared by the churches participating in the Inter-Lutheran Commission on Worship: Lutheran Church in America, the American Lutheran Church, the Evangelical Lutheran Church of Canada, and the Lutheran Church-Missouri Synod (Minneapolis, Minn.: Augsburg Publishing House, 1978), 66, 86, 107.

25.   *Catholicism*, ed. George Brantl (New York: George Braziller, 1962), 77.

26.   Garrison Keillor, *Lake Wobegon Days* (New York: Viking Press, 1985), 103.

27.   Ibid., 118-19.

Further Readings

Several works are helpful in clarifying concepts and definitions in the study of folk religion and religious folk tradition. A special issue of *Western Folklore* 33(1974), *Symposium on Folk Religion*, edited by Don Yoder, includes a useful discussion, "Toward a Definition of Folk Religion" and an introductory bibliography on folk religion, both by Yoder. Another article by the same author, "Official Religion Versus Folk Religion," *Pennsylvania Folklife* 15 (1965-66): 36-52, discusses the distinction between two major kinds of religious tradition and draws its illustrations from Pennsylvania Dutch folk culture. John C. Messenger, "Folk Religion," in *Folklore and Folklife: An Introduction*, edited by Richard M. Dorson (Chicago: The University of Chicago Press, 1972), 271-32, defines the topic from an anthropological point of view and illustrates his generalizations with examples from the Irish-Catholic folk culture of the Aran Islands.

"Religion as a Cultural System" by Clifford Geertz and "Religion:

Problems of Definition and Explanation" by Melford E. Spiro, in *Anthropological Approaches to the Study of Religion*, edited by Michael Banton (London: Tavistock Publications, 1966), 1-46, 85-126, are excellent theoretical explorations of religious culture. Similar discussions can be found in the *International Encyclopedia of the Social Sciences*, vol. 13 (n.p.: The Macmillan Co. and The Free Press, 1968), under the topics "Religion," "Religious Observance," "Religious Organization," and "Religious Specialists."

The well-known *Reader in Comparative Religion: An Anthropological Approach*, edited by William A. Lessa and Evon Z. Vogt (New York: Harper & Row, Publishers, Inc., 1965), contains many provocative ethnographic documents and articles about religious behavior, for example, myth, ritual, witchcraft, the function of religion, symbolism, and methods of analysis. Its topics range from Aztec sacrificial rituals to American Memorial Day customs.

The following references concern three selected religious groups well represented in folklore studies. They are not intended to provide a complete list of citations, but to indicate the range of materials useful in the study of religious folk tradition.

Voodoo beliefs and rituals in black-American culture have been described by anthropologists, folklorists, and nonacademic writers. Zora Neale Hurston in *Mules and Men* (Bloomington, Ind.: Indiana University Press, 1978), 193-252, provides a vivid account of her apprenticeship to hoodoo "doctors" in Louisiana. A more conventional scholarly approach can be found in Alfred Metraux's detailed anthropological study, *Voodoo in Haiti*, translated by Hugo Charteris (New York: Oxford University Press, 1959). The four-volume *Hoodoo-Conjuration-Witchcraft-Rootwork* (Hannibal, Mo.: Western Publishing, Inc., 1970-74), by Harry Middleton Hyatt, an indefatigable collector, is a treasure trove of raw data. For an interesting example of the relation between medical research and religious folk belief, see Claudia Wallis, "Zombies: Do They Exist?" *Time*, 17 October 1983.

Scholarly interest in American Pentecostal religious experience is well represented in recent folklore publications. Elaine Lawless, in

"Brothers and Sisters: Pentecostals as a Religious Folk Group," *Western Folklore* 42(1983): 85-104, explores the sociocultural boundaries used to maintain a coherent sense of group identity, and in "Shouting for the Lord: The Power of Women's Speech in the Pentecostal Religious Service," *Journal of American Folklore* 96(1983): 434-59, describes and analyzes traditional expressive verbal art in the Pentecostal service. "Ritual Possession in a Southern Appalachian Religious Sect" by Steven M. Kane, *Journal of American Folklore* 87(1974): 434-59, is one of many investigations of snake handling in Appalachian Pentecostal Holiness worship. William M. Clements examines Pentecostal healing traditions in "Ritual Expectation in Pentecostal Healing Experience," *Western Folklore* 40(1981): 139-48, and the rhetorical strategies of Pentecostal radio preachers in "The Rhetoric of the Radio Ministry," *Journal of American Folklore* 87(1974): 318-27. Documentary film is another source of information concerning religious experience and tradition, for example, the remarkable *Joy Unspeakable* (¾" videocassette, color, 59 min., available from the Audio-Visual Center, Indiana University, Bloomington, Indiana 47405).

The religious folk traditions of the Mormons, or Latter-day Saints, have been well documented by folklorists. Austin E. and Alta S. Fife survey the wide range of Mormon folklore and relate it to important events in Mormon history in *Saints of Sage and Saddle: The Folklore of the Mormons* (Bloomington, Ind.: Indiana University Press, 1956). Oral traditions concerning the three Nephites have been studied by Austin Fife, "The Legend of the Three Nephites among the Mormons," *Journal of American Folklore* 53(1940): 1-49, Hector Lee, *The Three Nephites: The Substance and Significance of the Legend in Folklore*, University of New Mexico Publications in Language and Literature No. 2 (Albuquerque, N.M.: University of New Mexico Press, 1949), and William A. Wilson, "Mormon Legends of the Three Nephites Collected at Indiana University," *Indiana Folklore* 2(1969): 3-35. Traditional Mormon songs, many related to Mormon legendry, can be found in Thomas E. Cheney's work, *Mormon Songs from the Rocky Mountains: A Compilation of Mormon Folksong*, American Folklore Society Memoirs Series, vol. 53 (Austin,

Tex.: University of Texas Press, 1960). *Mormon Folklore*, a special issue of the *Utah Historical Quarterly* 44(1976), edited by William A. Wilson, is a collection of essays which interrelate Mormon beliefs with Mormon folk tradition and includes an excellent survey of Mormon folklore scholarship.

Chapter 4
Occupational Folklore

Robert McCarl

The study of the lore and skills of work has paralleled changes in the ways in which Americans have historically adapted themselves to their environment. The occupational experiences of cowboys, miners, and lumberjacks generated work songs, jargon, and new skills which were collected by folklorists as examples of a uniquely American response to the frontier. As the variety and complexity of the work shifted from rural to urban settings, folklorists began to expand their investigations to include the lore of urban occupations such as mill and factory work. The study of occupational folklore today focuses not only on the verbal forms of occupational jargon and narrative, but also on the customs designed to mark an individual's passage through a respective career, as well as the various skills and techniques which must be informally learned and performed by a worker in any job. Together the techniques, verbal expressions, and customs of work comprise a wide-ranging way of life in the workplace which folklorists have termed occupational folklife.[1]

As any novice worker knows, the first days on the job can be a nightmare of new terms, actions, and techniques. Experienced workers sending new welders for a glass rod to weld a broken window, or apprentice meatcutters to find the meatcase stretcher for a load of roasts, suggests in a very forceful manner that in spite of what new workers think they know, there are traditional ways of doing things in the workplace which workers themselves create, evaluate, and protect. The *canon of work technique* refers to this body of informal knowledge used to get the job done; at the same time, it establishes a hierarchy of skilled workers based on their individual abilities to exhibit that knowledge. The canon of work technique is not a law or a written set of rules but a standard that workers themselves create and control. It lies at the heart of any work culture because it forms the technical base out of which workers must derive their satisfaction or dissatisfaction with a particular job. In order to understand the importance of the canon of technique performance, however, we must find a way to document the variety of ways in which workers themselves create and expand the canon in their daily work lives.[2]

Perhaps the most useful way to think of the technical base of any work culture (whether the inherited body of knowledge passed on by retail sales people in a department store or the techniques employed by a machinist to create a stamping die), is to look at the various levels of technique within each setting. Members of any trade generate a body of traditional work knowledge. The associated techniques range from the simplest to the most complex. Easily learned skills, like sizing dresses for sales persons and reading micrometers for machinists, lead eventually to very complex techniques like marketing a whole new design or creating a new milling procedure. The simplest mundane skills become unconscious reflexes whereas the more unusual innovations and techniques become near-legendary in the trade. Between these two extremes lie the central, daily technique performances in which the informally learned skills are performed by individuals under the scrutiny of co-workers who evaluate a worker's status in the culture on the basis of these acts. In order to understand how these performances can be documented, however, we need to look more closely into a specific technique performance and explore the ways in which folklore is expressed within such activity.

One of the more useful ways to document a performance in a work culture is to look for *cultural scenes*. A cultural scene is a recurrent social situation in which two or more people share some aspect of their cultural knowledge or folklore. An end-of-the-week get-together at the local bar after work, a coffee break during the day, a quick conversation in the teacher's lounge, or a critique of a particular fire while fire fighters clean up the equipment are all examples of cultural scenes. As daily work rituals, these scenes provide the folklorist with an excellent opportunity to see how the knowledge of the workplace is both acted upon and evaluated in a natural setting.[3]

In the following scene within fire fighting culture, we can see how folklore is actually performed within a contemporary work culture. Members of an engine (hose wagon) company and truck (ladder truck) company in the same firehouse have just returned from a tough fire on the fourth floor of a downtown office building. The fire, located in a small closet in a corner office, had been difficult to locate. It had also been difficult to extinguish since a lack of ventilation caused polyvinyl chloride fumes to fill the hall with odorless but deadly gas. This critique took place as the fire fighters washed out their face pieces from their Scott-Air backpacks and refilled the air bottles at the large, compressed-air tanks at the rear of the firehouse.

Officer to rookie: Kid, you worked your ass off tonight. Turn around here and let's see if it's still on.

1st fire fighter: Who ran out of air?

2d fire fighter: The guy who wouldn't leave when his bell rang. Had to hang in there and play big bimbo.

1st fire fighter: Hell, I could ring your bell with your mask not even on.

3d fire fighter: I want to tell you something, man [to the rookie]. We shoulda had it, buddy; we went right on by that damn fire. But that's what you got all them other guys for is to back you up when you can't find it, but we shoulda had it.

Rookie: I tell you I went into that room and looked around. I thought we were really gonna come into something there on the left.

3d fire fighter: I hung around as long as I could. But after the third "Get your ass out of here," by the white hat over there, I couldn't ignore him any longer.

1st fire fighter: Yeah, when it's time to get out you got to get out. Like those fires we caught on the other tour when W. knocked him on his ass trying to get out.

2d fire fighter: That was on Third Street, right? When I was on the pipe?

1st fire fighter: The one after that.

2d fire fighter: No, I wasn't on that.

1st fire fighter: What fire was it that W. either run out of air or whatever, but he about killed you when he came out of there?

Officer: Municipal Building.

2d fire fighter: Oh Municipal . . . oh man, I hadn't run out of air, I was just scared.

Officer: Oh you were? Well then you were the only one. Just because there was live ammunition and tear gas exploding everywhere . . . .

4th fire fighter: Yeah, I wasn't scared at all. I just decided I'd stroll out to the street and lay there on my face for fifteen minutes trying to get my breath. I think I only sucked up about six or seven inches of concrete off of that sidewalk trying to get some air.[4]

Even within this short cultural scene, we are provided with a variety of insights into the work culture of fire fighters through their expression and evaluation of the canon of technique performance. In the actual fire fighting situation itself, the rookie must have performed his job well, as illustrated in the recognition by the officer that he "worked his ass off." This compliment in front of the experienced members of the fire company suggests that the rookie or probationary fire fighter is progressing well in his on-the-job training. Notice as well that, when he does speak during the rest of the critique, he is careful to maintain a somewhat soft-spoken, self-effacing tone which is a clue that he recognizes the customary deference paid by novices to experienced workers.

The critique also illustrates the concerns that urban fire fighters have about adequate air supply in a burning building, and the lack of respect they have for a fellow fire fighter "who wouldn't leave when his bell rang. Had to hang in there and play big bimbo." An experienced fire fighter knows just how long he can safely push his air supply before the warning bell tells him that he has only three minutes of emergency air left and must exit the burning building. This knowledge is based not only on his previous fire fighting experience, but also on the accumulated technical knowledge he has learned from others through both example and narrative.

He is recognized as a positive example of the technique canon when he pushes the envelope of safety afforded by the air pack to only a safe and warranted extreme. If he were to violate this envelope and "hang in there and play big bimbo" to the point that he might have to be rescued himself, he would be ridiculed for having acted improperly, and his status in the culture would be diminished.

Finally, this scene illustrates the variety of contexts in which cultural information is linked over time and space to form the canon of technique performance. The specific fire critique about the events in the office building are connected to both the violation of appropriate technique by the lax fire fighter who stayed in the building too long, and to a fire in the Municipal Building in which a police storage room for ammunition and tear gas exploded. This linkage of current knowledge to the experiences of the past forms perhaps the most important aspect of the scene from a folklorist's perspective. It illustrates not only that a continuum of experiential knowledge forms the traditional canon of the trade, but also that verbal evaluations of these past techniques provide opportunities for members of the culture to experience events and evaluate performances they did not even witness. Both the fires of the past and the fire fighters' critiques of those fires form a collective standard against which individual fire fighters must measure themselves.

Technique forms the background of any occupational experience, from the proper way to grasp a tool to the development of a new procedure. Between these two extremes lie the central, daily technique performances and their verbal evaluations (such as the post-fire critique given above) which comprise what I have called the canon of technique performance. Yet even as we recognize the central importance of actual technical performances in the workplace, we are immediately confronted with the difficulty of documenting these complex human activities. The movements and interactions necessary to make a bed or to clean the house, for example, are very difficult to document without film or videotape. The situation is further complicated in the workplace because much of what goes on is either covert, occurs too quickly to be measured, or is impossible to document. Perhaps in the future we will be able to use less expensive

75

video equipment to record the processes that form the basis of work culture. But until that happens, we must rely more upon verbal evaluations of technique to document occupational culture.

This leads us to consider verbal art in the workplace because these more easily documented performances of critiques and narratives allow the folklorist to develop an appreciation of any work culture. As we saw in the cultural scene above, the terms and informal names used to describe elements in a work culture form a unique work language made up of informally passed jargon. References to ventilation (allowing super-heated smoke and gas to escape), bells going off (a sound indicator that the air pack is almost empty), the white hat (the color of hat worn by an officer), and tour (length of time on duty during one shift or six-day rotation) are all terms unique to the trade and understandable only to its members. Yet verbal expressions, even at this minimal level of naming things and people in the workplace, give insights into the fire fighter's unique cultural perspective.

The verbal arts in the workplace range from the naming of things and events in the occupation to complex, individual narratives. Between these two extremes lie the more common conversational forms of critique, joking, and narrative exchange that link and extend experience beyond the immediacy of a given moment. The vehicle through which all this takes place is *metaphor* and by starting with this aspect of occupational folklife, we can begin to develop the basis for a more systematic approach to the verbal arts in work culture.

A metaphor is simply a symbol that extends meaning by linking two previously unconnected ideas. A fire fighter, for example, might use the metaphorical phrase, "He laid out short," to describe the poor planning of a hose-line man who didn't have enough hose to reach a fire. Yet this same phrase can be used to describe any situation of insufficiency, such as not having enough bed sheets to go around during a night shift or enough steaks to serve for dinner: "Well, Jimmy, you sure laid out short for dinner tonight." This relationship between verbal expression and cultural terminology illustrates the way in which many occupations literally shape the cultural perspectives of their practitioners. In addition to creating a unique occupational jargon or language within each trade, these metaphors also provide the folklorist with an appreciation of how the culture of work can be most successfully approached. If researchers can participate in the trade, and observe the members of a work culture actually interacting, they will quickly perceive that these terms and metaphorical expressions form the basis for the more elaborate, extended verbal performances. An awareness of the impact of occupational experience at even this minimal level of cultural expression will also reveal that nicknames (derived from looks or stature ["short wheels," "the hook"]); work processes (like the replacement of the hose in the hose bed ["take up" or "rack hose"]); and even certain locations in the city (for example, Fourteenth Street ["the corridor"]) reflect a unique cultural perspective by metaphorically personalizing virtually everything that the members of the culture experience in their work. Fire fighters, doctors, houseworkers, and the members of any work culture perceive the world differently because their work forces them to describe their experiences in occupational terms and that description reinforces their unique vocational perspective.

Beyond this basic metaphorical level of verbal expression are the more central, conversational forms of interaction which draw upon and elaborate the basic metaphors cited above by weaving them into the fabric of collective narrative performances. If behavior is anything and everything that happens in a work culture, and conduct is simply behavior under the influence of cultural norms and rules, then performance suggests that members of the culture assume a responsibility to their audience of fellow workers to act or speak in a certain manner.[5] At the heart of any work culture, these genres of verbal performance vary from joking behavior to verbal critique and storytelling or "shooting the breeze," "telling lies," or whatever term is used in the particular trade. Beyond these central, conversational performances are the unusual yet highly significant occasions in a work culture when an individual performs an extended narrative that is not only unique in its length and complexity, but also unusual for its personal introspection. These extended accounts (what we might call full performances) will be discussed in more detail below.[6]

Robert McCarl

Joking behavior in any work culture is an extremely important form of social control. In the fire service, to be joked with, or "messed with" is a sign that the other members of the trade know you well enough to kid you or play pranks on you. These jokes and pranks create and reinforce a sense of community so essential in fire fighting culture. Usually, only members of equal status within a trade joke with each other or "rag" each other, because supervisors and those they direct actually live in two subcultural worlds within the workplace. Although members of these two groups might share a type of joking relationship, rarely is it as incisive as the type of verbal interaction which takes place between equals. The following account provides an illustration:

> [After the change of shifts in the firehouse at seven in the morning, a group of fire fighters are reading the morning papers and having a cup of coffee]:
> 1st fire fighter: [Finishes coffee and looks around at the other two men seated at his table] Anybody else want a refill?
> 2d fire fighter: [Slides cup over the table] Yeah, and see if you can get it right this time, will ya?
> 1st fire fighter: Why sure and is there anything else I can get you while I'm up?
> 2d fire fighter: Now that you mention it . . . .
> 1st fire fighter: After all, if you drink coffee the way you drive the damn truck [ladder truck], you need all the help we can give you. . . .
> 2d fire fighter: A rose among dandelions . . . .
> 1st fire fighter: Hey, Billy, got any training wheels for this cup? Wouldn't want any unnecessary P.O.D. [sick leave].[7]

Through joking exchanges like these, co-workers continue to monitor their changing moods and feelings. An artfully phrased comeback or witty sarcasm which either tests or reflects tension or apprehension (as in the assessment of the truck driver's driving abilities) allow members of the trade to evaluate serious subjects under the guise of humor. As fire fighters put it, you have to be able to throw as well as receive these verbal "darts." One of the first indications that something is wrong among the members of a work group is the absence of this type of banter. A close relationship also exists between one's position in the canon of work technique and joking relationships. A joke about technical ability (such as the one above about the truck driver) is only permissible when one has an established reputation as an accomplished worker. If this individual were not accomplished or were considered incompetent, then a joke about the need for training wheels would be no joke at all, but a message designed to force the incompetent worker out of the group, or at least challenge his right to the job.

In addition to joking behavior and the post-fire critique discussed previously, the most central form of verbal interaction in any work culture is simply telling stories. Referred to by many terms ("telling lies," "swapping war stories," or in the fire service as "pumping water"), these naturally occurring narrative exchanges lie at the heart of folklife. Through the performance of these work-related accounts, individuals reveal and confirm their position in the informal canon of technique performance. The following storytelling session provides a useful illustration:

> [It is late at night in the firehouse and a group of four fire fighters are sitting around the watch desk at the front of the firehouse drinking coffee and telling stories.]
>
> *Olson:* Another thing I learned is that when these garden-type apartment buildings were first being made, they had these metal doors that were supposed to be fire doors and all that. Well the walls were brick and just beyond the brick there wasn't nothing but Sheetrock. So if there is a fire in there, instead of tearing out the door — and tearing out any door is a lot of work; particularly if there is a dead bolt on it — just take that Halligan bar [forcible entry tool] and smack that corner brick right above where the doorknob is and smash it through the wall, reach around and unlock your door.
>
> *Saunders:* That's like the other night when we got off of the elevator. What I was looking for was, like a lot of times you can't get in coming from the elevator and you got to back up and go down to the floor beneath and come up the stairs . . . .
>
> *Olson:* That's what happened in that high rise fire — we couldn't-a gotten

it from the elevator. I tell ya, those elevators are great for saving time getting to the fire, but you can get tore up on an elevator. That's why if some guy gets on the elevator without a mask, it's his ass.

Saunders: You know it is usually pretty cool and nothing is really up there to worry about. But that one time if you get up there without a mask and all of a sudden the stuff comes down bad and you don't have a mask — you can be in big trouble . . . .

Olson: I remember at HEW one time — this is where I really learned my lesson. This guy Bill W. took a mask in and the officers who were along did not. So Bill says to one of these guys, "Here, take my mask." And I said, "Man, you're gonna be sorry you did that." And we were joking, you know, just joking . . . thinking that we had probably, you know, a pound and a half's worth of fire. [Gestures an explosion with two hands mushrooming out from his chest] *Puggghh!* Like a blast furnace, man. And he's crawlin' around underneath me because he didn't have anything to protect himself and we were all down with our faces to the floor sucking air.

Saunders: And if you're running the bar you have to have that mask on when you hit the street or else. The officer who we used to have here drilled that into our heads day after day. I tell you, we went to a fire around the corner here one night and we got on the elevator and neither one of us had one. Kinda deliberate because we had a kind of an attitude. And he goes, "Where's you all's mask?" And we went, "We don't have one." And this guy was tough, an ex-Marine. And he said, "All right. When we get there, if there is anything there, you two stay right beside me." So we're both grinning at each other knowing that it's probably gonna be false [a false alarm]. So we finally get to the floor and thought we smelled a mattress burning and they're always nasty. So anyway, the door opened and I mean the stuff was on the floor. And he grabbed both of us and threw us in there and man we took a whippin' trying to get those things out of there.

Olson: And the thing is that that was a hotel storage thing and they had a whole roomful of mattresses to take care of . . . .[8]

This narrative session illustrates the importance of storytelling in occupational culture. Unlike a critique in which the members of the work group simply relate their individual perspectives about a specific event, the storytelling session provides each member of the group with an opportunity to match his experiences with those of the other participants. The topic, in this case not taking an air pack or mask into the fire, provides each fire fighter with an opportunity to narrate a story that parallels in style, length, and substance the one that preceded it. Just as the rookie in the post-fire critique maintained a self-effacing tone in deference to the more experienced men in the company, both Olson and Saunders reveal aspects of their individual points of view through the stories they tell. Olson's story about not taking a mask into a fire and Saunders's account about challenging the authority of a tough officer, reveal more than simply lessons about fire fighting technique; they illustrate the importance of presenting and performing narrative in a prescribed manner. By telling these stories in front of other members of the trade, Olson and Saunders not only confirm their status as knowledgeable insiders who know the importance of the requisite technique, they also use their respective narratives to illustrate the results of nonprofessional behavior. These accounts are in a very literal sense lessons in proper cultural performance.

From the storytelling session to the more unusual extended personal narrative, we move from the more collective performance forms to the most individual. In extended personal narratives individuals draw attention to themselves over a long period of time. Lengthy stories do not occur in occupational folklore very often. Although we can learn a great deal from this type of verbal art, the extended personal narrative is usually performed in an interview context or during retirement or promotional dinners where old-timers congregate, and are provided with an opportunity to talk about the way things were done in their day. The following narrative provides an illustration of this type of story and also acts as an introduction to the final area of occupational folklife that will be discussed in this chapter, custom:

[The scene is the sitting room of one of the oldest firehouses in the city. The table in the sitting room is covered with white sheets, covered with the remnants of an elaborate meal of roast beef, potatoes and gravy, and homemade apple pie. A fire fighter in this house has just been promoted to the rank of sergeant and he and the nonretired pumper driver who broke him into the trade are talking over old times.]

Sergeant: Ya know, I can't believe all of the crazy things we've seen in the five and a half years I've been here . . . some of the things people do . . . .

Retiree: I was talking to Mac on the way in tryin' to remember your first fire when you got assigned over here. But one that I did remember was about four o'clock in the mornin' and it was fully involved when we got there. Black smoke just boiling out of there — second floor. As soon as we got the ladder up, we get a young couple down. And then we looked up in the other window and here was this old lady, and so you and I put up the ladder and that woman musta weighed about nine thousand pounds if she weighed an ounce. You remember that one? How you got her out of that window I'll never know, but she slid about halfway down and you had an arm and I had a leg, but she ended up on top of both of us and she musta weighed about four hundred pounds. I'm not kiddin'. Now this is the mother and father, young couple, right? Now those two-story rows up there aren't that big, right. Two windows up there with a little partition in between, and we took the couple out of that window and the old lady out of the other. But it wasn't until that big, fat woman hit the ground that they told us there was a baby up there. So we went back in there and neither one of us had a mask. The fire was in the rear, in the kitchen, burnin' real good. We crawled around in the damn room for what seemed forever and I thought I was gonna die. Finally we found the kid, between the windows in a crib. Either one of them could have picked him up and handed him out the window. But they waited until they were on the ground and told us about him.

McCarl: Dead?

Sergeant: No — smoked up pretty good, but he was tough, made it.[9]

The extended personal narrative combines not only the requisite awareness and critique of work technique, but also provides the narrator with an opportunity to extend personal points of view beyond the normal cultural boundaries. My presence as a member of the audience alters the context of the narrative event and forces the retiree to tell a story about the new sergeant and himself without appearing to be bragging or drawing unusual attention to his own abilities. Unlike naturally occurring critiques, storytelling, or joking sessions, the extended personal narrative (as full performance) is a much more self-conscious verbal form in which a narrator assumes full responsibility to an audience and consciously plays the part of storyteller until he has completed the account.

In the narrative cited above, the retiree recounts an event that occurred five years before. His story, however, is not told for self-aggrandizement but is performed within the context of this promotional dinner to celebrate the passage of the sergeant from a fire fighter to an officer. The structure of the account parallels the events as they unfolded in a manner typical of all fire experience stories. Within the context of the promotional dinner, the story acts as a tribute to the sergeant and a somewhat self-conscious linkage of the older man's teachings to the younger fire fighter's promotion. An important aspect of occupational folklore, the extended personal narrative is perhaps most important for the interpersonal and introspective insights it provides into the personalities of those who enliven the work culture. At the same time, however, their sensitivity to unusual performance contexts and interview-like performance frames makes such narratives informative but somewhat atypical folklore forms.

The setting in which the above narrative was performed calls attention to the subject of custom. Customs in occupational culture range from the simplest personal habits, like wearing a hard hat in a distinctive way, to more complex customs like ceremonial rites of passage. Between these two extremes lie the central forms of customary interaction in the workplace, the enforcement of daily norms and social hierarchies based on an individual's abilities and status within the trade. Customs, unlike verbal performances and work techniques, anticipate and sanction change in the workplace by providing the members of work cultures with mechanisms for negotiating the inevitable flow of individuals into, up through, and out of the trade.

Within each occupation, people develop recurrent methods of coping with the repetitive tasks of work which, over a period of time, become so habitual as to be almost totally unconscious. Routes through the plant, the lunch routine, a cup of coffee, and a snack between jobs are all individual customs that comprise the human maze that workers must negotiate during their workday. Techniques may informally determine how the work gets accomplished, and verbal expressions critically evaluate an individual's performance, but habitual customs dictate the style and pace with which an individual worker accomplishes a recurrent task and, at the same time, provide that worker with an opportunity to personalize the process.

At the heart of any occupational culture lie the customary forms of deference and respect earned through the performance of work techniques. Joking behavior, nicknames, and "perks" (like access to certain areas or pieces of equipment) are all customary recognitions of status. Officers in the fire service wear white hats and construction supervisors on work sites often wear distinctly colored hard hats. Journeymen and experienced workers often work by the job or assignment, whereas apprentices and helpers must keep to a strict hourly schedule, taking breaks only when authorized. The emotional temperature-taking of joking with new workers and giving them a hard time is a culturally sanctioned method of using customary forms of social control to continually monitor individual attitude and point of view. In many occupations workers depend on each other for survival in the workplace, and it is extremely important that these informal methods of establishing attitude are continually available.

The most elaborate form of custom in the workplace occurs when the collective will of the group is brought to bear on the vertical movement of an individual within the occupation. The symbolic passage of a worker through the group is marked with a celebration, in a very real sense a rite of passage from one stage of a career to the next. Initiations, promotions, and retirements are extremely important benchmarks in occupational life; the members of the culture engage in a symbolic marking of the transition to recognize the importance of the change.

Rites of passage in occupational culture are important because the ways in which the members of a work culture mark transitions or changes within the group reveal a great deal about their cultural values. In fire fighting culture, for example, rookies must spend a year on the job as trainees before they are actually considered members of the culture. At the end of this period, the rookie usually provides a meal for company members. Those members of the trade who have contributed to the rookie's informal training use the opportunity to verbally harangue the new fire fighter (as in joking behavior) and exhibit informal acceptance into the work culture by hurling at the individual a few choice "darts." Just as a rookie marks his passage from outsider to insider with a dinner, similar transitions from fire fighter to officer, lower rank to higher rank, and finally from active fire fighter to retiree are also celebrated with a ritual meal.

A retirement dinner is one of the most complex ritual occasions in any work culture because it celebrates the entire career of an individual and provides opportunities for fellow workers to comment on their individual relationship with the person leaving the trade, as well as to share a meal in his or her honor. In a typical retirement dinner in fire fighting culture, announcements are sent out to all the firehouses a month or so in advance. The members of the retiree's "home" or original company sell the tickets, prepare the retiree's favorite meal, and organize the event. Once everyone has eaten his or her fill, an emcee, usually another retired fire fighter, begins to verbally "roast" or recount all the individual's exploits on the job. The following transcript reveals just a portion of the type of verbal interaction characteristic of these ritual dinners:

[The post-dinner program has included a number of speakers who have trooped up to the microphone to tell their respective anecdote about the retiree. The volunteer firehouse is packed with over three hundred men who have come to participate in the dinner. At this point in the proceedings, a significant event occurs during the verbal roast of the retiree.]

Emcee: J.F. is an Italian. That's about as good a thing as you can say about him. J.F. is an Italian — *mango idioti dingolini* . . . get yerself up here. Let's have a big hand for J.F. . . . ain't he wonderful! [Applause] O *solo mio* . . . it's the only Italian song I know, Joe.

J.F.: And you don't know that one very well.

Emcee: Who the hell you think I am, Mario Lonzo?

85

J.F.: Well I don't know what the hell I'm doing up here.
Emcee: I don't know either.
J.F.: This particular presentation has to do with an incident at 24 engine
and a certain individual, but I think it would be better to turn the whole
thing over to Jerry and let him explain it himself. [Presents the retiree with
a galvanized bucket with a trip wire. It is a miniature version of the type of
buckets used by fire fighters to set elaborate traps for each other in the
firehouse, particularly during the springtime when the weather warms up
and the firehouses are hosed out for spring cleaning.]
Jerry [the retiree]: This undoubtedly . . . if there was anything that I've
ever done wrong . . . and I'll regret it until the day I die. Well at 24 engine
they had the usual thing with the water battles and all, and they used to
figure out all kinds of ways to get you with a bucket of water. Well I never
was in on any of those tricks, you know. [Laughter] So one night he says
that he's got a problem. And I thought, "Oh my God, what the hell is
wrong now?" So I went over there and just as I got there I looked up and
there must have been ten thousand gallons of water. I mean I was soaked
from my nose to my toes. And then, being a perfect ass, I got mad at Joe and
walked into it. And like I say. If there was any moment that I regret in this
fire department, it was that. I did live up to it later on, but like I say that
was terrible and I regret it to this day and until the day I die.[10]

Even in this short segment of the retirement dinner, we glimpse the
importance placed on this ritual transition of Jerry from active fire fighter
to retiree. The story elicited from him by Joe's "gift" of the toy bucket
illustrates the recognition on the part of all the participants at the dinner
that this is a celebration, but it is also an occasion to recall the good times
and the not so good times. Jerry's mistake of getting mad and "walk[ing]
into it" — pulling rank and taking the joke as a serious affront — must be
publicly acknowledged in front of more than three hundred of his peers.
This single illustration indicated how seriously the members of this
occupational culture view this rite of passage. If they didn't care enough
about Jerry to bring out these past mistakes, then the traditional
camaraderie and informally held ethics and values of the trade would
simply die out. The retirement dinner is the most complex form of

customary interaction. The stories told and the focused attention paid to the retiree exhibit a series of cultural performances unmatched in their strength in addressing and expressing the informally held canon of occupation.

The media continually present us with images of work that are suprisingly superficial and stereotypical. One important reason to the skills, stories, and customs which both reflect and participate in work culture is to exchange these vague stereotypes and misconceptions about how others make their living with concrete examples of what people really do and what meaning they derive from work activities. Not all work is satisfying or romantic, but we will never truly understand our neighbors, or even the members of our own families, until we have begun to appreciate what kind of work they do and how that activity shapes their outlook on the world.

Notes

1. There are many early works by folklorists who conducted research in work settings. See John Lomax and Alan Lomax, *Cowboy Songs and Other Frontier Ballads* (New York: Macmillan Publishing Co., Inc., 1948 [orig. 1910]); Earl C. Beck, *Lore of the Lumbercamps* (Menasha, Wis.: George Banta Publishing Company, 1948); Wayland D. Hand, "The Folklore, Customs and Traditions of the Butte Miner," *California Folklore Quarterly* 5(1946): 1-27, 153-78. A useful review of the development of occupational folklore studies can be found in Archie Green, "Industrial Lore: A Bibliographic-Semantic Query," in *Working Americans: Contemporary Approaches to Occupational Folklife*, edited by Robert H. Byington, Smithsonian Folklife Studies No. 3(Washington, D.C.: Smithsonian Institution Press, 1978), 71-102. [Reprinted from *Western Folklore* 37(July 1978): 213-44].

2. Robert McCarl, "Occupational Folklife: A Theoretical Hypothesis," in *Working Americans: Contemporary Approaches to Occupational Folklife*, edited by Robert H. Byington, Smithsonian Folklife Studies No. 3(Washington, D.C.: Smithsonian Institution Press, 1978), 3-18.

3. James Spradley and David McCurdy, eds., *The Cultural Experience:*

Ethnography in a Complex Society (Chicago: Science Research Associates, 1972), 23-37.

4. District of Columbia Fire Fighters' Project, Tape 9, November 1978, AI, log pp. 3-4B.

5. Dell Hymes, "Breakthrough into Performance," in *Folklore: Performance and Communication*, ed. Dan Ben-Amos and Kenneth S. Goldstein, (The Hague: Mouton, 1975), 18.

6. Ibid.

7. District of Columbia Fire Fighters' Project, field notebook II, March 4, 1979, log pp. 7-9B.

8. District of Columbia Fire Fighters' Project, Tape 10-11, November 1979, log pp. 7-9B.

9. District of Columbia Fire Fighters' Project, Tape 2-3, April 1979, AI, log pp. 3B-4.

10. District of Columbia Fire Fighters' Project, December 13, 1979, A, log pp. 2-6.

Further Readings

One of the most comprehensive overviews of occupational folklore can be found in Archie Green, "Industrial Lore: A Bibliographic-Semantic Query," in *Working Americans: Contemporary Approaches to Occupational Folklife*, edited by Robert H. Byington, Smithsonian Folklife Studies No. 3(Washington, D. C.: Smithsonian Institution Press, 1978), 71-102 [*Western Folklore* 37 (1978): 213-44]. Specific ethnographic studies of occupational culture include Michael J. Bell, *The World From Brown's Lounge: An Ethnography of Black Middle Class Play* (Urbana, Ill.: University of Illinois Press, 1983) and my fire fighters' ethnography, Robert McCarl, *The District of Columbia Fire Fighters' Project: A Case Study in Occupational Folklife*, Smithsonian Folklife Studies No. 4 (Washington, D.C.: Smithsonian Institution Press, 1985). Many folklorists have looked at specific forms of folk expression within occupational contexts, including Edward D. Ives, *Joe Scott: Woodsman Songmaker* (Urbana, Ill.: University of Illinois

Press, 1964); Patrick Mullen, *I Heard the Old Fisherman Say: Folklore of the Texas Gulf Coast* (Austin, Tex.: University of Texas Press, 1978); and Archie Green, *Only a Miner: Studies in Recorded Coal Mining Songs* (Urbana, Ill.: University of Illinois Press, 1972). Some of the classic genre studies concerned themselves with a variety of folklore forms in frontier and resource occupation. These include Horace Beck, *Folklore and the Sea* (Middletown, Conn.: Wesleyan University Press, 1973); Mody C. Boatright, *Folklore of the Oil Industry* (Dallas, Tex.: Southern Methodist University Press, 1963); and Ben A. Botkin and Alvin Harlow, eds., *A Treasury of Railroad Folklore* (New York: Crown Publishers, 1953). More recent work in this area can be found in Jack Santino, "Miles of Smiles and Years of Struggle: The Negotiation of Black Occupational Identity through Personal Experience Narrative," *Journal of American Folklore* 96(1983): 393-412. A comprehensive anthology of essays which include a number of articles on occupational lore and performance can be found in *"And Other Neighborly Names," Social Process and Cultural Image in Texas Folklore*, edited by Richard Bauman and Roger D. Abrahams (Austin, Tex.: University of Texas Press, 1981). Although there have been no comprehensive bibliographies compiled on contemporary occupational folklore, the Folklife Program at the Smithsonian Institution does have a well-organized and indexed library of hundreds of hours of occupational narrative recorded both in the field and as a part of the annual Festival of American Folklife. Additional information can be obtained directly from the program staff by writing Folklife Program, Suite 2600, L'Enfant Plaza, Smithsonian Institution, Washington, D.C.   20560.

Chapter 5
Children's Folklore

Jay Mechling

Although each of us has a unique constellation of folk group affiliations and identities within those groups, the one thing we all share is that we were children once. This fact makes the study of children's folklore so attractive and, at the same time, so difficult. The white, male folklorist recognizes that he will never really know what it means to be a black woman, but we all think we know what it means to be a child. Studying the child, therefore, has layers of motive and meaning often not present in other folklore inquiry, since we tend to project our own childhood experiences upon others and may attempt to recapture an especially pleasant period in our lives. We may even search for an image of "the child" that confirms certain of our ideological biases. A look at the folklore of children must begin, then, with a conscious stepping back from our preassumptions and emotional responses to the subject.

This is not to say that we must ignore all that is fun in the study of children's folklore. The material itself is enormously attractive and exciting, often appealing to our childish selves. When the adult hears an eleven-year-old girl recite a ditty, such as,

I pledge allegiance to the flag,
Michael Jackson is a fag.
Pepsi Cola burned him up,
Now he's drinking Seven Up.

the adult likely responds with a mixture of disapproval and delight.[1] An adult might well appreciate the cleverness of the rhyme and the fun it has with current events in the popular culture scene, but it seems unlikely that adults will include this rhyme in their repertoire of stories and jokes told among adult friends. Adults love parodies and seem to share the same anxieties about homosexuality and disfigurement by fire as children do.[2] Yet, there is something about the folk rhyme that identifies it as children's lore. Figuring out what that "something" is will take us a long way toward understanding what is distinctive and perhaps unique about the folklore of children.

Who are the "children" in children's lore? Children were among the first nonpeasant groups to be studied by folklorists at the end of the nineteenth century. These folklorists, guided by the Darwinian model that permeated social scientific thinking at that time, took seriously the cultures of children. They tended to see children as embodiments of an early stage in human and societal evolution. Consequently, the study of children had the same rationale as did the study of American Indian cultures — namely the collection and preservation of the representatives of the savage stage in human evolution. Yet, since this view was predicated on the notion of childhood as a simple, incomplete, uncivilized state, preparatory to civilized adulthood, scholars have also tended to "trivialize" childhood. Childhood is trivial, in this view, to the extent that it is merely an indication of the past or a potential for the future, not something whole and meaningful in its own right. This "triviality barrier" continues to plague the inquiry into the nature of children's folklife.[3]

It is only recently that we have come to understand that childhood is not a universal category across contemporary and past human cultures. Our own notion of childhood probably emerged in the sixteenth century, linked to such forces as the invention of printing (and literacy), the Protestant Reformation, the beginnings of a technological, industrial revolution, and the appearance of a sense of individualism. The category of adolescence was invented much later, appearing only at the end of the nineteenth century. Anthropological work since the turn of the century similarly demonstrates that our American notions of childhood are quite ethnocentric. Enlightenment and romantic era portraits of the child still dominate our imaginations, leading us to believe that our category "childhood" is a human universal.[4]

Our American commonsense understanding of childhood is that it is a period of separation, protection, preparation, and innocence. In a sense we are "stuck" with this intuitive understanding of children, but we need to be cautious about projecting our own experiences and our own intuition onto others. What is true for our commonsense notions about childhood is also true for our "scientific" theories about the child. The various schools of child psychology and the classics from those fields (e.g., by Sigmund Freud, Jean Piaget, Erik Erikson, and Melanie Klein) are all bound by cultural assumptions and biases. To be sure, cultural bias is difficult to put aside, but because our study of children's folklore carries so much ideological "baggage," it is a good idea to approach the child's folk group assuming very little.

The children's folklorist begins by taking seriously the folk cultures of children. The folklorist does not assume the "normative" model of socialization; that is, the folklorist does not view children as merely unsocialized adults whose main goal is to acquire the adult world view. Rather, the folklorist takes an approach that views children's folk cultures as if they were fully complex, developed, and autonomous.[5] This "as if" assumption means that we approach children's folk cultures just as we would any unfamiliar culture. We, the foreigners, will be able to study the child's folk culture mainly at those borders where our adult culture interacts with the child's culture, and we are resigned to the fact that portions of the child's culture and dimensions of that culture's meaning remain inaccessible to us.

Given that our concepts of childhood and adolescence are culturally specific, where shall we draw the line between childhood and adulthood for the purposes of defining our domain, "children's lore"? After all, our lives are continuous, even though we have cultural institutions which seem to create discrete periods of life and ceremonies punctuating the transition from one stage to another. It would be tempting to regard childhood's end at the transition into high school, but children's folklorists tend to be just as interested in adolescent lore and look for continuities between childhood and adolescence. We could use high school graduation as the transition from childlore to adultlore, but folklorists have found among college students many of the folk performances and folk customs (taunts, teases, pranks, graffiti, legends, and so on) we associate with adolescents or children. Indeed, one function of the formal education system in our post-industrial society is to prolong childhood; so there is some wisdom in saying that children's lore ends whenever the individual leaves school and enters full time the world of work, that eight-hour-a-day setting which spawns a folk culture of its own.

Along the way to the adult settings, the child is a member of several folk groups, face-to-face human groups wherein people use stylized communication to create the sense of a shared, meaningful world. The first folk group is the family, and much of the current interest in family folklore is relevant for understanding children's folk cultures. A child's first experience with a folk culture of peers may be with the siblings with whom the child shares a system of secret languages, nicknames, stories, riddles, jokes, traditional interaction routines, pranks, taunts, teases, toys, playhouses, secret hideouts, pets, clothing, dangerous play, obscene play, and forbidden play (e.g., smoking or drinking).

As the child's network of human contracts extends beyond the family, the neighborhood provides settings for additional folk groups. The "best friend" may become the partner in a folk dyad, and there may be a larger neighborhood group that coalesces as a "club" or "gang." These networks of friendships, and the dynamic system of "friendship" as a social process, are proper for study by the folklorist. The folklorist asks how it is these friends use their stylized verbal and nonverbal communication to create a sense of shared meanings. These are informal folk groups, of course, in some ways fragile and transitory, coalescing and dissolving. Yet, it is important to realize that the children's folk traditions bring some stability to these comings and goings. Play groups may change members, but the children bring to each new grouping some traditional rules and understandings that establish a continuity in their folk culture. Thus, a new girl on the block can be integrated swiftly into the group once she understands that the rules for jump rope in San Francisco differ from the rules she learned growing up in Philadelphia. Local traditions, however, are not immutable. The new girl can also introduce the rhymes, variations, and rules from Philadelphia into the repertoire of the California play group.

The formal school system becomes the next setting for children's folk cultures. This used to begin in American society at age five, with preschool or kindergarten, but the rise of daycare institutions now pushes the highly structured, institutional, social experience into very early childhood. These are settings in which, like the family, the adults hold the real power and set the institution's agenda for the children. In these formal institutions, the children become increasingly adept at creating folk cultures separate from and resistant to the adults' definition of the organization's culture.

With the onset of formal schooling, the child experiences the rigid age-grading of American childhood institutions. Neighborhood folk groups likely mix ages, gender, and (if it is a multicultural neighborhood) ethnicity. But the schools make sure that the classroom experience, hence any folk group that may emerge in the classroom, occurs among children within one year of each other's age. The primary and secondary schools keep together children within certain age ranges, so that even recess has a limited range of ages from which the children may regroup themselves into the folk groups of the playground.

Both within and outside of school, children belong to a range of formal and informal folk groups. These may be clubs, scout troops, organized athletic teams, summer camp cabins, bands, cheerleading squads, drama or debate groups, social fraternities or sororities, and even part-time work groups. The after-school organized youth activities also tend to be age-graded. Boy Scouts and Girls Scouts, YMCA and YWCA, swim teams, soccer leagues, organized baseball, softball, and football leagues, and a host of similiar settings in which children might discover ways to create a shared folk culture, all reinforce the age-grading of the schools and in some cases segregate the children by gender. The adults usually create and justify these age grades on the basis of psychological theories of child development, so the whole institutional structure of childhood tends to embody adult theories of childhood.

This age-grading is a powerful, limiting force on who shall constitute the child's folk peers. Furthermore, age-grading correlates somewhat with the popularity of certain genres of children's folklore. Stories, jokes, and riddles of certain complexity are found among certain age groups. For example, the urban belief legend seems to be primarily an adolescent genre. Thus, age affects both the membership of the child's folk group and the genres the children are developmentally prepared to master and use to create their shared, expressive culture.

In addition to the formally structured, age-graded institutions for children, there are informal settings for the creation of folk groups. Kids "hanging out" at the mall or at video game parlors or gathering for breakdancing on a street corner may constitute a folk group. The point is that a shared, created, emergent folk culture marks a group as a child's folk group, not the group's relative formal or informal status. We should not assume, for example, that the kids at a "pickup" game of softball constitute a folk group while the Little League team, formed and controlled by adults, does not. A folk group exists if a folk culture exists, and autonomous children's folk cultures can emerge within informal groups as well as in groups highly structured by adults.

Most folklorists would agree that folklore is expressive, stylized communication performed within and for a community of humans with whom an individual shares life experiences which form the bases for the creation of meaning. Given this general definition, we can think about the characteristic features of children's folklore and folklife by exploring four perspectives or issues folklorists have found especially useful when looking at the folk cultures of children. I shall characterize these perspectives as polar oppositions: order versus disorder, hierarchy versus equality, male versus female, and dynamic versus conservative. The oppositions appear useful in talking about children because children often seem to exaggerate each extreme in their folklore. Overall, these perspectives are meant only to serve as starting points in the conceptualization and characterization of children's folk cultures.

One perspective in the study of children's lore focuses upon the tension between *order* and *disorder*. Anyone who spends time around children knows their penchant for orderliness, despite the current condition of any one child's bedroom. A child will not permit a tired parent to skip over a few pages of Dr. Seuss's *Green Eggs and Ham*, and children playing with blocks tend to create orderly patterns, even if that means simply sorting the blocks by shape. I recall once that we gave our two-year-old daughter a bag of M&M candies, only to discover a half hour later that she had sorted them into piles of separate colors before beginning to eat them.

Perhaps it is against this backdrop of order that children can experiment with disorder. Children can be as fanatically attached to disorder as they sometimes are to order. Children's folklore is quite often *antithetical*.[6] Children are an underclass in most societies, including our own. But unlike racial, ethnic, gender, and other underclasses in American society, children as a group are perpetually in the one-down relation to adults. To be antithetical is to be posed against an official order of meanings, uses, and processes. Sometimes the audience for these folklore displays are adults, sometimes the child's peers.

The child's primary strategy for being antithetical in the world is to adopt the *play* frame in the folk performance. Adults play, too, of course, but play is an especially legitimate activity for children. An increasing tendency in modern America is for adults to organize children's play in the service of adult work, seeing play and games as the training ground for adult life in a bureaucratic, industrial society. The play of boys, especially, is much more ordered and institutionalized in the 1980s than it was at the beginning of this century.

Girls' play, thought by adults to be less important, escaped for a while this organizing impulse, in part because girls' play tends to be more verbal and private than the more physical and public play of boys. Girls' games generally are much less complex, less active, and less competitive than those of boys, and even in competitive games the girl players tend to use the play action and rules to maintain a collaborative network.[7] It is in girls' gaming that folklorists tend to find the most spontaneous play controlled by the participants. In the struggle between the children's and the adults' definitions of heavily organized play situations, folklorists find hints of autonomous children's folk cultures.

Because play is "not for real," "not serious," children can use play to engage in activities and to explore themes not open to them in the everyday, commonsense, taken-for-granted world. Playing can be a powerfully antithetical, subversive frame for action, and the child learns this very early. Cruel play, dangerous play, obscene play, and forbidden play are all antithetical modes that violate the adult's romantic notion of the child. Cruel play may be the setting for aggression, both verbal and physical, while dangerous play evokes heightened excitement for all the players. Dangerous play is usually one form of forbidden play, this latter category containing such activities as smoking, drinking, stealing, trespassing, drug use, and sexual activity.

Obscene play is an important antithetical category in children's folklore. People working in this field regularly confront expressive behavior filled with talk of sex, urine, menstrual blood, and feces. Developmental theories in child psychology, especially from the psychoanalytic tradition, may help explain the prevalence of these themes in children's jokes, riddles, songs, jump-rope rhymes, legends, pranks, stories, and other performed texts.

Yet, one need not adopt a Freudian perspective in order to recognize that the child's body is a powerful symbolic territory. The child endures early pressure toward the socialization of oral satisfaction and toward the control over the bowels and bladder, understanding early that these matters are important to adults and that these matters can become a source of power in a contest of wills with adults. Obscene lore, accordingly, has great expressive value for children, who will often display this lore with the intent of shocking the adult audience.

But the child's lore need not be cruel, forbidden, obscene, or dangerous to be antithetical. We find antithesis in even the most benign modes of play. While it is not possible here to describe fully the range of antithetical mechanisms in children's folk cultures, we can explore three of the most common ones — parody, nonsense, and secrecy.

Parody is a common antithetical device used by children in their expressive cultures. Sometimes they parody adult roles and values, as in "playing house." Sometimes the parodies are of the songs and rhymes the adults teach the children. The following parody version of the "Battle Hymn of the Republic" makes a frontal attack upon adults and the institutions they devise for children:

> Mine eyes have seen the glory
> Of the burning of the school,
> We have tortured all the teachers,
> We have broken every rule.
> We are marching down the hall
> To hang the principal,
> Our gang is marching on.
>
> Glory, glory hallelujah,
> Teacher hit me with the ruler.
> I hit her on the bean
> With a rotten tangerine
> And her teeth went marching on.

Like the Michael Jackson rhyme, this song parodies a sacred text in the adult American civil religion. The parody features fantasies of violent rebellion and revenge against the adult caretakers. But the parody is "not for real" and can even be sung in front of the teachers and principals who are its target. The original song establishes a rigid formula within which the parody must operate, but within that convention the children may exhibit a considerable range of inventiveness. One folklorist collected the following variant of the parody while she was visiting the Children's Asthma Research Institute and Hospital (known familiarly as CARIH) in Denver:

> My eyes have seen the glory
> Of the coming of CARIH,

We have tortured all the counselors,
We have ruined Mr. G.
We have tied up all the nurses
And we've taken all their purses
And our troops go wheezing on.

Glory, glory hallelujah,
Debbie hit me with a ruler.
Hid behind the door
With a loaded forty-four.
Debbie ain't our counselor anymore.[8]

These hospitalized children have created a parody of a parody, inventing lines that reflect their new institutional setting and even their shared ailment (i.e., "wheezing").

Nonsense is another important device in the child's arsenal of antithetical folk routines. Nonsense figures prominently in children's humor and strikes nicely at the heart of the adult's desire for sensibleness and rationality. Children learn about this strategy in such folk performances as riddling sessions, where children begin telling riddles, each riddle elicited somehow by a preceding one and all sharing certain themes. Parodic riddles sometimes enter these sessions, violating the conventions of riddling and the canons of common sense. Consider the following parodic chain of elephant joke riddles:

Q: How do you shoot a blue elephant?
A: With a blue elephant gun.
Q: How do you shoot a pink elephant?
A: Choke him until he turns blue, then shoot him with a blue elephant gun.
Q: How do you shoot a white elephant?
A: Tell him a dirty story; when he turns pink, choke him until he turns blue; then shoot him with a blue elephant gun.[9]

Some parodic riddles create nonsense by violating the riddling conventions altogether:

A: What's the difference

B: Between what?
A: On this one I'm giving you no clues.[10]

By violating and otherwise playing with the conventions of this folklore genre, children develop competence and mastery over a form. In other folk performances, children may use nonsense in their jokes, in their stories, or in their dramatizations. Nonsense paradoxically helps the child affirm orderliness by temporarily experimenting with disorder. Children are very rule-conscious. At the same time, they are always testing the rules and developing competence in "the rules for breaking the rules."

Children sometimes use the play frame to "mask" desires and motives not normally acceptable to adults and sometimes not even acceptable within the child's own group.[11] Nonsense may be an especially safe mechanism for masking forbidden topics. The following jump-rope rhyme is commonly collected from preadolescent and adolescent girls:

Cinderella, dressed in yellow,
Went upstairs to kiss her fellow.
Made a mistake and kissed a snake,
Came downstairs with a bellyache.
How many doctors did it take?
One, two, three . . . .

One way to account for the popularity of this rhyme is to see in it a disguised discussion of sex and pregnancy. The rhyme begins innocently enough with a fairytale character, probably known to children through the Disney film and storybooks. But the Cinderella story itself is about the sexual awakening of a young woman.[12] In the jump-rope rhyme, the young woman goes upstairs to kiss her boyfriend, but she kisses a "snake" instead, and one way to interpret the meaning of "kissing a snake" is in sexual symbolic terms. In the child's vague understanding of reproduction and the difference between the womb and the stomach, sexual contact could result in a "stomach ache" — that is, pregnancy.

Other variants of this rhyme make a sexual interpretation increasingly plausible. The following version seems to emphasize a different theme:

101

Cinderella, dressed in yella,
Went upstairs to kiss her fella.
On the way her girdle busted.
How many people were disgusted?

In this parody version, the rhyme would seem to find its fun in a comment on overweight girls, a topic that can be as serious as sex and pregnancy. On the other hand, the busting girdle might still be a reference to the swelling stomach of a concealed pregnancy.

Secrecy is a third antithetical device children regularly use within the play frame. A common element in children's lore is the secret. Adults have secrets, too, and to the extent that all folk groups have traditions shared only within the group as signs that "we are different from those others," secrecy will be an aspect of in-group folklore. But secrets are especially meaningful within a relatively powerless group. Children like secrets. Sensing that knowledge is power, children will create secret clubs with secret initiations and secret handshakes. They will write messages to one another in school in secret codes, speak secret languages, or will publicly whisper "secrets" as a way of bonding with confidants and separating themselves from the unincluded.

Secret languages, sometimes called "play languages," provide a good example of the child's love of secrecy. Children from quite different cultures have play languages they invent partly for the fun of the speech play but partly to exclude outsiders, including adults. "Pig Latin" is probably the secret language most familiar to Americans; and it is one of the simplest, with words constructed by moving the first letter (or letters) to the end of the word and adding "-ay." Thus, "pig Latin" becomes "igpay atinlay." Children's secret languages, however, can be much more complicated than this, including elaborate written codes and symbols. Children can use these secret languages to communicate with each other even in the presence of adults, much as slaves of the American South used coded languages in the presence of their white masters.[13]

These, then, are the several manifestations of the antithetical nature of children's lore. Children use the play frame to establish a shared,

102

expressive folk culture distinct from and often resistant to what they perceive as the adult sense of order. Children's play may often be cruel, dangerous, forbidden, and obscene. Even when it is not, children have at their disposal devices like parody, nonsense, and secret codes to serve in their opposition to the adult world.

A second perspective we bring to the study of children's folklore focuses upon *hierarchy* and *equality*. Children's folklore is at times hierarchical, at other times egalitarian, and sometimes simultaneously both. Again, this dimension is not unique to children. Adults at times work very hard making their folklore serve hierarchies, and at other times rely upon their folk cultures to give them a comforting sense of belonging among equals. Once more, the folklore of children seems to exaggerate these dimensions.

Many psychologists and folklorists claim that children seem to have a high need for affiliation, a strong impulse to belong to a group and to conform to its norms. There is plenty of evidence of this in the folklore of children. Anthropologists and folklorists often remark on the social experience of homogeneity and comradeship that they see in certain cultural rituals. These experiences of egalitarian community stand against and in contrast to the more everyday experience of social institutions filled with hierarchies and distinctions.[14]

Children's folk groups often employ their folklore to create a feeling of egalitarian community against the structured world adults create for them.[15] At the same time, the folk groups of children are quite often very hierarchical. The children put much of their folklore to use establishing differences among the group members and classifying members according to those differences. For example, some children assume supervisory positions in assigning dramatic roles (of mother, father, child, dog) to the other members of an imaginary play group, or explicitly rank individual abilities in the process of "choosing up" teams.

Much of children's lore is "about" their relationships, including dominance and submission. Consider the prevalence of teases and taunts in children's folk cultures. Teases, which come in verbal and nonverbal varieties, are relatively harmless forms of folklore. In older children and adolescents they may paradoxically serve as much to cement the folk group as to create hierarchies within it. That is, teasing among friends may serve their sense of close friendship. Teasing of this sort seems to involve a mutual frame something like the "license to joke" anthropologists find in "joking relationships."[16] Two children may have a secure and close enough relationship that they may give one another the license to tease. It is also quite common for adolescents to learn to interpret teasing as an expression of affection, "reading" the tease as a symbolic inversion of the real message.

Taunts, on the other hand, are more aggressive verbal strategies meant to create social distance between folk groups or hierarchy within a folk group. Taunts often focus upon the target's deficient skills or physical features and usually appear in those rhyming forms we've come to expect in the briefer children's genres: "Fatty, fatty, two-by-four/ Can't get through the kitchen door." Ritualized taunts may begin to lose their power for older children and become more like play, as in the case of the rhymed or other formula taunts we find in children's games and in Little League baseball.

Even in the case of taunts, however, we find the paradox that these aggressive messages can be framed in a way to communicate social closeness rather than distance. Conventionalized insults among teenagers, for example, are an important expressive component in the solidarity of the male adolescent folk group. Urban black youths seem to have the most stylized formula insults in their "playing the dozens," but white teenagers engage in "cut wars" that serve similar purposes.[17]

Playfighting is a physical form of folklore within some children's folk groups, and it is no doubt related to teases, taunts, tricks, and pranks in a causal chain of offense and response. One folklorist found in his study of the boys at a group home for juvenile delinquents that playfighting was a very important form of communication among the boys; it was the only available means for them to show intimacy and physical affection.[18] Similarly, the game of "cootie tag" involves physical contact within the context of a game based on a tease — "Ohhh, you have cooties!" — and the game can be either a mask for cross-gender touching or the occasion for scapegoating and cruelty. "Cootie catchers," those folded paper devices for removing "cooties" from an infected peer, are another variant in this complex of teases.[19] These various play forms of touching are the children's way of exploring and violating the very complicated rules of touching we have in American culture. If the child's body is a salient model for the child's understanding of what the adults say about control and release, clean and dirty, and inside and outside, then it is not surprising that so much children's lore entails their suspending in the play frame the adult rules about the body.

Children take power when they establish themselves in a hierarchy, and they consciously give power or share power when they create nonhierarchical affiliation. Children sometimes use their folklore to experiment with power, to try out power roles that might not be available to them in the normal course of the day.

"It" games and other "central person" games, for instance, permit children to take turns being the most powerful player. In simple tag, a central person game common among younger children, the game provides the central person with high power and helps to protect that player against low skill. As the gaming group matures, the central person games begin to shift the power away from the "it" role to the other players, who become more of a cooperative collective against the central person.[20]

The popular game of kick-the-can is a good example of a hierarchical central-person game with a solitary "it" pitted against an egalitarian community of players. In larger versions of the game, the "it" is badly outnumbered by players who hide, sneak around, and madly dash to kick the inverted tin can before the central person can touch the can and holler "one-two-three on [name of player spotted]." Then there are prisoners and "jail breaks" for the central person to control. Although the "it" in this game may on occasion be a scapegoat in the group, the players usually will seek a relative balance of power, finding the game most fun when the central player is neither too weak nor too strong.

An important qualification to the above generalizations is that there appear to be significant gender differences in patterns of hierarchy and affiliation within the child's folk group. Our understanding of these differences is still in its early stages, since so many previous generalizations about children's folklore were grounded in male-oriented assumptions about children's culture rather than in ethnographic studies of how children actually conduct their lives in their folk groups. Folklorists with firsthand experience in children's folk cultures find that girls tend to use their folklore to create conditions of egalitarian community within their folk cultures, whereas boys tend to make hierarchies. Interestingly, this gender pattern seems to cross ethnic and cultural lines.[21]

The third perspective on children's folklore focuses on this question of gender, on distinguishing *male* from *female*. Children commonly use their folklore to create and sustain gender differences, even in the face of an adult culture increasingly blurring those differences. American children acquire early a sense of appropriate play for girls and boys. These gender-specific activities change over time, but what stays constant is the child's tendency to associate certain verbal and nonverbal activities with a specific gender.

There really is a dialectic between the folklore and the gender construction. Children come to attribute certain activities to one gender or the other, but it is also true that a child is constructing his or her gender through participating in those activities. Human gender is as much a social construction or accomplishment as a biological given, and adults expect the child to have accomplished the appropriate gender identification by the onset of puberty.

The thematic content of children's lore reinforces the distinctions made through the gender segregation of folk groups and their activities. Prevalent in the obscene lore mentioned earlier are sexual matters. The adolescent boys in the Scout troop I studied have a repertoire of taunts, jokes, songs, stories, games, and rituals — some of it virulently misogynist — which establishes clearly for them what it means to be male in American culture. At the same time, folklorists studying girls' folk settings, such as pajama parties or Girl Scout camps, find an equally rich repertoire of legends, jokes, songs, games, and rituals that help construct and sustain a "female culture" within the larger, generally patriarchal American social structure.

Adolescents, especially, use their jokes, personal narratives, and urban legends to explore difficult questions of sexual identity. The male adolescent belief legend of "The Promiscuous Cheerleader," documented in its several variants, features a female high school or college cheerleader who has fellatio with all the members of an athletic team. She becomes ill and is rushed to the hospital, where the doctors pump enormous amounts of semen out of her stomach. By telling the legend among themselves, the male adolescents share expressive materials which punish sexually aggressive women, which reinforce male fantasies of sexual potency, and which serve social ends in those cases in which the legend is told about a rival school.[22]

My own junior-high-aged daughter came home one afternoon to announce seriously that she heard in school that rock singer Rod Stewart, said to be bisexual, had collapsed in the middle of a concert and had to be rushed to a hospital, where the doctors pumped two quarts of semen from his stomach! Apparently female adolescents had found a use for this kernel legend, transforming the central character into a bisexual male. The story had become more complex, addressing a new adolescent concern of the 1980s. It is important for the story, I think, that Rod Stewart be the rock star named. His image and the lyrics of his songs reflect powerfully masculine heterosexuality, but the teenagers also "know" that he is bisexual, thereby amplifying the meanings of this legend. An exclusively homosexual rock star would not work well as the protagonist. Bisexuality is a far more puzzling ambiguity to teenagers than is homosexuality. The ambiguous status of the central character in the legend thereby reflects a larger concern about bisexuality and gender confusion in American society of the 1970s and 1980s.

The fact that my daughter heard this legend at her junior high school in the early 1980s makes great sense. The junior-high-school years are powerful years of physical and emotional transition for American children. Their "developmental task" (as the child psychologist might say) is to achieve their appropriate gender role identification, which includes not only directing their attention toward the opposite sex but also establishing the repertoire of clothing, hairstyles, body ornament, talk, and other elements of style appropriate to their gender.

What interfered with this adolescent "identity workshop" in the late 1970s and early 1980s were mass-media images and stories of gender confusion. Teenagers are crucial consumers of American popular music, television, theatrical films, and body ornament (including clothing, makeup, hairstyles, and jewelry). Popular "style" in these realms tended toward androgyny. These messages pose no problem for young children and adults, the former because gender is not yet really problematic for them and the latter because they have settled on a gender identification that governs their interpretation of the mass-media images (even if just to label them "perverted"). But for the twelve-year-old, gender is still a tentative accomplishment and "style" appears to be a major strategy toward becoming male or female. Bisexuality suddenly offers a third choice just when two seem more than enough to handle. Moreover, the Rod Stewart paradox — supposed bisexuality under an image of aggressive heterosexuality — would seem to present a further problem to the adolescent girl. Can she trust external appearances in her world of masculine and feminine?

Significantly, the legend remains a morality tale, punishing promiscuity and bisexuality. Its morality is conservative, a trait common in the lore of children and adolescents. And, as we have seen, it is loyal to the formula story it borrows. The dynamism lies in the legend's transformations, changing the gender and the social roles of the characters in a changing cultural context.

Further into adolescence, the belief legends of American teenagers turn from concern with sexual identity to concern with sex itself. A classic example of the latter is "The Hook." In that legend the kernel story features a pair of teenagers "making out" in a car in lovers' lane. Suddenly a male announcer interrupts the program of music on the radio with a news alert that a sex maniac with a hook in place of his hand has escaped from a nearby mental institution. Frightened, the girl asks her boyfriend to take her home. When they reach the safety of her driveway and he comes around to open the car door, the boy discovers a hook hanging on the door handle, apparently wrenched from the maniac's arm as the car sped away from lovers' lane.

Folklorists see in this legend much about teenage concerns. The story is most often told by girls to girls, so it is likely the story addresses the young woman's anxieties about her first sexual explorations. The automobile and the "lovers' lane" in the legend are presented in a context of threat and danger. In the middle of their "necking" and the background of their own music, a male voice warns the pair of danger from a sex maniac. If we interpret the radio voice as the girl's conscience speaking through her father's voice, then the warning may be about the "sex maniac" boyfriend who has "escaped" the normal institutional controls of home. The teenagers cease their sexual exploration just as they are about to receive the punishment dispensed by a retributive adult. From a psychoanalytic perspective, the maniac's hook is a symbolic phallus, so the additional threat is violent rape. Appropriately, the hook is torn off just in time, a symbolic dismemberment (castration) that preserves the sexual virtue of the girl. [23]

The gender perspective permits us to ask a broad range of questions about the ways in which children and adolescents use their folklore to name and describe appropriate and inappropriate sexual identities, to construct appropriate identities for themselves, and to address the anxieties and puzzles they have regarding sexual behavior.

A fourth perspective relevant to children's folklore is that of *dynamism* and *conservatism*, the twin forces that combine to create a specific variant of a folk performance. [24] The Michael Jackson rhyme provides a good example of the fundamental paradox of children's lore — namely, that it is simultaneously so inventive and so conservative. Rhymes are a particularly rigid, formulaic, conventional form, and we encounter a great deal of rhyming in children's genres. Rhyming acts as a conservative force in children's lore, providing mnemonic devices for the child to pass on the rhyme pretty much as heard. At the same time, however, the Michael Jackson rhyme is highly inventive within the formulaic constraints, responding to current events in the mass media.

Children's inventive raiding of the mass media for their own folklore raises some very important questions around this issue of dynamism and conservatism. On the one hand, children have become the quintessential passive audience in modern American society. An increasingly common scene is the solitary child parked in front of a television set. As we have noted earlier, children are important consumers in the marketplace, and adults direct a considerable amount of advertising at children.[25] This passivity suggests a very traditional, conservative role for children in the process of production and consumption.

On the other hand, however, is the argument that the media do not seem to have the adverse effects upon children's folk cultures that the media critics predict. Put differently, the cultural "hegemony" the mass media are supposed to inflict upon our society, wiping out "local cultures" of all sorts, does not seem to be happening among children. Children's folk cultures turn out to be very resilient, according to this perspective, entering into a dialectic with the mass media and appropriating for their own uses its materials and forms. The jokes and campfire skits of the Boy Scouts I studied incorporated all sorts of television material, from well-known sitcoms to game shows. And folklorists have found that the plots of children's spontaneous trickster stories are transformations of the Bugs Bunny cartoons they watch on television.[26]

In fact, the commercials themselves are often the targets of the children's parodies. Folklorists are forever collecting from children parodies of commercial slogans or jingles, such as,

> Everything tastes better
> With Blue Vomit [i.e., Blue Bonnet Margarine] on it![27]

or,

> Comet, it tastes like Listerine
> Comet, it makes your mouth so clean
> Comet, it makes you vomit,
> So get some Comet and vomit today![28]

A great deal of children's antithetical folklore centers on commercial foods. McDonald's, in children's folklore, would seem to symbolize all fast foods, and we find a considerable amount of parody of McDonald's commericals. The Boy Scouts I studied had a favorite campfire song, "Gopher Guts," to which they added (increasingly, by tradition) tag lines referring to fast food establishments:

Gopher Guts (Tune: "The Old Gray Mare")

Great green gobs of greasy grimy gopher guts
Itty bitty birdy feet,
Mutilated monkey meat
One pint portion of all-purpose porpoise pus,
And me without my spoon!
(But here's a straw!)
(Have it your way, have it your way!) [sung as Burger King commercial]
(Take that, McDonalds!)

There is even more concern about food contamination in the following parody of a McDonald's jingle:

McDonald's is your kind of place;
They serve you rattlesnakes,
Hot dogs up your nose,
French fries between your toes,
And don't forget those chocolate shakes,
They're from polluted eggs.
McDonald's is your kind of place;
The last time that I was there,
They stole my underwear,
I really didn't care,
They were a dirty pair.
The next time that you go there,
They'll serve my underwear.
McDonald's is your kind of place.
Scoo-oobie.[29]

We see in this commercial jingle parody the connection between food and feces (i.e., the "dirty" underwear), between clean and dirty, that we find elsewhere in children's foodlore and that confirms how rich a symbolic resource is the human body and its excretions.

Adolescents in high school continue the assault on fast food establishments by circulating legends about local taco stands where the tacos are made from stray cat meat, about the earthworms that give Wendy's hamburgers that extra juiciness, about the kangaroo meat in McDonald's hamburgers, and about the Kentucky Fried rat.[30] Adolescents have plenty of anxieties about their bodies and what they eat, but these bits of lore also suggest some anxiety about relying upon impersonal restaurants for their meals. Perhaps the adolescents who tell these tales and sing these parodies are lodging a protest against the lack of nurturant family food preparation and eating occasions.

The dialectic between children's folklore and the mass media works both ways. Many themes which begin in children's folklore find their way into the mass media. Theatrical horror films such as *Friday the Thirteenth*, *Halloween*, *When a Stranger Calls*, and their multiple sequels, are adolescent urban belief legends converted into cinema stories. Popular music lyrics sometimes build on teen narratives (e.g., "Teen Angel"), and the "breakdancing" phenomenon makes a nice case study of a folk performance genre that enters the popular culture.

A last, startling implication of the dynamism/conservatism oppostion in children's lore is that, far from being the conservator of tradition, it is often avant-garde. There is a sense in which the creative flexibility and adaptability of children gives them an advantage in a rapidly changing, post-industrial society. Margaret Mead was fond of pointing out how unusual is American culture, where the parents learn from the children. In a world of microchips and radically redefined social relations, children are at the cutting edge of the future.

Perhaps we are ready to return to that little Michael Jackson ditty with which we began. We see now in the text the conservative formula of the rhyme, infused with a creative, dynamic response to immediate and particular events. The folk rhyme empowers the child to engage in the commentary, not matter-of-factly, but through a stylized, antithetical rhyme that parodies both what adults take seriously (the Pledge of Allegiance and "product market segmentation," as the advertisers say) and the popular entertainment that the kids take seriously. This rhyme tackles content bound to provoke anxiety in pubescents, since male homosexuality adds great complexity to the world of gender identification they are just entering, and since disfigurement by fire holds a special meaning for young people in a mass-media culture that puts a premium on the face and on physical attractiveness.

This rhyme has one more feature typical of some folklore — its timeliness. The audience's ability to understand the meaning of the rhyme depends heavily upon shared knowledge about the person Michael Jackson and the fact that he was injured during the filming of a television commercial for Pepsi Cola. While its themes touch upon general anxieties, the rhyme is so particular to a time (1984) and to specific events that it is likely to be meaningless to eleven-year-olds five years hence. By then, children will have new media events to appropriate for their folk rhymes and jokes.

The Michael Jackson ditty also helps us see some of the themes pervading children's folklore. One such theme is *power*, something children generally do not have in their institutional settings. So they take power, or play at taking power, through their folklore. This is a rebellious grasp for power motivated out of their subordinate positions in the family and in school. Sometimes the power helps the child create and sustain a personal identity through competent performance. This is the power of mastery and maturity. Knowledge is power, so an important function of the children's lore is to help them acquire the knowledge that adult members of the culture take for granted. Sometimes the power helps the child establish relations with others. Sometimes the power is purely antithetical and subversive.

Another prevalent theme in the children's lore is the child's *body*. So much of the child's biological and psychological developmental drama centers on the body that it is little wonder that no bodily function escapes the child's folk repertoire. Sex, food, and excretions appear prominently in the lore, but so do other bodily themes like illness, mutilation,

113

exaggerated body parts, and death. Physical play and lore, the assortment of punching, probing, and poking we find in children's cultures, explore the body and our complex adult rules of touching. And this focus on the body is as common in the innocent folk texts as in more obscene ones.

An old truism in anthropology and sociology says that "marginal" folks, people who stand near the border between the insiders and the outsiders, make especially good cultural informants. What is so taken for granted by people at the center becomes problematic for people at the periphery. Marginal people often see the cultural paradoxes and contradictions invisible to most others. This suggests that children may be the most insightful commentators about American culture. They are "marginal" in many senses, lacking at the outset the power and knowledge they need to be at the center. What seems clear to us mystifies them. Furthermore, the fact that most children *want* to be at the center, want to achieve the power and knowledge of adults, means that they work hard at learning the culture. They violate rules as a way of learning them, they exaggerate cultural traits or values as a way of understanding them, and they explore under the "masks" of innocence and play some of the most troubling and horrifying issues in American life.[31]

By paying serious attention to children's folklore, we may learn something about ourselves. Nostalgia is probably a poor motivation for the adult's study of children's lives. The search for fresh sources of cultural criticism would seem a better place for the adult to begin. The children will do the rest.

Notes

1.   I am indebted to folklorist Priscilla Ord for this text. She collected it from an eleven-year-old girl in Pennsylvania in 1984. The Pepsi Cola company executed a major coup in its market battle with Coca Cola when it signed popular music star Michael Jackson to do a series of television commercials. Jackson was injured during a taping when fireworks temporarily ignited Jackson's hair and he required hospitalization. The commercial's fame was ensured by its frequent use during the 1984 Los Angeles Olympics.

2.   Evidence of this is a joke circulating among adults shortly after the Michael Jackson incident: "Did you hear? Richard Pryor and Michael Jackson are going to do a concert tour together for a new charity — the Ignited Negro College Fund." This joke depends upon the audience's knowledge that black comedian Richard Pryor was badly burned and scarred while allegedly free-basing cocaine, and upon the audience's familiarity with television commercials for the United Negro College Fund.

3.   The notion of "the triviality barrier" is Brian Sutton-Smith's, proposed first in his "Psychology of Childlore: The Triviality Barrier," *Western Folklore* 29(1970): 1-8.

4.   See Philippe Aries, *Centuries of Childhood: A Social History of Family Life,* trans. Robert Baldick (New York: Random House, Vintage Books, 1962) and Joseph F. Kett, *Rites of Passage: Adolescence in America 1790 to the Present* (New York: Basic Books, 1977). Still a classic is Margaret Mead and Martha Wolfen-stein, eds., *Childhood in Contemporary Cultures* (Chicago: The University of Chicago Press, 1955).

5.   Robert W. Mackay explains the distinction between the "normative" and "interpretive" approaches to children. See his "Conceptions of Children and Models of Socialization," in *Recent Sociology No. 5,* ed. Hans Peter Dreitzel (New York: Macmillan Publishing Co., Inc., 1973), 27-43; reprinted in *Ethnomethodology: Selected Readings,* ed. Roy Turner (Middlesex, England: Penguin Books Ltd., 1974), 180-93.

6.   Brian Sutton-Smith coined the term "antithetical" to describe children's play and folklore.

7.   On these matters of gender and children's play, see Helen B. Schwartzman, *Transformations: The Anthropology of Children's Play* (New York: Plenum Press, 1978) and Brian Sutton-Smith, "The Play of Girls," in *Becoming Female,* ed. C. B. Kopp and M. Kirkpatrick (New York: Plenum Press, 1979), 229-57.

8.   This text is from Roberta Krell, "At a Children's Hospital: A Folklore Survey," *Western Folklore* 39(1980): 223-31.

9.   Alta Jablow and Carl Withers, "Social Sense and Verbal Nonsense in Urban Children's Folklore," *New York Folklore Quarterly* 21(1965): 250-51.

10.   Ibid., 249.

11.   Brian Sutton-Smith and Diana Kelly-Byrne, eds., *The Masks of Play* (West Point, N.Y.: Leisure Press, 1983).

12.   For a variety of interpretations of Cinderella, see Alan Dundes, ed., *Cinderella: A Casebook* (New York: Garland Publishing, Inc., 1982).

13.   See, for example, Joel Sherzer, "Play Languages: Implications for (Socio) Linguistics," in *Speech Play: Research and Resources for Studying Linguistic Creativity*, ed. Barbara Kirshenblatt-Gimblett (Philadelphia: University of Pennsylvania Press, 1976), 19-36, and R. Berkovits, "Secret Languages of School Children," *New York Folklore Quarterly* 26(1970): 127-52.

14.   Victor Turner introduced the term "communitas" for the egalitarian sense of community experienced in some rituals. See his *The Ritual Process: Structure and Anti-Structure* (Ithaca, N.Y.: Cornell University Press, 1969).

15.   Samples of my study of this Boy Scout troop are my essays, "The Magic of the Boy Scout Campfire," *Journal of American Folklore* 93(1980): 35-56; "Patois and Paradox in a Boy Scout Treasure Hunt," *Journal of American Folklore* 97(1984): 24-42; and "Male Border Wars as Metaphor in Capture the Flag," in *The Many Faces of Play*, ed. Kendall Blanchard (Champaign, Ill.: Human Kinetics, 1986), 218-31.

16.   A. R. Radcliffe-Brown, "On Joking Relationships," *Africa* 13(1940): 195-210.

17.   Chapter Two of Roger D. Abrahams's *Deep Down in the Jungle: Negro Narrative Folklore from the Streets of Philadelphia* (Chicago: Aldine Publishing Company, 1970) offers an excellent introduction to black ritual insults ("dozens") in context. For ritual insults and "cut wars" among white male adolescents, see Simon J. Bronner, "'Who Says?' A Further Investigation of Ritual Insults among White American Adolescents," *Midwestern Journal of Language and Folklore* 4(1978): 53-69.

18.   This is from the dissertation work of Robert Horan at the University of Pennsylvania.

19.   Sue Samuelson, "The Cooties Complex," *Western Folklore* 39(1980): 198-210.

20.   Brian Sutton-Smith, "Play, Games, and Controls," in *Social Control and Social Change*, ed. J. P. Scott and S. F. Scott (Chicago: The University of Chicago Press, 1971), 73-102.

21.   The new, ethnographic approach to girls' play is represented by Linda A. Hughes's "Beyond the Rules of the Game: Girls' Gaming at a Friends' School" (Ph.D diss., University of Pennsylvania, 1983), and by Marjorie Harness Goodwin's "The Serious Side of Jump Rope: Conversational Practices and Social Organization in the Frame of Play," *Journal of American Folklore* 98(1985): 315-30.

22.   Gary Alan Fine and Bruce Noel Johnson, "The Promiscuous Cheerleader: An Adolescent Male Belief Legend," *Western Folklore* 39(1980): 120-29.

23.   The following interpretation relies heavily upon that offered by Alan Dundes in his essay, "On the Psychology of Legend," in *American Folk Legend: A Symposium*, ed. Wayland D. Hand (Berkeley, Cal.: University of California Press, 1971), 21-36.

24.   Barre Toelken discusses the "twin laws" of dynamism and conservatism in his textbook, *The Dynamics of Folklore* (Boston: Houghton Mifflin Co., 1979), 34-39. Making this point for children's lore and inserting the term "Newell's Paradox" into the field is Gary Alan Fine's "Children and Their Culture: Exploring Newell's Paradox," *Western Folklore* 39(1980): 170-83.

25.   On solitary play, see Brian Sutton-Smith, *Toys as Culture* (New York: Gardner Press, 1985). I am characterizing the media critic's perspective from my reading of Neil Postman, *The Disappearance of Childhood* (New York: Dell Publishing Co., Inc., 1982).

26.   David M. Abrams and Brian Sutton-Smith, "The Development of the Trickster in Children's Narrative," *Journal of American Folklore* 90(1977): 29-47.

27.   Text from Mary and Herbert Knapp, *One Potato, Two Potato...The Secret Education of American Children* (New York: W. W. Norton & Co., Inc., 1976), 162.

28.   Steve Bartlett, "Social Interaction Patterns of Adolescents in a Folklore Performance," *Folklore Forum* 4(1971): 58.

29.   Knapp and Knapp, 163; Bartlett, 59.

30.   Gary Alan Fine has done the most work interpreting urban legends regarding food contamination. See, for example, his "The Kentucky Fried Rat," *Journal of the Folklore Institute* 17(1980): 222-43.

31.   It may be, for instance, that children were using their "dead baby

joke" cycle as coded commentary on abortion long before the adults moved into the heated public discourse that now surrounds that topic. See Alan Dundes, "The Dead Baby Joke Cycle," *Western Folklore* 38(1979): 145-57.

Further Readings

The most comprehensive collection of scholarly essays on children's lore is the volume, *Issues in Children's Folklore* (Washington, D.C.: Smithsonian Institution Press, in press), recently completed as a project of the Children's Section of the American Folklore Society. Edited by Brian Sutton-Smith, Jay Mechling, and Thomas W. Johnson, this collection of fifteen essays covers children's folklore issues, methods, genres, settings, and applications. The volume has the most complete bibliography of children's folklore to date.

The classic beginnings of this field lie in such collections as William Wells Newell, *Games and Songs of American Children* (New York: Dover Publications, 1963 [1883]); Alice B. Gomme. *The Traditional Games of England, Scotland, and Ireland*, 2 vols. (New York: Dover Publications, 1964 [1894-98]); and Stewart Culin, "Street Games of Boys in Brooklyn, N.Y.," *Journal of American Folklore* 4(1891): 221-37. British folklorists Iona and Peter Opie continued this collecting tradition in their several volumes, such as *The Lore and Language of Schoolchildren* (Oxford: Clarendon Press, 1959), *Children's Games in Street and Playground* (Oxford: Clarendon Press, 1969), and *The Singing Game* (Oxford: Clarendon Press, 1985). Still in this collecting tradition, though they add more analysis than the others, are Mary and Herbert Knapp, *One Potato, Two Potato...The Secret Education of American Children* (New York: W. W. Norton & Co., Inc., 1976).

There are excellent studies of children's verbal play. A good place to start is Barbara Kirshenblatt-Gimblett, ed., *Speech Play: Research and Resources in Studying Linguistic Creativity* (Philadelphia: University of Pennsylvania Press, 1976). Martha Wolfenstein's *Children's Humor: A Psychological Analysis* (Bloomington, Ind.: Indiana University Press, 1954)

118

is a worthy psychoanalytic classic, and Paul E. McGhee's *Humor: Its Origin and Development* (San Francisco: W.H. Freeman & Co., 1979) is a more broadly psychological successor. John Holmes McDowell's *Children's Riddling* (Bloomington, Ind.: Indiana University Press, 1979) and Brian Sutton-Smith's *The Folkstories of Children* (Philadelphia: University of Pennsylvania Press, 1981) are two good genre studies. The great virtue of these studies is that they are ethnographic, collecting not only texts but also the contexts of children's folk cultures. The essays collected in P. Gilmore and A. T. Glatthorn, eds., *Children in and out of School: Ethnography and Education* (Washington, D.C.: Center for Applied Linguistics, 1982) confirm the fruitfulness of this approach.

Helen B. Schwartzman's *Transformations: The Anthropology of Children's Play* (New York: Plenum Press, 1978) offers a superb view of the subject and includes a comprehensive bibliography. Bernard Mergen's *Play and Playthings: A Reference Guide* (Westport, Conn.: Greenwood Press, 1982) is an indispensable research tool. Brian Sutton-Smith's *A History of Children's Play: The New Zealand Playground, 1840-1950* (Philadelphia: University of Pennsylvania Press, 1981) and his earlier *The Folkgames of Children*, American Folklore Society Bibliographical and Special Series, vol. 24. (Austin, Tex.: University of Texas Press, 1972), are models for the historical work still to be done. R. E. Herron and Brian Sutton-Smith assembled in their edited volume, *Child's Play* (New York: John Wiley & Sons, Inc., 1971), a number of excellent essays by the best scholars in the field. There is an emerging tendency for play theorists to gravitate toward Gregory Bateson's understanding of play as a particularly paradoxical communication frame for interpreting messages. See his "A Theory of Play and Fantasy," in his collected essays, *Steps to an Ecology of Mind* (New York: Ballantine Books, 1972), 177-93.

The Association for the Anthropological Study of Play (TAASP) publishes a *Newsletter* and an annual volume of essays, many devoted to children. See, for example Helen B. Schwartzman, ed., *Play and Culture* (West Point, N.Y.: Leisure Press, 1980).

Much of the good work in children's folklore appears in essays far too numerous to list here. In addition to the essays cited in the footnotes for this chapter, good beginning readings are the following: the essays collected as a special "Children's Folklore" issue of *Western Folklore* 39(1980): 159-265; Herbert Halpert's "Childlore Bibliography: A Supplement," *Western Folklore* 41(1982): 205-28; Gary Alan Fine and Barry Glassner, "Participant Observation with Children," *Urban Life* 8(1979): 153-74; and Danielle Roemer, "Children's Verbal Folklore," *The Volta Review* 85(1983): 55-71.

Chapter 6
Folk Narratives

Elliott Oring

"Narrative" is another word for story. Narrating is a method by which an experience is transformed into a verbal account. Experience is recapitulated by matching a verbal sequence of statements to some sequence of events which is purported to have occurred. For example:

(1) At first he refused the drink that she offered.
(2) She persisted in her demand that he at least taste it.
(3) He finally consented and drained the glass.
(4) Suddenly, he felt a searing pain in his stomach.
(5) He knew that he had been poisoned.

There are, indeed, other ways of communicating this same information which do not depend upon a re-presentation of the temporal sequence of events. For example, "He knew that he had been poisoned when he felt the searing pain in his stomach from draining the drink that she insisted that he taste, but which he had first refused." Although this second formulation is perfectly logical and communicative, we will not consider it a narrative because it does not re-present experience in the order in which the events took place. Maintaining the order of events in the verbal recapitulation is basic to our definition of narrative. This distinguishes a narrative from other kinds of event reporting.[1]

A narrative is conceptualized as a whole, not as a mere list of clauses or sentences. A sentence links words together, whereas a narrative links actions and events. The individual sentences in our example above could possibly be regarded as a random list of sentences for parsing in a grammar exercise. However, once we perceive that they are *related* ("narrate" comes from the Latin word for "relate," a word we also use to characterize the telling of a story), these sentences are transformed into powerful, cognitive and affective verbal organizations. Even in our rather anemic example, the temporal sequence of events assumes significance. Consequently, we may respond to the man's initial refusal of the drink as wise and founded upon a just suspicion, but to his subsequent succumbing to the woman's entreaty as foolish. We surmise that the pain in the man's stomach is the result of a poison which perhaps an evil or vengeful woman has pressed upon him. As a whole, the narrative might imply that people in general, or women (or some particular woman), are dangerous and not to be trusted. However, none of the constituent sentences bear these messages. They can be derived only from a consideration of this narrative sequence as a whole.

Note that narrative has the ability to ensnare us. It engages us intellectually and causes us to make demands of it. Why did the woman put poison in the drink? What did the man do when he realized that he was poisoned? Did he survive? What, if any, was his revenge? Narrative has affective import as well. That is, it engages the emotions as well as the mind. We may feel anger, fear, joy, sorrow, suspicion, hope, despair, or triumph — the full range of human emotions. Indeed, narratives may serve as important vehicles to communicate emotion.

All in all, a narrative is a medium for communicating experience. Its ability to engage the mind and arouse the emotions greatly depends upon the sensitivity and artistry of the narrator. A good narrator may engage his audience totally, directing or redirecting their thoughts, emotions, and perhaps their future behavior as well.

What makes a narrative a "folk" narrative poses a somewhat different question. The notion of folk narrative is based upon a conceptualization of what folklore is, and there is no unanimity among scholars about the basic defining characteristics of folklore. Suffice it to say that folk narratives are generally conceptualized to be those narratives which circulate primarily in oral tradition and are communicated face-to-face. Since they communicate through oral rather than written channels, such narratives tend to exhibit certain other characteristics: (1) Folk narratives tend to exist in multiple versions. No single text can claim to be the authoritative or "correct" one. Rather, different narrators perform narratives differently in different circumstances. A folk narrative, in other words, must be re-created with each telling. (2) As a result of this process of re-creation, the folk narrative reflects both the past as well as the present. Narrators must draw upon past language, symbols, events, and forms which they share with their audience for their narrations to be both comprehensible and meaningful. Yet because each narration is a creation of the moment, it crystallizes around contemporary situations and concerns, reflecting current values and attitudes. A folk narrative is something of a renovation; the past is made to speak in the present. (3) A folk narrative reflects both the individual and the community. The narrator shapes the narratives he re-creates in accordance with his own dispositions and circumstances. Yet his creativity is not unlimited. His narrations depend upon a measure of community acceptance. The re-creation of a narrative relies upon a negotiation between the narrator and his audience. The narrator's individuality must find outlet in a narrative acceptable to the community if he is to be confirmed in his role as narrator and if he is to be permitted to perform again in the future.

Obviously, the process of folk narration evolved sometime after the development of language and has continued unabated until the present day. It is often necessary to point out that folk narration is not characteristic of just primitive or peasant groups, but is characteristic of all known human groups at all stages of civilization — ourselves very much included.

Folklorists have tended to divide folk narrative into a host of subvarieties, and it is not unusual for the folklorist to be familiar with a large folk-narrative terminology: origin myth, Saint's legend, memorate, fabulat, novella, aetiological tale, magic tale, joke, jest, animal tale, catch tale, clock tale, formula tale, personal experience story, and life history, just to name a few. In truth, the terminology often leads to more confusion than clarification, but it also reflects some of the distinctions which folklorists have perceived as important within the larger body of folk narrative.

Three major prose narrative categories regularly distinguished by folklorists are myth, legend, and tale. These terms do not refer to the *forms* of narrative so much as to the *attitudes* of the community toward them.[2] Thus, myth is a term used for a narrative generally regarded by the community in which it is told as both sacred and true. Consequently, myths tend to be core narratives in larger ideological systems. Concerned with ultimate realities, they are often set outside of historical time, before the world came to be as it is today, and frequently concern the actions of divine or semi-divine characters. Indeed, through the activities of mythological characters, the world has come to take the form that it has today. The story of Adam and Eve in the Garden of Eden might serve as an appropriate example of a myth, even though it takes a written rather than an oral form. For those who hold the story to be both sacred and true, the activities of this primordial couple, in concert with beguiling serpent and deity, explain fundamental aspects of world order: why the serpent is reviled, why a woman is ruled by her husband and suffers in childbirth, why man must toil to live, — and most importantly — how sin entered the world and why man must die. It should be noted that nowhere in this definition is myth held to be untrue — rather, that the narrative is held by someone to be ultimately true enables its characterization by the folklorist as a myth. Myths are frequently performed in a ritual or ceremonial context. There may be special personnel designated to recite the myth; the time and manner in which it is performed may also distinguish it from the other forms of narration in the society. Indeed, the language of a myth may be as sacred as its message.

There are few, if any, folk narratives in our own society which could be readily categorized as myths according to our definition. Those narratives that deal with ultimate truths are generally safeguarded through a written, indeed printed, tradition. Consequently, they are read rather than re-created anew with each performance. Changes in the texts of these written myths may also occur, but major changes come about primarily through retranslation and reinterpretation rather than through the oral re-creation of the text itself.[3]

Another category of narrative to which the folklorist frequently refers is the legend. Legends are considered narratives which focus on a single episode, an episode which is presented as miraculous, uncanny, bizarre, or sometimes embarrassing. The narration of a legend is, in a sense, the negotiation of the truth of these episodes. This is not to say that legends are always held to be true, as some scholars have claimed,[4] but that at the core of the legend is an evaluation of its truth status. It might be that a particular narrative is regarded as false, or true, or false by some and true by others. This diversity of opinion does not negate the status of the narrative as legend because, whatever the opinion, the truth status of the narrative is what is being negotiated. In a legend, the question of truth must be *entertained* even if that truth is ultimately rejected. Thus, the legend often depicts the improbable within the world of the possible. The legend never asks for the suspension of disbelief. It is concerned with creating a narrative whose truth is at least worthy of deliberation; consequently, the art of legendry engages the listener's sense of the possible.

The legend is set in historical time in the world as we know it today. It often makes reference to real people and places. The full range of associations to these people and places often remains implicit, however. Their identity and significance is not usually addressed in the narrative proper but is generally assumed to be known to the audience. What follows is an example of a legend that circulated widely in St. Petersberg, Russia, in 1890 and was eventually reported in the newspaper:

> There is a story going about town that is worthy of attention. The only question is whether it is true, and to what extent. The other day, somewhere on Sergievskaya Street, or near it, a priest carrying the holy sacraments came to a certain apartment after mass. A young man answered the door.
>
> "I was asked to come here and give the sacraments to a sick man," said the priest.

"You must have made a mistake. Nobody lives here except me."

"No, a lady came up to me today and gave me this very address and asked me to give the sacraments to the man who lives here."

The young apartment dweller was perplexed.

"Why look, that is the very woman who asked me to come," said the priest, pointing to a woman's portrait hanging on the wall.

"That's the portrait of my dead mother."

Awe, fear, and terror seized hold of the young man. Under the impression of all of this he took communion.

That evening he lay dead.

Such is the story.[5]

In this account, we can see that the question of truth is raised explicitly within the body of the narrative itself.

Legends may be artfully told, but their raison d'etre is rarely the creation of an aesthetically satisfying story so much as the creation of a story which requires the audience to examine their world view — their sense of the normal, the boundaries of the natural, their conceptions of fate, destiny, and coincidence. Thus, the appearance of a legend in normal conversation may not be readily apparent, for the verbal artistry of the legend may not be distinguished significantly from the artistry of the conversation in which it is embedded.

A folktale is a narrative which is related and received as a fiction or fantasy. Such narratives, unlike myths, are not sacred, nor do they challenge the world views of the audience in the same manner as the legend. Folktales appear in a variety of forms. They are encountered only rarely in the oral traditions of our own society, although many have been adapted for children's entertainment in hundreds of illustrated books and scores of films. One of the most popular sources for this children's literature is the collection of German folktales compiled by Wilhelm and Jacob Grimm in the early decades of the nineteenth century. The Grimms first heard these tales orally performed (their analogues circulate widely in oral tradition), but the Grimms also edited and freely embellished the oral tales included in their famous collection.

One such tale, the fifth in the Grimm collection, is "The Wolf and the Seven Young Kids" ["*Der Wolf und die sieben jungen Geisslein*"]. This tale, which has regularly found its way into children's books, concerns a mother goat and her seven kids. As the mother goat has to go into the forest, she cautions her kids not to let the wolf into the house. She further cautions that he often tries to disguise himself but that he can be identified by his gruff voice and black paws. No sooner does the mother depart than the wolf comes to the door pretending to be the mother returning. The kids refuse to let him in, recognizing his gruff voice. The wolf buys a piece of chalk, eats it, and returns to the house again, pretending to be the mother. The kids see his black paw through the window and send him away. The wolf then gets a baker to put dough on his foot and a miller to sprinkle the dough with flour so it appears white. When the wolf returns this time, he shows his white paw through the window. The kids open the door, and when they see the wolf, they all rush to hide. The wolf, however, devours them all, except for the youngest, who hides in the clock case. The wolf leaves the house and falls asleep under a tree in the meadow. When the mother goat returns home, she finds her youngest, who tells her what has happened. She follows the wolf, finds him asleep, and sees something stirring in his stomach. Hoping that her children are still alive, she sends her youngest to fetch scissors, needle, and thread. She cuts open the wolf's stomach, from which her children emerge alive and whole, fills the wolf's stomach with stones, and sews it shut. When the wolf awakens, he feels thirsty and goes to the well. As he bends over to drink, the weight of the stones pulls him into the well and he drowns. The mother and kids dance together in celebration.[6]

    This rendition is only a synopsis of the Grimm tale. Space does not permit the printing in full of even this brief tale. Prominently absent in this synopsis is the sense of drama created by the dialogue in each of the encounters of the major characters — goat, wolf, and kids. And if our synopsis is only a shadow of the Grimm version, it is well to keep in mind that the Grimm version is only a shadow of an orally performed folktale. Nevertheless, this synopsis can still serve to illustrate some aspects of this type of narrative.

    Folktales place little emphasis upon character development.

Characters, be they animal or human, are generally known through their actions or by their physical attributes. No attention is paid to internal conflict or complex motivation. Folktale figures are two-dimensional characters rather than three-dimensional personalities. The wolf is large, voracious, and wily. The kids are small, innocent, and gullible. These traits are givens. The folktale does not concern itself with explaining the wolf's behavior in psychological or philosophical terms. Instead, the folktale plays upon the polarization of these two-dimensional characters and their attributes. That is to say, the figures of folktale are depicted in terms of extreme contrast: the wise versus the foolish, the strong versus the weak, the rich versus the poor. In the Grimm tale above, the characters are literally contrasted in black and white terms. The wolf is black and he must whiten his paw in order to assume his disguise as the mother goat. The contrast of sweet and gruff is also employed; the wolf has to sweeten his voice as part of his disguise. (Since the wolf sweetens his voice with chalk, it is possible to view the contrast between sweet and gruff as a subset of the white/black contrast. By using chalk, the wolf is, in effect, "whitening" his voice.) All in all, the drama of this folktale, as well as many others, depends upon the encounter between characters who stand at opposite poles of some attribute scale.

As the representations of character in the folktale are flat and two-dimensional, so are the interactions of these characters. Only two characters interact in any particular scene: for example, the wolf with the kids (they can be regarded as an undifferentiated single character in their relation to the wolf); the goat with her kids; the goat with her youngest, who hid in the clock case. When more than two characters appear in one scene, the extra characters tend to be silent and inactive. They do not constitute separate and salient identities in that encounter.

The plot of a folktale proceeds as a logical sequence of events. Each event in the tale logically conditions the events that follow: the kids are left at home; the wolf fools them and gains entry to the house; all except one are eaten; the mother returns home and learns of their fate; the kids are rescued from the wolf's stomach; they are replaced with stones; the wolf drowns when he goes to drink; the goat and her kids celebrate. The sense of the tale would falter if the mother and kid celebrated after the kids had been eaten by the wolf. Indeed, this is what is meant by "plot." One of the reasons that many of our dreams seem so strange to us is that often they are difficult to conceptualize in terms of plot. The order of events is merely a chronological sequence, the logical connections between these events often obscure. All folk narratives can be said to be governed by plot. The plot of folktales, however, can be further described as single stranded. The tale tends to follow the actions of a single character from beginning to end. We know where that character is and what he is doing throughout the story. Rarely will a folktale follow a thread of action whose relation to the central character emerges only at the end of the story. Furthermore, the folktale does not rely on flashbacks. Past information required to further the plot will be revealed in the course of action through dialogue or deduction. In "The Wolf and the Seven Young Kids," we must learn that there is some potential for the kids to be alive in the wolf's stomach. Otherwise, we could make little sense of the goat sending for scissors to cut open the wolf's stomach. In the scene in which the wolf gains entry to the house, the tale merely states that the "wolf gobbled them up one after the other." But when the mother goat sees the wolf sleeping in the field, she sees his stomach stirring and quivering. "Dear God," she thought, "can my poor children that it gobbled up for supper still be alive?" This deduction on the part of the mother goat logically conditions the remaining action of the tale. The expectation that the kids are alive and whole could be created in several other ways. (For example, it could have been witnessed and reported by the kid hiding in the clock case.) However, a scene will not be omitted from its chronological position to be reenacted only later in the story.

The action of the folktale is often stereotyped and repetitive. The progress of the story is alternately delayed and stimulated as characters replay some typical scene until it culminates in some transformation of circumstance or situation. In "The Gold Bird" ["Der goldene Vogel"], the fifty-seventh tale in the Grimms' collection, brothers set out on successive nights to guard the golden apples on a tree belonging to their father. The first two brothers are overcome by sleep during their attempts. Only on

129

the third night does the youngest brother succeed in snatching a feather from a bird that has been stealing the apples. When the first two brothers set out, in turn, to find this bird, they ignore the advice of a fox sitting by the road, and they are diverted from their quest. The youngest son heeds the fox's advice, however, with consequences significantly different from those of his siblings. Even in the tale of the wolf and the kids, the wolf repeatedly approaches the house, with only slight variations in disguise, until he gains entrance on the third attempt. The consequence of that third effort is, of course, crucial for the remainder of the story. European and American tales tend to rely on the threefold repetition of action, but fourfold, fivefold, and even sevenfold repetition may be utilized in the folk literatures of other cultures.[7]

Although folktale plots depend upon logic, it is not always the logic of the everyday world. Ordinary logic might question the plausibility of the kids not demanding more evidence than a whitened paw before opening the door to the house, especially after so many attempted deceptions by the wolf. Ordinary logic might also question the fact that wolves and kids are talking and behaving like human beings. Fictional narratives demand a logic, but this logic may operate upon a set of extraordinary premises: talking animals, powerful magical objects, and impossible obstacles. Furthermore, many behaviors of the characters may seem exceedingly contrived — as when a poor peasant sells a magic wallet which can never be emptied of gold. But contrived is not the same as illogical, and in the folktale it is required only that an action logically condition further action. Indeed, the peasant's sale of the magic wallet does condition the remainder of the tale, which is occupied with the sequence of events through which that wallet is eventually returned. In other words, if the poor peasant had not acted so stupidly by selling his magic wallet, there might have been no tale to tell.[8]

Folktales no longer occupy a central place in the oral traditions of western urbanized society. This does not suggest, however, that we have no oral fictional narratives. The joke as a fictional form currently enjoys wide oral circulation. A great many jokes are fictional narratives like the folktale, although a good number may take the form of riddles, proverbs, gestures, or drawings. Unlike the folktale, however, a joke narrative subordinates the ordering of events in a plot to a higher ordering, the creation of humor. The resolution of a joke is worlds away from the resolution of a tale. A tale's climax is the logical result of an episodic sequence. If the folktale hero pursues a woman, he can win or lose her; if he seeks a treasure, he can acquire it or fail in his attempt; and if he confronts a villain, he can triumph or be defeated. (The folktale is generally resolved according to the first of these alternatives.) The range of tale conclusions is generally finite and predictable because the events described permit only so many logical consequents. Whatever the particular tale outcome, however, the climax must relate to the preceding events in a logical sequence of cause and effect. The joke, on the other hand, diverts the flow of the narrative into unpredictable courses. It uses a host of techniques to short-circuit the story narrative so the outcome will be totally surprising and unexpected without being totally irrelevant. For example:

> An American man-of-war was cruising in the Mediterranean in the days of the Barbary Pirates. The captain is walking on the main deck when his first mate comes running up to him yelling, "Captain, captain! Pirate ship off the starboard bow!"
>
> The captain says to his mate, "Bring me my telescope." The mate brings the scope and the captain looks to starboard, and sure enough, there is the pirate ship. The captain says to his mate, "Call the men to their battle stations. Bring me my sword and my red cape." The mate brings the sword and red cape as he is instructed, the ship engages the enemy, and the enemy is defeated.
>
> The next day they are sailing along when the mate comes rushing up again crying, "Captain, captain! Pirate ship off the port bow."
>
> The captain says, "Bring me my telescope." The mate brings the telescope and the captain looks to port and spies the pirate ship. "Bring me my sword and my red cape," the captain shouts to his mate. The sword and red cape are brought, they engage the pirates, and once again are victorious.
>
> As the smoke from this last victory clears, the mate approaches the

131

captain and asks, "Captain, I understand why you call for your sword before we engage the enemy, but why the red cape?"

The captain replies, "I wear the cape so that in case I am wounded during the course of the battle, blood will not show against the cape, and thus my men will not know of my wounds and will not become demoralized." The mate nods in understanding.

The next day, the mate comes rushing up to the captain yelling, "Captain, captain! There is a pirate *fleet* off the starboard bow."

"Fetch me my telescope." The mate brings the telescope, the captain looks to starboard and sure enough, an entire pirate fleet is bearing down on the ship. The captain looks down at his mate and says, "Fetch me my sword and brown pants."

This contemporary joke uses the threefold repetition of action which has already been described for the folktale. However, in the tale such repetition intensifies and ultimately furthers the action toward a conclusion. In the joke, we are in fact quickly distracted from the major action which is taking place to the details of clothing that the captain wears during his military engagements. The significance of this clothing becomes the focus of the joke, not the outcomes of the military engagements themselves. In this joke, as in many others, the events are merely the backdrop against which the joke takes place. Here the shift from a characterization of the captain as brave and noble to his characterization as a rank coward is suddenly and economically achieved. Furthermore, tabooed or other rebellious thoughts are brought to mind without any explicit expression of them. The joke uses the action of the narrative to discourse about other things, and usually it is not until the end of the joke, in the punch line, that the topic of the joke becomes clear. Only then can the listener perceive what is major and what is minor — which elements are central and crucial and which are inconsequential background.

The points which have been made about folk narratives have several implications. First, folk narratives are not necessarily ancient or even very old. Folk narration is an ongoing process. Although there exist today many narratives which can be shown to reflect long traditions of development — traditions dating back centuries — innumerable narratives appear as exceedingly contemporary and do not reflect such deep historical roots. It is not possible to determine whether a particular narrative has such roots by the mere examination of the narrative alone. Narratives which seem exceedingly contemporary in their settings and details may be part of a much older narrative tradition. For example, some jokes which seem exceedingly contemporary can be traced back to the fourteenth-century tales of Giovanni Boccaccio or the fifteenth-century facetiae of Poggio Bracciolini.[9] The lineage of a particular narrative can be established only by exhaustive historical research. In any event, the antiquity or novelty of a particular narrative cannot be established simply by examining the text alone. Old narratives often appear in modern guise, and recently created narratives may carry with them the aura of venerable age.

Second, folklore in general, and folk narrative in particular, does not necessarily represent all that is good, beautiful, or noble in the world. Folk narratives are reflections of the societies and individuals which create and transmit them; consequently, they reflect a wide range of human ideas and emotions. Often one must get used to the fact that folk narratives do not just document the triumphs of good over evil and injustice, the sacrifices and martyrdoms in the pursuit of a righteous cause, or acts of humility and charity for which supernatural rewards are bestowed. Certainly such tales exist, but we must remember that folk narratives represent themes of violence, hatred, cruelty, racism, prejudice, sexuality, obscenity, and scatology as well. Those who wish to study and examine folklore which reflects only one or another of these sets of themes are not truly interested in the study and understanding of folklore as an expression of the human condition, but rather are interested in justifying, rationalizing, or exemplifying a philosophy or world view to which they are already committed. They are not truly interested in learning about the world; they are primarily interested in confirming what they think they already know.

Of course, folklore and folk narrative have been used in this way, they are used in this way, and they will continue to be used in this way.

But there is a difference between the *use* of folklore and the *study* of it. The student of folklore assumes that from the collection, analysis, and interpretation of folk narratives something is to be learned. Users of folklore are generally interested in folklore because they believe it illustrates something they wish to teach.

A corollary of the above discussion is that folk narratives are not the exclusive property or even the primary property of children. In our society, we often remember with great nostalgia the tales we read or had read to us as children. The enjoyment we derived from this very select group of tales, perhaps augmented by the attention our parents paid to us when they took the time to read or tell them, leads us to believe that folk narratives are particularly appropriate for children. Most of the research done on folk narrative in our own as well as in other societies indicates that such is not the case. Although children may attend narrative performances and occasionally participate actively in them, folk narration seems to be an activity primarily performed by adults for adults. Therefore, folk narrative is not de facto a children's literature. A great many folk narratives are not performed by children nor would they be performed by adults for children.

A third point concerns the discussion of the distinctions drawn between myth, legend, and tale. The central criteria which folklorists have brought to even the distinction of these varieties of folk narrative rely to a great extent on the perceptions and attitudes of the people who tell them. Do the people regard the narrative as sacred? If so, then it would seem to be a myth. Do they entertain the narrative as a potentially accurate recounting of actual events? Then it is a legend. Do they regard the narrative as a total fiction with a requisite suspension of disbelief? Then it is one form of the tale. The central point is that the folklorist is primarily concerned with the place of folk narrative in some larger context of belief and behavior. The folklorist recognizes that folk narratives are the productions of individuals, produced during social interactions, and informed by surrounding cultural traditions. The entire sense of folktale is not sandwiched in between "Once upon a time" and "they lived happily ever after." A tale is much larger than that. The folklorist must attempt to understand why people tell stories in the first place, why listeners appreciate them, and why they favor some stories over others. The problem is not only to understand how a text "hangs together," but also to understand why a particular individual or group of people would find such a text meaningful, worthy of attention, and deserving of repetition.

The answers to such questions can be sought only through a holistic study of narrative. The folklorist must seek to discover the structure or organization of the narratives, the possible explicit and implicit meanings to the people who tell them, and the functions of narration in the life of the group. The study of these structures, meanings, and functions can be accomplished only by examining the relations of particular folk narratives to larger contexts. There are four major contexts which have regularly served as the backgrounds for the understanding of folk narrative: the *cultural* context, the *social* context, the *individual* context, and the *comparative* context. In the analysis and interpretation of folk narrative, the folklorist must refer to one or more of these contexts.

The cultural context encapsules the system of ideas, symbols, and behaviors of the group in which particular folk narratives are found. The cultural context is often essential in the understanding of the narrative at the most basic level, but it is a context against which deeper layers of meaning in a narrative may be uncovered. Consider a folktale told in 1974 in the Tuscan region of Italy. It concerns a recently married woman, Genoveffa by name, whose husband, a prince, goes off to war. Before her husband leaves, she becomes pregnant. A cousin, whose own suit had been spurned by Genoveffa, accuses her falsely to her husband's parents, saying that she would give birth to a beast. Genoveffa gives birth to a lovely male child, but the queen mother orders her huntsman to take Genoveffa into the woods with her baby and kill her. The huntsman takes pity on Genoveffa and lets her go free, killing a deer and bringing its eyes to the queen as proof that he killed her son's wife as ordered. The tale continues with the husband's return and his discovery that Genoveffa is still alive. He seeks her out, asks her forgiveness and punishes his own wicked mother who condemned her. They are married once again, and when the king dies, he becomes king, with Genoveffa as his queen.

The folklorist who collected this tale as part of a larger study of folklore in Tuscany noted the Tuscan belief that the birth of monstrous children was to be a punishment brought down upon a woman, whereas a child who resembled the husband was thought of as a blessing. It was presumed that if at the moment of conception a woman thought of her husband, her child would have his features. Thus, the narrative motifs concerning the looks of the child are direct comments on the love of Genoveffa for her husband, according to Tuscan conventions.

The folklorist also stressed how much the situation depicted in the tale of Genoveffa reflected the family drama in the patriarchal Tuscan family. The wife has no status in her husband's family until she bears her first male child, at which point her husband generally begins to call her "mother" rather than by her Christian name. This is the point at which the wife supplants her own mother-in-law — inherits her position, so to speak — as Genoveffa does in the tale. Indeed, as her son grows up and takes a wife, she too will become a mother-in-law. This conflict, which is resolved in favor of the daughter-in-law in this fictional tale of Genoveffa, may end tragically in other Tuscan tales of wives falsely accused. Indeed, the unjust accusation of the bride is one of the most widespread motifs in Tuscan tales concerning married couples.

This relation of a tale to its cultural context cannot but affect the sense that the folklorist will make of the tale. Given this context, the interpreter of the tale of Genoveffa is likely to view it as directly related to Tuscan family structure and the opposition that exists between descent and marriage. It is likely to be regarded as a stage upon which active sociocultural forces are externalized, examined, manipulated, and played out.[10]

Narratives are performed in specific social contexts. These contexts are constituted by a specific group of people, by a specific set of principles governing their interrelationship, by a specific set of behaviors and conversations in which the narrative is embedded, and by a specific physical and symbolic environment present at the time of narration. The understanding of a narrative is governed to some extent by an understanding of the specific situation or situations in which it is told. How this social context shapes the use and informs upon the meaning of narrative can be illustrated by the following Jewish joke:

> A man once came to a rabbi to ask a *shayle* [question] regarding ritual purity.
>> He (the rabbi) says, "What is it? What did you do?"
>> He says, "I didn't say the prayer before the meal."
>> He says, "How come?"
>> He says, "Because I didn't wash my hands."
>> He says, "Well, why didn't you wash your hands?"
>> He says, "Because I wasn't eating Jewish food."
>> He says, "How come you weren't eating Jewish food?"
>> "Because I was eating in a Gentile restaurant."
>> He says, "How come?"
>> "Because it was *Yom Kippur* [The Day of Atonement] . . . and the Jewish restaurants were closed."

Orthodox Jews ritually wash their hands before saying the blessing over the bread that commences a meal. Yom Kippur, the Day of Atonement, is the most solemn day in the Jewish ritual calendar, a day devoted entirely to fasting and prayer. This joke concerns the confession of a small sin which ultimately reveals the existence of much more serious transgressions. What begins with the seeming oversight of failing to say grace before a meal is gradually transformed into a violation of Jewish dietary law and the prescribed fast on the Day of Atonement. While the understanding of this story requires considerable familiarity with its cultural context, its performance on one occasion can be understood only with reference to aspects of social context. This joke was used as a parable to comment upon the behavior of the teller's brother, who had repeatedly promised his children that he would take them to the movies only to renege each time. He finally agreed to take them to the show very late in the evening. By that time, the children no longer wanted to go and were angry with him. He couldn't understand why they were angry and asked his sister, "What have I done?" She responded with the above story. The

137

sister used this strategically in the course of a social interaction to make a comment about the events which had transpired and to characterize her brother's behavior. Had she criticized him directly, he might have responded with all kinds of rebuttals or rationalizations, and the argument in the family would have continued. As it was, he laughed heartily, thus acknowledging the joke as an appropriate characterization of his behavior. His laughter communicated, if only indirectly, his acceptance of responsibility for the family discord. As a result of this story and the responses to it, the atmosphere in the household was transformed and harmony was restored.[11]

Some folklorists' emphasis on social context in the recording and analysis of folklore expression has contributed to a conceptualization of folklore as *performances*. What we call a narrative "text" is merely a report about only one of the many behaviors which take place during storytelling. Indeed, a narrative is a report of only the verbal behavior of a single person. The study of performance, however, would attend to the full range of ideas and behaviors that bear upon a communicative interaction. Narration is conceptualized as an *event* taking place in time and space. It is more than a text and its constituent elements.

By individual context I refer to the particular individuals who perform and appreciate any particular narrative. Within the body of narratives traditional to a particular society and appropriate for performance on any particular occasion, why does a performer choose to perform a particular narrative? Why does he favor certain narratives over others? What is the nature of his relationship to the narrative as an individual? Here we must begin to examine the dispositions and life experiences of the narrators themselves. We must look at them as more than the mere representatives of particular cultural traditions or social statuses and begin to situate the narratives which they tell in the context of unique individual histories.

We may illustrate the individual context with another example drawn from Tuscan folk narration. The tale was told during a *veglia*, a ritualized evening gathering of family and friends by the fireplace. Storytelling formed an important part of the *veglia*. On one occasion, when several stories had already been told, a woman in her forties, who had come with her two children, requested that the one about Rolando and Brunilde be told. The story concerns a mother and her daughter, Brunilde, who was engaged to be married to Rolando, a young man of her village. One day, a passing magician sees Brunilde, who is quite beautiful, and asks for her hand. She refuses him because she is very much in love with Rolando. The magician kidnaps her, takes her to his castle, and shows her all his riches, but she doesn't care for any of it. The magician locks her up in his castle in a room near his bedroom, and because he is a sound sleeper, he makes an effigy with thousands of bells on it, so if anyone bumps into it during the night, he would be awakened. Meanwhile, the mother encounters a fairy in the form of an old woman who tells her of Brunilde's plight. The fairy shows the mother how to slip into the magician's castle and stuff the bells with cotton. After many nights, when all the bells are stuffed with cotton, the fairy tells the mother to take Rolando with her into the castle. Rolando is given a sword and told to cut off the left ear of the magician, since that is where all the powers of the magician reside. Rolando cuts off the magician's ear and the entire castle crumbles into dust. The couple takes all the gold and treasure which belonged to the magician, becomes rich, marries, and lives happily ever after.

The woman who regularly requested that the tale of Rolando and Brunilde be told was recognized as having something of a personal investment in it. She had lived with her widowed mother and was engaged to be married to a charcoal man. The padrone of the estate, who gave employment to everyone in the village, including the mother and charcoal man, had the woman come and work for him in his house. He never let her out. He made advances to the woman, but she could not leave his house since all three of them were dependent upon him for their livelihoods. The head housekeeper of the padrone's house was sympathetic to the woman, and helped her to arrange her marriage to the charcoal man. When she was ready to leave the house to marry her fiancé, the padrone did not want her to leave his service. The charcoal man came and had quite an argument with him. In the end, all of them lost their

139

employment. The charcoal man had to find work in another area; the mother, daughter, and housekeeper all lived together in town.

The similarities between the tale and the experiences of this individual are quite remarkable. Only the resolutions differ. In the tale, the heroes are rewarded with riches. In real life, the characters lose their employment and their home on the padrone's estate. It is apparent that the woman who constantly requested this tale at the *veglia* identified with it quite personally, and that its meaning to her was qualitatively different than its meaning to other members of the community. Exactly what the tale meant and how it functioned for this woman would require further investigation and discussion.[12]

The final context within which folk narrative may be analyzed and interpreted may be called the "comparative context." This context is different from the others mentioned thus far in that it is not a context that immediately bears upon the performance of the narrative itself. Rather, "comparative context" refers to the world of folk narrative which extends beyond the immediate situation of performance, perhaps beyond the society and culture as well. Nevertheless, this context may inform the analysis and interpretation of any particular narrative. Folklorists compare tales with other tales in order to unravel aspects of their history, structure, and symbolism.

There are numerous ways in which a comparative perspective can contribute to the interpretation and understanding of narrative. Once again, the narrative of Adam and Eve in the Garden of Eden may serve as an example. During the early decades of this century, the English folklorist, Sir James George Frazer, noted a peculiarity in this famous narrative. Although there were two trees in the garden — the Tree of Life and the Tree of the Knowledge of Good and Evil — and although they both get equal billing, only the latter tree plays any significant role in the tale. The Tree of Life, as it were, stands to one side, out of the limelight, while the cast of characters — Adam, Eve, and Serpent —seem to drape themselves about the other tree. In effect, Frazer asks why the Tree of Life should be introduced if it has so little consequence in terms of the story's plot. Frazer sees this biblical account as a possible transformation of an earlier tale in which there were two trees: a tree of life and a tree of death (rather than a tree of knowledge). As we have already seen, this fundamental polarization of attributes — in this case, life versus death — is characteristic of narratives in many oral literatures. Indeed, since this myth is about the origin of death in a very substantial sense, the notion that the Tree of Knowledge may have originally been a tree of death is not a farfetched claim. This would put the biblical myth in a wider class of world myths about the origin of death, the original story from which the biblical tale derives being an analogue of such stories in other cultures. Thus, underlying the biblical myth, Frazer suggests, is a common narrative of wide distribution in which a deity gives man the choice as to whether he is to live or die. He sends a messenger with the advice that man should choose life (in this case that he should eat from the Tree of Life rather than from the Tree of Death), but the message is falsified or otherwise perverted in the transmission so that man eats from the wrong tree and therefore must die. In some myths of this type, the messenger wrongly gives the message to man that he must die and to serpents that they are to live by shedding their skins and renewing their youth. In the context of world folklore, serpents are frequently symbols of immortality, not of evil.[13]

It is not difficult to see, whatever the merits of this particular interpretation, that viewing narratives comparatively within the context of world narrative cannot help but alter perspectives and provide possibilities for interpretive commentaries unobtainable through the investigation of cultural, social, and individual contexts alone.

In truth, when the folklorist approaches the interpretation of a folk narrative, he rarely restricts himself to only one of the four interpretive contexts which have been described. Usually, the approach to the narrative is multicontextual, since these contexts inform one another. There is no sharp division between the individual and the social, the social and the cultural, the cultural and the comparative. They all blend imperceptibly into one another. It would be foolish to believe that one could come to a full understanding of narratives and narrating by exploring only one of these contexts.

Elliott Oring

Folk narratives have been scrutinized since the days of the Brothers Grimm. As societies change, however, so do the kinds of narratives which tend to predominate. Attention paid in the past to myths and folktales is being redirected to jokes, legends, and personal experience stories, to those kinds of narratives that tend to infiltrate our common everyday discourse and pass by us almost unnoticed. These changes in focus and emphasis, however, do not alter the fact that the basic mysteries of narrative remain. The discovery of how and what folk narratives communicate will concern folklorists for generations to come.

Notes

1. William Labov and Joshua Wiletzky, "Narrative Analysis: Oral Versions of Personal Experience," in *Essays on the Verbal and Visual Arts*, ed. June Helm, Proceedings of the 1966 Annual Spring Meeting of the American Ethnological Society (Seattle: University of Washington Press, 1967), 20-21.

2. William Bascom, "Forms of Folklore: Prose Narratives," *Journal of American Folklore* 78(1965): 3-20.

3. For a representation of English translations of the Bible through 1948, see Hugh Pope, *English Version of the Bible* (St. Louis: B. Herder Book Co., 1952). For the National Council of Churches' retranslation and reinterpretation of "God the Father" as "God the Father and Mother" in response to recent feminist viewpoints, see *New York Times*, 16 October 1983, I: 27; 12 November 1983, I: 24.

4. The problem of defining legend in terms of belief has been addressed by Robert A. Georges, "The General Concept of Legend," in *American Folk Legend: A Symposium*, ed. Wayland D. Hand (Berkeley, Cal.: University of California Press, 1971), 4-5, 15-18.

5. Jan Harold Brunvand, *The Vanishing Hitchhiker: American Urban Legends and Their Meaning* (New York: W. W. Norton & Co., Inc., 1981), 34.

6. Grimm Brothers, *German Folk Tales*, trans. Francis P. Magoun, Jr., and Alexander H. Krappe (Carbondale, Ill.: Southern Illinois University Press, 1960), 20-22. It is a version of Aarne-Thompson Type 123. See Antti Aarne and

142

Stith Thompson, *The Types of the Folktale*, Folklore Fellows Communication No. 184 (Helsinki: Suomalainen Tiedeakatemia, 1964).

7.   For an example of sevenfold repetition in the folk literature of Land Dyaks, see W. R. Geddes, *Nine Dyak Nights* (London: Oxford University Press, 1969), xxx, 79n, 82.

8.   These characteristics of the folktale have been described by Axel Olrik, "Epic Laws of Folk Narrative," in *The Study of Folklore*, ed. Alan Dundes (Englewood Cliffs, N.J.: Prentice-Hall, Inc., 1965), 129-41; and Max Luthi, *Once Upon a Time: On the Nature of Fairytales* (Bloomington, Ind.: Indiana University Press, 1976), 47-57. The tale about the peasant and his wallet may be found in Kurt Ranke, ed., *Folktales of Germany* (Chicago: The University of Chicago Press, 1966), 104-6. It is a version of Aarne-Thompson Type 564.

9.   Giovanni Boccaccio, *The Decameron*, trans. Richard Aldington (New York: Garden City, 1930) and *The Facetiae of Poggio and Other Medieval Storytellers*, trans. Edward Storer (London: George Routledge and Sons, n.d).

10.   Alessandro Falassi, *Folklore by the Fireside: Text and Context of the Italian Veglia* (Austin, Tex.: University of Texas Press, 1980), 148-52.

11.   Barbara Kirshenblatt-Gimblett, "A Parable in Context: A Social Interactional Analysis of Storytelling Performance," in *Folklore: Performance and Communication*, ed. Dan Ben-Amos and Kenneth S. Goldstein (The Hague: Mouton, 1975), 105-30.

12.   Falassi, *Folklore by the Fireside*, 48-52.

13.   Sir James Frazer, *Folk-Lore in the Old Testament: Studies in Comparative Religion, Legend, and Law*, abriged ed. (New York: Tudor, 1923), 15-33.

Further Readings

Many people are familiar with the collection of folktales edited by the Brothers Grimm which has seen numerous English editions, including *German Folk Tales*, translated and edited by Francis P. Magoun and Alexander H. Krappe (Carbondale, Ill.: Southern Illinois University Press, 1960). Few are familiar with their collection of legends *The German Legends of the Brothers Grimm*, 2 vols., translated and edited by

Donald Ward (Philadelphia: Institute for the Study of Human Issues, 1981), which has only recently been translated. A volume of essays that explores concepts and theories of myth is Alan Dundes, ed., *Sacred Narrative: Readings in the Theory of Myth* (Berkeley, Cal.: University of California Press, 1984). The same editor provides a similar survey of perspectives on a single folktale in *Cinderella: A Casebook* (New York: Wildman Press, 1983). For essays addressing the concept of legend, see Wayland D. Hand, ed., *American Folk Legend: A Symposium* (Berkeley, Cal.: University of California Press, 1971). Personal experience stories are addressed by Sandra K. Stahl in " The Personal Narrative as Folklore," *Journal of the Folklore Institute* 14(1977): 9-30, as well as by other essays in that journal issue.

A number of excellent collections explore the text and context of narrative forms in different cultures. Alessandro Falassi, *Folklore by the Fireside: Text and Context of the Italian Veglia* (Austin, Tex.: University of Texas Press, 1980), explores storytelling occasions in northern Italy. Roger D. Abrahams, *Deep Down in the Jungle: Negro Narrative Folklore from the Streets of Philadelphia* (Chicago: Aldine, 1970) discusses the narrative traditions of urban black males. An extensive description of cultural context is provided by Jerome R. Mintz in his collection *Legends of the Hasidim: An Introduction to Hasidic Culture and Oral Tradition in the New World* (Chicago: The University of Chicago Press, 1968). A collection of African folktales and commentary are found in Peter Seitel, *See So That We May See: Performances and Interpretations of Traditional Tales from Tanzania* (Bloomington, Ind.: Indiana University Press, 1980). This collection is also concerned with the aesthetics of the folktale and addresses the question of how oral tales should be rendered in print.

A collection of children's nonfolk narrative is Brian Sutton-Smith's *The Folkstories of Children* (Philadelphia: University of Pennsylvania Press, 1981). This collection can provide a sense of how narrative competence develops with age. A collection of modern urban legends is provided in Jan Harold Brunvand, *The Vanishing Hitchhiker: American Urban Legends and Their Meaning* (New York: W. W. Norton & Co., Inc., 1981). For a detailed, yet comprehensible analysis of the humorous narratives of another culture, see Elliott Oring, *Israeli Humor: The Content and Structure of the Chizbat of the Palmah* (Albany, N.Y.: State University of New York Press, 1981). A focus on social context appears in Barbara Kirshenblatt-Gimblett, "A Parable in Context: A Social Interactional Analysis of Storytelling Performance," in *Folklore: Performance and Communication*, edited by Dan Ben-Amos and Kenneth S. Goldstein (The Hague: Mouton, 1975), 105-30, and Alf Walle, "Getting Picked Up Without Being Put Down: Jokes and the Bar Rush," *Journal of the Folklore Institute* 13(1976): 201-17. An emphasis on the individual context of narrative can be found in Elliott Oring, ed., *Humor and the Individual* (Los Angeles: California Folklore Society, 1984) [*Western Folklore* 44:1(1984)] and in Elliott Oring, *The Jokes of Sigmund Freud: A Study in Humor and Jewish Identity* (Philadelphia: University of Pennsylvania Press, 1984). How mythological and folktale motifs are employed in written literature is addressed from a quasi-Jungian perspective in David J. Burrows, Fredrick R. Lapides, and John T. Shawcross, *Myths and Motifs in Literature* (New York: The Free Press, 1973).

Chapter 7
Ballads and Folksongs

Barre Toelken

A folksong begins its life like any other song: as a musical and poetic expression of some person's feelings or ideas. A song *becomes* a folksong when it begins to be passed along and rephrased or used by others for whom it also functions as a way of articulating shared attitudes or feelings. Because the song's ability to trigger a group's feelings is more important than the practical matter of who the composer was, a folksong usually loses its direct connection with its maker and becomes the ward of those who sing it. It becomes a folksong not simply because a lot of people like it or because thousands have listened to it, but because some have persisted in singing it among themselves, and in their own way. It picks up the colorations, nuances, and styles of the group among whom it circulates, and gets continually rephrased to suit their responses to time, place, rhetoric, and performance. Such a song is seldom memorized word-for-word the way we were taught to memorize a literary text in school (in which we were not encouraged to improve on the poet's skill or demonstrate our own capabilities at composition), but rather it is comprehended and continually recomposed, in much the same way we pass on jokes, rumors, or family anecdotes.

As we pick up the songs of our family, of our age-mates, of our profession, we also learn by example the "knack" of how and when to sing them, how to join in on the chorus, or how to harmonize. Since the main idea of the song is often more important than specific wording or particular tunes, various kinds of changes occur constantly. Variations in local custom or phrasing, personal taste, creative ability, poor memory, variations in social and historical context, all bring about continual adjustments during the normal transmission of a folksong through generations of singers. Just as some people can tell a joke well and some can't, some people remember and sing better than others. In one family only Grandma sings, in another family no one sings (except for "Happy Birthday"), and in a third family everyone sings (except that Uncle Ken sings the parodies, Cousin Martha sings the old ballads, and everyone joins in on favorite hymns).

While someone in one place is forgetting a verse or phrase, someone in another place is singing it memorably (although perhaps only her family may hear it). While one culture tends to stress a hope for reunion in its songs about lovers' parting, another culture across the river savors the melancholy of the departure itself. Folksongs, like other genres of traditional expression, do not have to be ancient, or rural, or backward, or quaint in order to be called folklore; they are characterized by absorption into a group's expressive performances, by shaping of presentation and meaning brought about by the group's values, and by constant change and development. Some songs change more than others and some change very little, but the typical condition of folksong is one of flux.[1]

Who sings folksongs, and why do some change more than others? A brief recollection of songs we commonly sing or hear may suggest a few answers. We all sing folksongs at one time or another, and usually the occasion, plus local and family custom, will determine how we sing them. In America, songs sung by people joining in together are usually less apt to change than those sung by a single person; thus, "Happy Birthday," "Home on the Range," and "You Are My Sunshine" (often reinforced by mass media and popular culture) tend to change less than solo performances of a narrative folksong (ballad) such as "Barbara Allen," which has hundreds of different versions. Children's songs and obscene songs — perhaps because their effects are achieved by the use of certain key words — tend to remain very stable over long periods of time, whereas love lyrics in oral tradition may vary with each singing. We may never fully account for this wide range of possible variation, but it confirms "oral tradition" as a complex, common, and ongoing phenomenon.

Today, with the help of copyright laws, personality cults and fan clubs, media identification and glorification of stars and composers, royalty provisions and the like, the bulk of new songs retain their connection to their composers and achieve very little if any dynamic change. (Typically, change in such "owned" songs is limited to new arrangements by professional musicians.) In addition, Americans generally do not sing for themselves as much as they used to, and some smaller communities in which singing was common have changed so much that the context and expectation for singing are no longer present. Thus, many Americans get the bulk of their musical expressions not from each other under informal conditions, but from professional strangers who are skilled (often highly trained) performers and artists. It should be clear, then, that the distinction between folksongs and other kinds of songs is not based on quality, whimsy, purism, or commercial popularity, but rather on the basic characteristic ways in which musical and poetic expressions are created and transmitted among the members of various cultures and groups. We can say that folksongs are perpetuated by being constantly used and modified by their singers whereas commercial songs usually resist modification and remain identified with their owners. But these are not opposed or mutually exclusive kinds of propositions. Some songs which have been very resilient in oral tradition have also been widespread in various mass-mediated forms: many eighteenth-century broadside ballads, for example, were taken from oral tradition and achieved wide popularity in print, just as many songs composed for broadside publication became so well known that they developed into folksongs and were perpetuated in oral tradition long afterward.[2] Songs in oral circulation became popular hits in the 1950s when Burl Ives, The Weavers, Pete Seeger, and others began singing them for city audiences and on records. There has been a constant interaction between formal and informal music. Indeed, the works of many classical composers testify to the frequent borrowing from traditional folk music.

149

What kinds of songs become folksongs? Hypothetically, a folksong takes up and re-expresses any topic of human concern, but — like jokes and folktales — they tend to cluster around certain kinds of highly charged human values and activities. Some work songs (like chain-gang songs and some sea "chanteys") are sung in such a way that a work leader can organize and pace the rhythm of the work being done, while expressing through the words a longing for folks at home, recollections of a lady friend, distaste for the work, hatred for the boss, or the anticipation of returning home. Military cadence counts, by which the two basic rhythms of marching (4/4 and 6/8) are regulated and alternated, are usually sung as group responses to solo verses by the drill instructor and express shared concerns ("You had a good home but you LEFT!" "You're RIGHT!") or frustrations with life in the service ("Ain't no use in lookin' down; Ain't no discharge on the ground! Sound off!").

But other kinds of traditional songs are also alive and well: Children's parodies like "On Top of Spaghetti"; camp songs and ditties for passing the time on long bus rides ("Found a Peanut," "Ninety-Nine Bottles of Beer"); drinking and rugby songs; congratulatory songs ("For He's a Jolly Good Fellow," "Las Mañanitas," "Happy Birthday"); fraternity and sorority songs (not the ones in the official handbook); obscene songs ("The Big Red Wheel" or "Columbo"); and cowboy songs ("Streets of Laredo"). There are love songs like "Who's Gonna Shoe Your Pretty Little Foot" and "Turtle Dove," household songs like "Come Butter Come," "Life is a Toil," "Today is Monday," and play-party/dance songs like "Skip to My Lou" and "It's the Same Old Pig in the Garden." There are songs to be sung at the Passover Seder meal and around the Christmas tree which may or may not come from oral tradition, but their usage and meaning are determined by the customs which dictate when, where, and by whom they are sung. There are sung table graces (as well as parodies of the same); pow-wow songs sung by American Indians for intertribal dances; blues sung not only by blacks (who originated the genre) but by many others who have picked it up as an important mode of musical and poetic expression.[3]

Some folklorists have felt that a song qualifies as a folksong only when it has been sung and internalized over a considerable time by members of an identifiable folk group. To some extent this consideration makes sense, for it is usually the group's values which account for the constant "polishing" of a folksong as it goes on its way. Certainly, a black chain-gang song not only sounds different when sung by the Vienna Boys' Choir, but it is different because it both functions and communicates differently. But does it become more "authentic" when Harry Belafonte and a chorus of black singers perform the same song? This is more difficult to answer. Although black professional singers are not chain-gang laborers and thus do not sing from that experience or formally address themselves to those who do, they are nonetheless closer to it in a cultural and metaphorical sense by being related in color and political history to others who have lived in chains and have done forced labor. One single criterion is thus not enough to create a clear and distinct boundary between folksongs and other songs. We also know, moreover, that a song can go in or out of folk tradition for reasons quite remote from the attitudes of earlier audiences and singers. Surely, the London city folks who heard "The Unfortunate Rake" as a broadside popular song in the eighteenth century never dreamed that it would be sung by cowboys a hundred years later as a folksong called "The Streets of Laredo." As far as we know, loggers in the Pacific Northwest never sang "The Frozen Logger" as a logger song in the woods, but several generations of young people who have learned it as a campfire song (totally oblivious to its 1930s composition by James Stevens, author of many of the Paul Bunyan stories), sing it as part of their traditional repertoire around campfires. They, and not the loggers, have started to use it as a folksong, even though it has not yet started to pick up the variations we expect to find in traditional songs. (There is, however, an obscene parody of it sung by modern loggers.) Do we have to be parents to sing an authentic lullaby? No, but the experience of being a parent and the action of lulling a child to sleep repeatedly (not just on scattered occasions) create a deep personal connection to a culturally shared context. A song which refers to this shared system may articulate a tremendous range of understood meaning, nuance, implication, and feeling.

Not only are folksongs different according to their topics, singers, and performances, but they also differ greatly in structure and focus. The possibilities range from the incredibly simple but emotionally charged tune for "I know Billy's girlfriend"/"Billy is a sissy"/"Billy got in trouble" (which needs only to be hummed at the right moment to start young boys punching) to the pleasant repetitions of "Happy Birthday," to the metaphoric subtleties of love lyrics, to the narratives of English-Scottish ballads, to the stunning tours-de-force of Yugoslavian epic singers (who can lay out a narrative of 20,000 lines while entertaining their friends in a corner coffee shop).[4] The point is not simply that a Yugoslavian epic is longer than a ballad, or that a ballad is longer than a lyric, because quantity in and of itself is not the defining feature of performance. A short story is not simply a would-be novel that ran out of words, but a story which intentionally focuses on a single, intensified cluster of actions. A novel, on the other hand, usually combines a number of actions into a large and complex network of meaning. A love lyric may dwell intentionally on a particular image because of what the poetic elaboration can say about love that is inexpressible in everyday language. An epic may focus — as does the *Iliad*, for example — on a broad panorama of cultural actions in order to overwhelm the listener (nowadays the reader) with an avalanche of meaningful adventures which in the aggregate represent a cultural history of families and nations.

In the United States, the most commonly found folksongs (and thus the most commonly studied and discussed) are narrative and lyric folksongs, normally referred to respectively as ballads and folksongs. Actually, as will be abundantly clear by now, "folksong" includes both, but for convenience, most people refer to the narratives as "ballads" and to the remainder as "folksongs." The terminology should not become more cumbersome than it needs to be; the terms simply remind us of the principal differences in characteristic focus and style. The ballad develops an episode in which action takes place and is concluded, whereas the other folksongs focus on the articulation of feelings, ideas, fantasies, and attitudes without utilizing a narrative thread to achieve their ends. In a ballad, the story itself carries much of the meaning, and we as audience "watch" and "listen" to the characters as they interact meaningfully. If we interpret a ballad, we tend to do so by finding a sense in the actions and words of the ballad characters within the framework of a story.[5] In the case of folk lyrics, there are greater ambiguities and multiple possibilities. The listener identifies a topic or a motif that is meaningful and — using this personal context — responds to the implications and nuances. These inferential features are not less real than the more obvious narrative thread of a ballad, but they are more difficult to articulate in informational terms. For instance, a ballad can tell a story in which a young man takes the selfish advice of his father, marries the wrong young woman, and brings disaster upon his family — a fairly obvious theme of bad consequences following upon bad choice, with the nice irony of the flawed advice having come from someone who should have done better by his son. But how would one interpret the feelings of a loved one left behind for a prolonged period? Some of the deepest and most important human concerns, and the most delicate relationships, resist dramatization. Lyric folksongs explore and give voice to the ambiguities of such subjects.

Let us take a close look at a few representative ballads and lyrics, trying to read all we can out of them. One version of a well-known British ballad (#73 in the Francis James Child collection) is called "Lord Thomas and Fair Annet."[6] Note the dramatic presentation, in which there is little description, and where most of the action is understood inferentially through dialogue. We do not even know who the first speaker is until well into the story, when we can begin "adding up" the details into a meaningful pattern. We are also aware that some aspects of description and action might have to do with customs not altogether clear to us, but which could be established with a bit of research into the folkways of Britain a hundred or more years ago.[7]

1.   "Father, oh Father, come riddle this riddle,
       Come riddle it all as one:
       What must I do, marry Fair Eleanor,
       Or bring the Brown Girl home?"

2.   "Oh, that Brown Girl, she has houses and land,

Fair Eleanor, she has none;
So for your own blessed good, my son,
Go bring the Brown Girl home.''

3. So he dressed himself in silk so fine,
    His clothing all was in green;
    And every town that he rode through,
    They took him to be some king.

4. He rode up to Fair Eleanor's gate,
    And he lightly twirled at the pin;
    No one was so ready as Fair Eleanor
    To arise and let him in.

5. "What news, Lord Thomas, what news?'' said she,
    "What news do you bring to me?''
    "Well, I've come to ask you to my wedding.''
    "That's very bad news!'' said she.

6. But she dressed herself in silk so fine,
    Her clothing all was in green,
    And every town that she rode though,
    They took her to be some queen.

7. She rode up to Lord Thomas's gate,
    And she lightly twirled at the pin;
    No one was so ready as Lord Thomas
    To arise and let her in.

8. "Is this your bride? Is this your bride?
    She looks so very dark brown!
    And you might have married the fairest young girl
    As ever the sun shone upon!''

9. Well, the Brown Girl took her little pen knife,
    It was both long and sharp;
    And between the long ribs and the short
    She jabbed Fair Eleanor to the heart.

10. Lord Thomas then he up and spoke:
    "What makes you look so pale?

You used to wear as red rosy cheeks
As ever shone under a veil."

11. "Oh, are you blind that you can't see
Your bride has murdered me?
I can feel my own, my own heart's blood
Come trinklin' down by my knee."

12. Well, he took the Brown Girl by the hand,
And he led her down through the hall;
And with his sword, he chopped her head off,
And he kicked it against the wall.

13. Then he put the sword against the wall,
The point up against his breast,
Sayin' "Father, oh Father, here's three true lovers,
God send our souls to rest."

14. They buried her in the old churchyard,
Lord Thomas's grave was nigh her;
And from her mouth there grew a red rose,
And from his mouth a briar.

15. They grew and they grew up the old church wall,
'Til they couldn't grow no higher;
And there they tied a true lover's knot;
The red rose 'round the briar.[8]

In verse one, we note the stereotype, of long standing in northern Europe, that fair and dark complexions can be contrasted in value. Knowing that the stereotype held lighter-skinned people to be more virtuous than darker, and noting that Lord Thomas feels obliged to inform Fair Eleanor that he is marrying someone else, we conclude that he would rather have married her — the obvious culturally acceptable choice. How do we know that the Brown Girl is so named because of her coloration and not because her family name is Brown? Look again at verse 8. In verse 2, the father advises marriage to the "wrong" partner simply because she is wealthy. Although verse 3 is not grammatically clear about it, it is

155

dramatically clear that "he" refers to Lord Thomas, and not his father. When he arrives, in verse 4, he makes a noise at the gate and Fair Eleanor (not a servant) herself comes to open it, presumably showing her affections for him (as well as preserving the typical ballad economy on the number of actors who appear in each scene). Notice how much more meaningful the same action is when Thomas, presumably in the midst of wedding preparations, goes out and opens the gate for the woman to whom he is not getting married. Would this not make the prospective bride a bit upset? Would a ballad singer need to mention that possibility to us, or should we perceive it readily? Of course, the very first thing the disappointed candidate does is to insult the bride by referring to her color. In still other variants, she demands to know how someone can be so brown, and the Brown Girl responds by demanding to know where Eleanor got her white skin. Her reply indicates that she got it naturally, in the womb, driving home even more thoroughly the biological coloration differences between them. Incidentally, these need not be interpreted as racial slurs (although in later times they no doubt were understood that way); northern Europeans often referred to southern Europeans or Mediterranean people as "black" or "brown." In any case, the term carries the meaning "outsider," and hence not a proper choice for marriage. Does verse 9, with its sudden appearance of the knife and the violent (though provoked) actions by the Brown Girl, indicate that our suspicions are confirmed — that indeed the Brown Girl comes from a fiery people whose behavior does not exhibit proper self control? And why does Lord Thomas seem so stupid in verse 10? Is he really blind to what is happening, or could we see his question as a dramatic device which leads to Fair Eleanor's lament for her own demise? Perhaps both, since up to this point he *has been* blind to the consequences of taking his father's advice. And it is presumably his sudden shock at the turn of events that explains — or makes believable —his violent actions in verse 12 and his suicide (note the pointed address to the guilty father) in verse 13. The burial scene is understandable enough, for the woman buried in the churchyard is undoubtedly Fair Eleanor, and the common practice of burying suicides outside the church wall would have been recognized by the audiences of earlier years. We can now imagine the scene with even more clarity and focus: the plants grow up opposite sides of a wall (suggesting the barrier which existed between them but is now transcended in death) and reach each other at the top.[9] The idea of plants as representative of departed souls is widely known, both in folk tradition and in classical literature. In the ballads, plants usually appear on the graves of people who have been separated by the action of the story; thus we can surmise that the image has a recognizable function in the resolution of the narrative events. Not all plants grow out of the corpse's mouth, but since we also know that the soul was believed to have left the body by way of the mouth, we can infer that perhaps some singers sought to make the connection between the plants and departed characters even more intimate.

In all these interpretive remarks, the discussion proceeds from the narrative, plus what we can discover about the cultural and historical contexts in which the ballad was sung. Thus far, we have done essentially the same kind of analytical job we would have done with any good poem: we have tried to pick up as much of the potential meaning as possible and have tested its validity against the events within the narrative itself. The ballad is also a song, however, and therefore the musical stanza, rhythm, and rhyme must be considered meaningful parts of the expression, in addition to the words. Finally, we need to remember that this is only one version of a ballad which has many other recorded performances: our task here would be to consult all the other versions to see if the same story is told with the same kinds of implications.[10] For example, of one hundred different versions, do all — or most — feature a contrast between women of different complexion? Does the action always proceed from selfish or socially inappropriate advice from an adult family member? Is there always a dialogue between the two female characters? Do murder and suicide always conclude the action? Do the two lovers always reunite in the form of plants? These questions allow us to see what the main concept of the song has been through time and then to recognize the various departures, regional specializations, and singers' preferences which have had an effect on the ballad through time and across space. Nothing is as central to the critical study of folklore as this often cumbersome but obligatory investigation of variant expressions of the same basic item, whether the subject be ballads, barns, quilts, legends, or recipes for potato salad.

The same kind of scrutiny is given lyric folksongs, of course, but here we do not have the structure of a narrative to help us in determining meaning. In a story, we know certain things almost in advance: of course Fair Eleanor will attend Lord Thomas's wedding, for otherwise, the rest of the action cannot take place. Of course Bluebeard's wife will look in the forbidden room, and Jack will climb the beanstalk, and the Prince will discover that the glass slipper fits the beautiful girl in the corner rather than the first ugly sister. Traditional stories are based on traditional logic, much of which we share through having learned it in a myriad of traditional forms. A lyric is more ambiguous; in fact, it thrives on ambiguity and allusion. Lyrics gain much of their meaning from the *way* they are sung, and the situations in which they are sung. Thus the ambiguity inherent in a lyric actually enhances its capability of being personalized and made compatible with and appropriate to the live scene in which it is performed. For these reasons, when we study lyric folksongs, we need to know more about the context and style of the actual performance. We must also be ready to allow the lyric words and music to evoke responses in us which we can use in the formulation of potential meanings. We need to be ready to admit, and even appreciate the fact, that a lyric can mean more than one thing, even to the same singer, and that this possibility for complexity and richness in meaning is precisely why we sing lyrics — they often communicate a feeling or idea that cannot be articulated so well in any other fashion. In short, they are lyrics not because they are short, or because singers have a poor memory, or because they are songs *lacking* a narrative structure; they are lyrics because they focus on the intense and distilled performance of unstructured thoughts and feelings.

An especially good example of this focus and ambiguity is a folksong often heard in the United States which actually descends from a British ballad called "The Lass of Roch Royal."[11] It would be tempting — but wrong — to assume that this brief set of verses represents the erosion of a once complete story. For one thing, the lyric, as it stands, is too self-contained, too symmetrical; it does not show signs of forgetfulness or lack of poetic capability. It does demonstrate compassion and ambiguity in a way that suggests a high level of poetic competence on the part of singers who have passed it along. In the older ballad, the lyric forms the early part of a story in which a woman attempts to follow and be reunited with her lover. The unmarried but pregnant young woman essentially is asked by her family, "Who will take care of you, now that you're in this condition?" In the American version, pregnancy is not hinted. Let us look at the lyric text, without reference to any context, to see what the text itself suggests.

> Who's gonna shoe your pretty little foot?
> Who's gonna glove your hand?
> Who's gonna kiss your ruby red lips?
> Who's gonna be your man?
>
> *Chorus*
> Who's gonna be your man?
> Who's gonna be your man?
> Who's gonna kiss your ruby red lips?
> Who's gonna be your man?
>
> Poppa's gonna shoe my pretty little foot.
> Momma's gonna glove my hand.
> Sister's gonna kiss my ruby red lips.
> I don't need no man.
>
> *Chorus*
> I don't need no man.
> I don't need no man.
> Sister's gonna kiss my ruby red lips.
> I don't need no man.[12]

On the surface, this simple and apparently repetitive song conveys a rather simple meaning — someone is courting the person, but that person isn't interested. Although the song does not explicitly say so, we assume

159

that the speaker of the questions must be a male, and that the answerer must be a female. Nothing in the song requires this interpretation, for this could easily be viewed as a homosexual invitation, but our cultural assumptions are in gear before our conscious awareness of this other possibility is engaged. Now we are left with the text, which leads off with mention of shoes and gloves. Is this the love song of a haberdasher? — a fetishist? — a fast talker who plans to bribe his way to the ruby red lips with gifts of clothing? Nothing else in the song conveys alarm or trickery, so we may safely infer that shoeing someone's pretty little foot and gloving her hand are figurative expressions for "who is going to provide for you?" The third point in the triad suggests that the offer to provide is more than altruistic and apparently connected to the idea of romance. "Who is going to take care of you physically, financially, and emotionally; that is to say, who is going to be your man?" When we paraphrase such a good poem and see how dull and tawdry the everyday expression would be, we gain a substantial insight into the reason for the existence of poetry and song. The singer further intensifies the real romantic burden of the question by repeating its principal message in the chorus. The woman replies that her family will provide for her on both counts, and therefore she needs no male companion; she drives the idea home with a repetition of the principal image — the only age-mate I need emotionally is my sister. One way to decode this song is to add up all these impressions and conclude that a male has proposed a serious relation-ship (marriage perhaps?) and that the lady of his intentions has turned him down, not because she doesn't like him, but because she does not want to leave her family. Fairly simple, or is it? Let us now view it in three different contexts to see what its meaning may turn out to be.[13]

Context A: a gathering in a rural home in the mountains of North Carolina. People are sitting in the kitchen, most of them taking turns singing. A young man from "down the branch" drops in and makes flirtatious gestures with his eyes at one of the sisters in the family. Her younger sister then sings the song, and everyone breaks out laughing, including the young man, who leaves shortly afterward.

Context B: a family gathering in Salt Lake City, Utah, where close family friends are bidding goodbye to a young Mormon missionary about to leave for two years abroad. He sings the song, looking earnestly at his fiancée. Afterwards, to ease the awkwardness, another friend comments, "Well, you know they say when you go away on a mission, you'll lose either your hair or your girlfriend!" The young man runs his hand through his hair and says, "Wonder what I'd look like bald." Everyone laughs.

Context C: a group of friends gathered for singing in a small town in Massachusetts. A married man sings the song, looking playfully at his wife of some twenty years. When the line "I don't need no man" occurs, she nods in mock agreement, kicks him on the side of the shin, and says louder than the song, "I told you that before; don't complain about it now!" Everyone laughs, including the husband who lovingly kicks her in return.

What are the meanings of these three performances? In Context A, the implication is that a family member is helping to reject the (serious?) flirtations of an acquaintance *as if* he had asked to provide for her sister. In Context B, the young missionary wants the song to mean that his fiancée's family will provide for her while he's away and that she will not need other (rival) male companionship. A young woman singing the song in the same context might be saying "Yes! I'll wait for you." In Context C, no real courtship or substantive question is being phrased or considered, but rather a happily married couple is pretending that there is some reluctance about their relationship, knowing that their friends know otherwise but still expect the woman to hold her own and speak her piece.

Now a fourth possibility: in a railroad yard outside Eugene, Oregon, where a number of nonstandard rail travelers are cooking a liberated Salvation Army chicken over a fire, a young man is singing a series of railroad songs, Bob Dylan hits, and a few nondescript and unconnected obscene verses. Then he sings:

I was standing on a dirty platform
Smokin' a cheap cigar —
Waitin' for the first freight train
To carry an empty car.

161

I got caught in a coon-can game
And couldn't hardly play my hand,
All for thinkin' about that woman I love
Run off with a railroad man.

She said ''Poppa's gonna shoe my pretty little foot,
And Momma's gonna glove my hand,
And Sister's gonna kiss these rosy, rosy lips,
But I won't need no man.

''I won't need no man,'' she said,
''I won't need no man.''
''Sister's gonna kiss these rosy, rosy lips,
But I won't need no man.''[14]

The general response is not laughter, but sighs of resignation and concurrence. Implied meaning: you can't trust women to keep their word (and the rival is the disliked man who has a job on the railroad that the rest of us have to catch on the fly).

In each of these cases, essentially the same song has touched off a different set of understood meanings. Obviously this would not have been possible unless the text had an inherent ambiguity which can be particularized in situations where values, emotions, frustrations, fears, and hopes await the opportunity for expression.

Many lullabies have the capacity to communicate several messages during the same performance. In this kind of ambiguity, there is a distinct difference between what the singer does with the song and what the song itself says, and both of these opposed messages will be communicated at one and the same time. In a lullaby, the presumed aim is to sing the baby to sleep, or at least to quiet the baby down. The tunes are often simple and melodic, and many parents use the rhythm of the song as a guide to how fast they should rock or swing the baby back and forth, their bodily actions participating with the tune in a concerted effort to soothe, hold, and lull the baby. But as Bess Lomax Hawes has shown, the words of lullabies are seldom designed to communicate soothing ideas to the baby.[15] In some, attention is called to the father's absence, often coupled with the hope that if he comes back, he'll be bringing gifts (sometimes

162

qualified by suspicions that the mocking bird won't sing, that the ring will be of brass, or that the billy goat won't pull). "Aunt Rhody" describes the death of a mother goose and the lamenting of her goslings, certainly not the most comforting imagery for a small child. Even more puzzling are such common songs as "Rock-a-bye Baby," which predicts the child falling from a tree (sometimes accompanied by a falling motion with the baby in the parent's arms while singing), obviously a way of creating fright rather than allaying fear. We can reduce the problem of ambiguity somewhat by noting that the smallest babies cannot understand the words, so these ideas register chiefly with the adults and older children in the audience. This brings us then to the crux of the issue: why do adults express disturbing ideas with words while soothing babies with tunes? Is there a relationship between these apparently opposed messages which might make sense of these most common of lyrics? Let us consider other common lullaby texts before trying to decode these ambiguities:

> Go to sleep, my little pickaninny;
> The bears will get you if you don't look out![16]

The first verse of the following song became rather well known during the folksong revival of the 1950s and 60s. The second verse, sung in a different stanzaic form, does not conform to the pretty, childish images of the first:

> Hush-a-by, don't you cry,
> Go to sleepy little baby;
> When you wake, you shall have
> All the pretty little horses —
> Blacks and bays, pintos and greys,
> Coach and six-a little horses.

> Way down yonder in the meadow
> Lies a poor little lamby;
> Bees and butterflies pecking out his eyes —
> Poor little thing cryin' "Mammy!"[17]

Another very common lullaby on the western frontier was a focused selection from a previous broadside ballad once popular in England. "The Children in the Wood," also known by several other titles, was such a great favorite in the eighteenth century that our phrase "innocent as babes in the woods" may derive from it. In America it was characteristically shortened to focus primarily on the dilemma of the two lost children, and the longer, overly moralistic and melodramatic plot of attempted murder by two hired thugs was dropped. The result is an intensified foregrounding of the image of lost children abandoned in the forest — not a very placid topic for a lullaby.

> One day, as I remember, a long time ago,
> Two sweet little babes, their names I don't know,
> Were stolen away one bright summer's day,
> And left in the woods, or so people say.
>
> And when it was night, so sad was their plight:
> The stars came out, but the moon gave no light;
> They sat side-by-side and they bitterly cried:
> Two babes in the wood, they lay down and died.
>
> And when they were dead, the robin so red
> Brought strawberry leaves and over them spread,
> And say them a song the whole night long,
> Two babes in the wood, two babes in the wood.[18]

Perhaps it is best to start the discussion of this kind of folksong with this last piece because it exemplifies several processes going on constantly in folklore. First, it comes originally from a composed popular song that went into oral tradition because there was something about it people liked or responded to. That something began to appear more clearly as people weeded out the parts of the story which were less important, details about a greedy and murderous uncle and about how many pounds per year the departed parents had allocated to the support of their surviving children. The plight of the children, the disturbing image of the innocent and defenseless away from the protection of the adult world, the compensatory image of nature's concern for the departed innocents are apparently the areas upon which subsequent singers wished to concentrate. Who are these children? They have become generic children, innocents lost who find their home in death and in nature. Why was it used as a lullaby in the American West? We can imagine that the fear of losing one's children in the forest must have been great. Many families had to bury their dead children in unmarked graves along the westward trails. When they arrived in the northwestern forests, the trees and underbrush were so thick that a child could easily wander away and get lost. It is easy to imagine that while a mother lulled her child to sleep, the comfort being immediately given was belied by the dangers and threats of the world outside the cabin. Concomitant with raising a child and stilling its fears was the adult awareness of how cruel and unpredictable, how dangerous and remote, how alien and anxiety-provoking the world could be. The double image of baby asleep surrounded by a hazardous world is indeed difficult to "explain" in mundane and precise language, but the oxy-moronic possibilities of the lullaby make such simultaneous expression possible. In figurative terms, the mother is worried about her child being "gotten" by bears; and the same mother who can promise a dreamy world in which the child can have all the pretty little horses, also knows of the world where the dead, unable to get help from their mammies, have their eyes pecked out by natural forces not envisioned by the child. Perhaps the most bothersome aspect of parenthood is this "double vision" of the world; perhaps the best indicator of how powerfully complex lullabies can be is this capacity to capture and express such a vision in song.

Still another form of folksong is the parody; this genre is so extensively found in modern times that its vitality must be seen as one of several signs that folksong transmission is far from moribund. In the case of a parody, the tune and the text must resemble a well-known original so closely that no doubt exists about what song is being referred to. Among other things, parodies are indicative of how well those other songs are known. But the function of parody goes much deeper: a conscious discrepancy is set up between the remembered original and the new set of words. Often the point of creating the discrepancy is to imply some

165

comment on the original or to suggest some parallel or contrast between the new and the original.

A common college song in the late 1950s was a comment on the sanctimonious, protective attitudes of college Deans of Women:

> Dean Jones is the good girl's doom:
> Intense whispers in the gloom;
> Suddenly there falls a hush:
> Dean's inspecting underbrush.
>
> Yes, Dean Jones loves me,
> Yes, Dean Jones loves me,
> Yes, Dean Jones loves me,
> My handbook tells me so.[19]

The implied parallel to "Jesus Loves Me," with its religious overtones, along with the suggestion of childish subordination to higher authority, make a complicated statement about how students felt concerning nosy deans and their moral assumptions about student activities. Not many years later, the colleges and universities began to abandon their parental and moral role in students' lives.

Labor and protest songs of the late 1930s often used the tunes and even the rhyme schemes of the better-known hymns. Juxtaposed to "Hallelujah, Thine the Glory" was "Hallelujah, I'm a Bum"; over against "In the Sweet Bye and Bye" was "You will eat bye and bye/in that glorious land above the sky"; and "Life is Like a Mountain Railroad," with its precept, "Keep your hand upon the throttle and your eye upon the rail," found a mirror image in the miners' union song which advised, "Keep your hand upon the dollar and your eye upon the scale." Suggesting parallels with religious themes or contrasts to religiosity gives these parodies a range of meaning that emerges *between* the texts, so to speak, rather than found manifestly in the content. Here, one set of meanings (the original) has been detoured and co-opted, transformed into another set through the contrast or similarity of the words. Clearly, in parodies, if the tunes were to change along with the words, this possibility for double-level irony would be quickly eroded.

Imagine you are a relatively religious westward pioneer who joins other folk occasionally in singing a hymn around the campfire. Many of your favorite hymns employ the imagery of a heaven with agricultural plenty — a kind of hopeful pun through which you envision your future home in a western valley as resembling the fields of heavenly plenty. Then you lose all your money, or your family, or your livestock in a hot, dry badland area of the Dakotas. Certainly, the song you had been singing as Beulah Land:

> I've reached the land of corn and wine,
> And all its riches now are mine;
> Here shines undimmed one blissful day,
> For all my night has passed away.
>
> Oh Beulah Land, sweet Beulah Land,
> As on thy highest mount I stand:
> I look away across the sea
> Where mansions are prepared for me
> And view the shining glory shore,
> My heaven, my home forevermore.[20]

might seem a bit empty to you now, and a parody that went something like the following might better serve to express the discrepancy between the real and the ideal:

> I've reached the land of dying wheat,
> Where nothing grows for man to eat,
> Where the wind it blows the fiery heat
> Across the plains so hard to beat.
>
> Oh Dakota Land, South Dakota Land
> As on thy burning soil I stand,
> I look away across the plains
> And wonder why it never rains

167

'Til Gabriel blows his trumpet sound
And says the rain's just gone around.[21]

Here is the burning landscape of Hell instead of the balm of Heaven; here, instead of seas of water, the rainstorms can be seen dropping on others' property far away; here, instead of growing, things are dying. Yet the optimism and joy of Beulah Land are echoed by the familiar tune. The irony is unmistakable. But more complicated yet is the fact that it was not (as far as we know) the disappointed settlers themselves who made up the parody, but their heirs, the succeeding generations, who used the song as a way of demonstrating a sense of triumph over privation, as if to say, "We're Dakotans, b'God, and proud of it!" Again, context, usage, nuance, feeling, shared history, and privation — these are the electrodes between and among which meaning takes shape.

Parodies lean heavily on recognizable tunes to cue our responses to the altered ideas produced by the new wording, and this is a solid demonstration of the importance of music as an element of meaning in folksong. In an essay like this, music itself is difficult to discuss in any great detail, but some important things can be said which will help us understand the role of musical meaning. To get a feel for the importance of music in folksong, consider the difference in quality between those things which are sung and those which are recited. For example, recite the words to a favorite popular song, leaving no words out. What is the effect? Recite the words to "Happy Birthday," "Silent Night," "Auld Lang Syne," or any of the song texts given in this essay. What do they lack in feeling when you simply say them? What do they gain in resonance when you sing them? Singing involves a personal, bodily involvement with a text which — because of the demands of tune, range, melody, and harmony — requires more from us than conveying lexical meaning. In addition, the tune itself may have an emotional charge to it; many people get tears in their eyes when they hear the tune of "Auld Lang Syne," or "Two Babes in the Wood," or "Las Mañanitas," the Mexican birthday song. This kind of emotional dimension is enhanced and intensified when a certain song is associated with a relative who sang it customarily, or with a family situation in which everyone sang it together, or with a deeply important ritual. The tune itself can trigger a wave of nostalgia, emotional commitment, personal experience, and intimate recollection.

Structurally, of course, folksong tunes are usually arranged in verses and choruses which help to organize the thoughts into meaningful clusters — paragraphs if you will — and to regulate the alternation of the singers (leader sings the verses, audience joins in on the chorus, for example). In this regard, the music may be said to be part of the rhetorical organization of the song, as well as the "vehicle" by which the song is conveyed. Furthermore, many people can remember immense amounts of poetry when it is accompanied by music. The rote memorization of words alone is often more difficult; the musical phrase helps singers retain the words they want and provides a rhythmic and tonal frame in which variations can be introduced without transforming the song beyond recognition.[22]

The singing of a folksong is intimately a part of its meaning and its reason for being. By singing, we come closer to experiencing the possible emotional dimensions and cultural meanings of a song, and we continue to deepen our own capacity to resonate to these important but often unexplained ingredients of our culture. Through the singing of a song we share more than verbal information. We provide a living voice for the concerns of others (who may be far distant in time or space) who have also sung the songs. According to the famous Japanese folklorist, Yanagita Kunio, by participating in folklore we achieve a personal and deep experience with the ongoing social history of the culture to which we belong. Surely, folksongs are an excellent example of this postulate.[23]

Notes

1. It will be clear from other essays in this book that the constant variation in folk expression has shaped the nature of folklore scholarship, which studies the changes in relation to the stable elements. For a book-length discussion of the interaction between conservatism and dynamics in folklore, see Barre Toelken, *The Dynamics of Folklore* (Boston: Houghton Mifflin Co., 1979).

2.   The basic study of this process is Malcolm G. Laws, Jr., *American Balladry from British Broadsides: A Guide for Students and Collectors of Traditional Song*, Publications of the American Folklore Society, Bibliographical and Special Series, vol. 8 (Philadelphia: American Folklore Society, 1957).

3.   Jan H. Brunvand, *The Study of American Folklore: An Introduction*, 2d ed. (New York: W. W. Norton & Co., Inc., 1978) devotes a whole chapter (Chap. 10) to folksong, another (Chap. 11) to ballad, and still another (Chap. 12) to folk music. Each chapter has a full, updated bibliography for further reading. See also Appendix D in the same book: "Structure and Meaning in the Folk Blues," by David Evans.

4.   A fine collection of folksongs ranging from occasional ditties to hymns to lyrics to ballads is found in Vance Randolph, ed., *Ozark Folksongs* (Columbia, Mo.: State Historical Society, 1946-50; [rev. ed., Harper & Row Publishers, Inc., 1980]). An excellent single-volume collection of ballads is Albert B. Friedman, ed., *The Viking Book of Folk Ballads of the English-Speaking World* (New York: The Viking Press, Inc, 1956; [repr. Penguin Books, 1982]). A view of the Yugoslavian epic singer may be obtained in Albert B. Lord, *The Singer of Tales* (Cambridge, Mass.: Harvard University Press, 1960).

5.   M. J. C. Hodgart, *The Ballads* (London: Hutchinson University Library, 1950; [repr. Norton, 1962]), uses the parallel of film montage to clarify the way a ballad narrative is built.

6.   Francis James Child, ed., *The English and Scottish Popular Ballads* (Cambridge, Mass.: Harvard University Press, 1882-98; [repr. Dover, 1965]), in five volumes, is the standard scholarly collection of ballad texts, though many of its individual items are open to question and its omissions are puzzling.

7.   The standard discussion of folk traditions in balladry is Lowery C. Wimberly, *Folklore in the English and Scottish Ballads* (Chicago: The University of Chicago Press, 1928). Helpful with historical and social detail as well as with rural figurative language are James Reeves, *Idiom of the People* (New York: Macmillan Publishing Co., Inc., 1958), and Roger deV. Renwick, *English Folk Poetry* (Philadelphia: University of Pennsylvania Press, 1980).

8.   Sung by "Grandma" Mary Spivey, at Buckeye Cove, North Carolina, in July of 1952; collected by Barre Toelken.

9.   For discussion of this and other traditional beliefs in ballads, see Wimberly, cited above.

10.   Child lists eleven versions and Randolph presents ten; the ballad appears prominently in virtually every collection of ballads in the English-speaking world.

11.   This ballad appears as #76 in the Child collection, where thirteen versions are given.

12.   This text collected by Barre Toelken from Clif Bushnell in Buckeye Cove, North Carolina, in July 1952; it is essentially the same in wording and structure as the versions discussed below.

13.   The three contextual situations discussed here are summarized from actual experiences I encountered while collecting folksongs. In each case, the situation lasted longer and was somewhat more complex than noted, but the singing of the song in each, and its relation to live context, are recollected as accurately as possible.

14.   Collected by Barre Toelken on Thanksgiving Day, 1980, under a bridge north of Eugene, Oregon.

15.   Bess.Lomax Hawes, "Folksongs and Function: Some Thoughts on the American Lullaby," *Journal of American Folklore*, 87(1974): 140-48.

16.   Text from an anonymous informant, housed in the Fife Folklore Archives folksong collection, Utah State University, Logan.

17.   Recollected from the singing of her mother by Pamela Renz, a student at Utah State University.

18.   Collected by Barre Toelken from Herb Arntson, Pullman, Washington, October 1958; these words are fairly typical of the song as it is sung throughout the United States, although one Oregon version uses "maple leaves."

19.   Text recollected from the author's memory; the song was common during the 1950s and 60s and was heard at Washington State University, Luther College (Iowa), the University of Utah, and the University of Oregon.

20.   The full text of this hymn can be found in almost any standard Protestant hymnal.

21.   Brunvand discusses this song briefly in his folksong chapter, and a somewhat more detailed view, including texts from Kansas, New Mexico, and Oregon, can be found in Barre Toelken, "Northwest Regional Folklore," in Glen Love and Edwin Bingham, eds., *Northwest Perspectives* (Seattle: University of Washington Press, 1979), 21-42.

171

22. For discussions of the relations between music and words, see Bertrand Bronson, *The Ballad as Song* (Berkeley and Los Angeles: University of California Press, 1969); Bronson, *The Traditional Tunes of the Child Ballads with Their Texts, According to the Extant Records of Great Britain and America*, 4 vols. (Princeton, N.J.: Princeton University Press, 1959-72); Roger D. Abrahams and George Foss, *Anglo-American Folksong Style* (Englewood Cliffs, N.J.: Prentice-Hall, Inc., 1968).

23. The extensive works of Yanagita Kunio remain mostly untranslated and thus unavailable to most Americans. A small book of essays about his work which includes some translated passages is J. V. Koschmann, Oiwa Keibo, and Yamashita Shinji, eds., *International Perspectives on Yanagita Kunio and Japanese Folklore Studies*, Cornell University East Asia Papers, Number 37 (Ithaca, N.Y.: Cornell University Press, 1985).

Further Readings

Since ballads and folksongs have been among the most intensely studied of folklore genres in England and America, there exists an overwhelming bibliography of important studies, collections of texts, essays, and notes — far too many in number and specialization to be presented fairly in a general study. The following references were chosen because they are particularly interesting or engaging, and because they provide ample citations of other important scholarly works. Check the bibliographies of any books listed here to find collections and seminal studies which have led to current views on folksong; read closely the footnotes in the articles listed here to see the wonderful variety of ongoing speculations, conversations, and arguments about the nature of folksong.

The works of Reeves, Wimberly, and Renwick, mentioned in the footnotes to this chapter, are especially valuable to those who wish to approach the question of folksong meaning (in contrast to structure, rhyme scheme, and other textual matters), for they provide the kinds of cultural backgrounds which are absolutely necessary for understanding the frames of reference and metaphor used by those who have shaped the genre. These are good antidotes for the tendency to read our own meanings into the songs (or to overlook the local meanings which are already there).

For understanding the ways in which folksongs and ballads travel and change, basic works are Tristram P. Coffin and Roger de V. Renwick, eds., *The British Traditional Ballad in North America*, rev. ed. (Austin, Tex.: University of Texas Press, 1977); Holger O. Nygard, *The Ballad of Heer Halewijn*, Folklore Fellows Communication No. 169 (Helsinki: Suomalainen Tiedeakatemia, 1958); Eleanor Long, *"The Maid" and "The Hangman": Myth and Tradition in a Popular Ballad*, Folklore Studies No. 21 (Berkeley, Cal.: University of California Press, 1971). Unfortunately, there is no equivalent study for folk lyrics that matches Gordon Hall Gerould's *The Ballad of Tradition* (Oxford: Oxford University Press, 1932; [repr. Galaxy, 1957]). An excellent ballad study using recent scholarship and reevaluation of older texts is David Buchan, *The Ballad and the Folk* (London: Routledge and Kegan Paul, 1972). A good single-volume edition of British broadside ballads is V. de Sola Pinto and Allen E. Rodway, eds., *The Common Muse* (New York: Philosophical Library, 1957).

A number of essay collections can be found, but two very important ones are MacEdward Leach and Tristram P. Coffin, eds., *The Critics and the Ballad* (Carbondale, Ill.: Southern Illinois University Press, 1961; [repr. Arcturus, 1973]) and Carol L. Edwards and Kathleen E. B. Manley, eds., *Narrative Folksong: New Directions* (Boulder, Colo.: Westview Press, 1985). The latter is international in scope and does not limit itself to ballads. (Indeed, Tristram P. Coffin presents therein a study of lyric classification which includes comments on "Babes in the Wood.") For folksong scholarship overall, see D. K. Wilgus, *Anglo-American Folksong Scholarship Since 1898* (New Brunswick, N.J.: Rutgers University Press, 1959); it is limited only insofar as its date of publication preceded much of the important work of recent years.

Nearly every state or region has produced collections of local folksongs; they need not be listed here. Rare but interesting is Robert W. Gordon's *Folk Songs of America*, published in mimeographed format in 1938 by the Works Progress Administration. John and Alan Lomax have published a number of folksong gatherings over the years, some of the texts more accurate than others (in terms of what actually occurred in the oral presentation), but all providing a rich overview of the variety and vitality of traditional singing in America. Students of folksong should also consult the major folklore journals for articles on folksong: The *Jahrbuch fur Volksliedforschung* [Yearbook for Folksong Research], published by the German Folksong Archives in Freiburg, West Germany, specializes in folksong and — though its articles are chiefly in German — often presents pieces in English. Since the term "folksong" has often been used in recent years to sell books of children's songs, topical and political songs, and popular songs accompanied by guitar, it is well for the student to take a close look at the way in which any collection of folksong texts is presented: if it is clear that the songs have been collected from oral tradition (including details of collection, notes on context, names and addresses of informants), then the reader can be reasonably certain that the contents will relate to the study of traditional folksong.

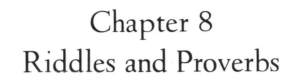

Chapter 8
Riddles and Proverbs

F. A. de Caro

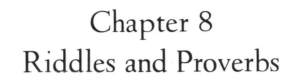

Readers of J. R. R. Tolkien's fantasy novel *The Hobbit* may recall Bilbo Baggins's dangerous encounter with Gollum in a dark and damp underground cavern where the latter lives. The hobbit, Bilbo, and his companions, the wizard Gandalf and a troop of dwarves, on their way to capture a treasure guarded by a dragon, are being stalked by goblins. The goblins swoop down, Bilbo is knocked unconscious and wakes up alone in the cave, where he soon runs into the sinister, slithery Gollum, who desires to make a meal of Bilbo. The two enter into deadly combat, not physical combat, but a war of words and wits. They exchange riddles, each posing and answering in turn. If Bilbo misses an answer, Gollum suggests, the little hobbit will be devoured.

> What has roots as nobody sees,
> Is taller than trees,
> Up, up it goes,
> And yet never grows?

asks Gollum, but Bilbo correctly answers, "Mountain, I suppose," and comes back with:

> Thirty white horses on a red hill,
> First they champ,

175

Then they stamp,
Then they stand still.

Gollum is not outfoxed, however, and says, "Teeth! Teeth!" and counterposes:

Voiceless it cries,
Wingless flutters,
Toothless bites,
Mouthless mutters.

This riddle competition is, of course, a fictional one in a much loved literary work,[1] but it may serve to demonstrate something about riddles as a folklore genre. Folklorists try to look at folklore in context, and the fictional context just given approximates in some ways some of the real social contexts of riddling (the exchanging of riddles). Riddling and riddle competitions are known in many of the world's cultures, and this exchange from Tolkien's novel is by no means the only example found in literature or folk literature. There is Samson's riddle in the Bible. In the Oedipus myth, Oedipus saves Thebes and becomes king when he answers the riddle of the Sphinx. In some folk narratives characters may even save their lives by posing a "neck riddle," one based on knowledge which only the character has and which an opponent, who would otherwise kill him, cannot guess (it is actually a "neck-saving" riddle). That, incidentally, is partly how Bilbo saves himself from Gollum in the end. This kind of riddle is at the center of the following English folktale (an example of a widespread tale type):

There was once a lady, very beautiful and wellborn. For some reason or other she was condemned to die a cruel death. She pleaded her case, and her beauty and her great goodness touched the judges, till they so far relaxed their severity, as to promise that she should save her neck if she could propose a riddle which they could not answer in three days. She was given a day to prepare. They came to her in her cell to know the riddle. She said:

Love I sit
Love I stand;
Love I hold
Fast in hand.
I see Love,
Love sees not me.
Riddle me that
Or hanged I'll be.

The judges could not guess, so she was acquitted. Then she gave them the explanation. She had a dog called "Love." She had killed it, and with its skin had made socks for her shoes — on these she stood; gloves for her hands — and these she held; a seat for her chair — on that she sat; she looked at her gloves and she saw Love; but Love saw her no more.[2]

Riddling in narrative presents an interesting topic to which we will have reason to return, but first we must address the riddle itself as a folklore form. For example, what exactly is a riddle from the folklorist's standpoint? In ordinary speech, of course, the word can mean a puzzle or something mysterious or difficult to understand. In folklore studies, the riddle is a particular verbal genre which consists of a question or an implied question and an answer to that question. One person poses the question and another tries to answer it. However, the riddle is more complicated than that, and a more precise definition is called for, though folklorists have argued over what the best definition should be.

One definition proposed by two folklorists says that the riddle is "a traditional verbal expression containing one or more descriptive elements, a pair of which may be in opposition to each other; the referent of the elements is to be guessed."[3] They add that "a descriptive element consists of both a *topic* and a *comment*." Such a definition may seem more confusing than enlightening until we understand that this is a "structural definition" or structural description. Structural approaches to folklore aim at reaching an understanding of a genre of folklore. Structuralists attempt to set forth the characteristics which are fundamental to all individual examples of a genre. A structural analysis should reveal a basic,

177

underlying pattern which accounts for all the parts of a whole and how they relate to each other in forming the whole. (Many riddles traditionally begin with an opening formula like "Riddle me, riddle me, ree," but this is not a fundamental aspect of how a riddle "works.") Furthermore, determining the basic structure is seldom, if ever, a question of just looking at surface elements; generally, these are considered merely variables of style or content, outward manifestations, and that to reach the fundamental elements we must look to a "deeper" level by carefully examining the individual examples and then reasoning to something more abstract. The definition of the riddle just given certainly may not be the best possible one,[4] but looking at what its authors meant by it *can* give us interesting insight into the nature of riddles.

By a "descriptive element," they simply mean that riddles start off by describing something. In Bilbo's riddle the descriptive element is "thirty white horses on a red hill" which "champ," "stamp," and finally "stand still." The *topic* is the basic object being described ("horses"); the *comment* (or comments) modifies and expands by giving more information (the horses are "white," "champ," and so on). However, people who are riddling understand that the topic is only an "apparent referent," that it is *not really* horses which are being referred to, but *something like* the horses as they are described. One is supposed to use the descriptive element as a clue to guess the "real referent," in this case "teeth." This example is entirely metaphorical; there is no "opposition," but in some riddles an oppositional element is added, for example in "It has a head but can't think." We associate having a head with being able to think, so there is an opposition or seeming contradiction here, though one which is resolved by the referent "cabbage"; "head" is taken metaphorically and "think" literally. The riddle question is, of course, meant to be puzzling and confusing; opposition is one way of adding to this confusion.

A riddle, to judge by the examples given, seems to depend on *metaphor*, on a kind of poetic comparison drawn between the thing actually described and the referent to be guessed. This process is indeed central to riddles, though folklorists use the term "true riddle" to refer to riddles which work in this way. However, other kinds of folklore called riddles do not operate on this principle of metaphorical description. For example, there is the "pretended obscene riddle," which consists of a question that seems to call for an obscene answer, but really has an innocent answer ("What is it that a woman does sitting down, a man does standing up, and a dog does on three legs?" "Shake hands."), and there is the "conundrum," a question/answer which relies on word play ("What is black and white and red [read] all over?" "A newspaper."). But the "true riddle" stands at the heart of any discussion of riddling and has evoked the greatest interest and curiosity among folklorists.

In modern American society, we tend to think of riddles mostly as amusement for children, and it may be difficult to imagine that riddles could be seriously studied. However, if riddles could tell us something about society and culture and the way the human mind "works," a consideration of them could be very fruitful. To determine whether they might, we ought to look at the process of riddling as it actually exists in several cultures or as it exists in one or more contexts cross-culturally to see what social or psychological functions riddles have. (In folklore, to give a simplified explanation, the term *function* refers to the *use* or *effect* which some particular kind of folklore has. Does it teach? Promote social cohesion? Express a sense of group identity?)

For example, a number of contexts and functions for riddles have been noted in Turkish society, contexts and functions which someone familiar only with riddles in American society might find surprising. In Turkey riddles aided in local defense (guards kept themselves awake at night telling riddles). They were also part of festivals, because it was believed that riddling brought good luck. In Istanbul riddles were an important part of social life. Neighborhoods had riddling teams, there were professional and semi-professional riddle makers, and riddle contests brought rewards to winners, penalties to losers, and sometimes ended up in fist fights. A riddle could be posed by writing it and posting it on the wall of one of the coffeehouses which are centers in Middle Eastern male social life; those who sought to answer it had to pay money to post their answers and the one who guessed it won the cash. And in Anatolia riddles still play a role in wedding ceremonies. The party bringing the bride to

179

the village of the groom stops at the edge where it is met by a local group and riddles are exchanged by the flag bearers of each group. When one of them fails to answer, he must surrender his flag and his group must buy it back or forfeit any say over the ensuing wedding festivities.[5]

The Dusun are an ethnic group in Borneo whose culture exhibits a high degree of tension in interpersonal relations which sometimes breaks out into open violence. It is not uncommon for people to engage in fist fights or even deadly knife fights over real or supposed wrongs. However, instead of starting a fight, a person will sometimes approach an enemy and pose a riddle to him, in a tone of voice generally reserved for teasing and shaming a person. If the supposed offending party cannot correctly answer it, the riddler walks away triumphant, perhaps commenting on the other's stupidity. Thus, in this case the riddle has served to channel hostility into a physically harmless outlet which is not socially disruptive.[6] Among the Venda of South Africa, riddles have an educational function for the young (though it is not the obvious one of training their minds by trying to figure out the answer because the Venda merely memorize riddles and answers both and don't try to guess an answer they don't know). Venda riddles have a form similar to sacred formulae called milayo, which must be learned in the "initiation schools" which prepare people for full participation in adult social life. The playful riddles prepare youth for learning the more important milayo.[7]

Riddling practices vary from society to society. There may be informal exchanges or formal competitions; individuals may compete or there may be teams; or riddling may be an activity taking place only at a certain time of the year. But, whatever form it takes, riddling is a widespread phenomenon and we could examine innumerable examples. The few examples just given, however, should indicate that riddling can serve various purposes and that riddling may, in some times and places, be a more central part of life than it seems to be in most modern Western cultures (though it is not absent even there). A survey of the cross-cultural data reveals that riddling falls into six broad situational areas: (1) leisure-time riddling, in which the purpose, or at least ostensible purpose, is entertainment; (2) riddling in folk narratives; (3) occasional use as a kind of greeting formula; (4) use in an educational context in which a teacher poses them to a pupil; or riddles may appear (5) in the context of courting or (6) in rituals, especially those of initiation or death.[8]

The explanation for the appeal and importance of riddles, however, probably lies in basic human thought processes, specifically in the way in which riddles draw, point out, or perhaps even call into question relations between categories. Take riddles in the context of courtship and of death rituals. In courtship a suitor or his surrogates may have to answer riddles in order to "win" the prospective bride. There is a moving toward the joining of two disparate entities or sets of entities (two people, two families, possibly two villages or other communities), as well as the joining of what may be perceived as two fundamentally opposite categories, male and female. Likewise the riddle "joins," through metaphor, two disparate, even contradictory entities, such as horses and teeth. At death rituals people also find themselves in a situation emphasizing different categories, the world of the living and that of the dead. A wake is a vigil held over the body of a dead person prior to burial, which in some societies includes feasting, entertainment, and other forms of socializing. The ritual itself often seems to be an attempt to symbolically transport the deceased's soul from one world to the other. (It may be believed that the wake ensures that the dead person will stay in the land of the dead and not return to haunt the living.) Those involved in the ritual are in a sense standing on a borderline where two opposites meet. In a sense they are joining these opposites together. Hence riddles seem appropriate here, too. In both courtship and death rituals, the very essence of the riddle seems to mirror the situation and to symbolically express the process taking place. Even the actual riddles themselves may suggest this joining of life and death. For example, at West Indian wakes erotic riddles are common. Although an emphasis on sex at such an occasion may seem inappropriate or even appalling to a middle-class European or North American, we can see this as an attempt to focus on life and the life force in the midst of the opposite, death. And a number of West Indian wake riddles metaphorically describe "the living emerging from the dead, or the living carrying over the dead."[9]

It is enlightening to see how the parameters of situations like courtship or a wake mirror the nature of the riddle, how situations which seem to involve the merging of the disparate or the opposite may call forth the use of a genre which does the same thing intellectually. However, we must go beyond the insights gained by looking at such situations to see if these insights point to an understanding of the riddle generally.

One major way, perhaps *the* major way in which human beings create order and structure reality, is by creating categories and placing entities in these categories. We think of things as either animate or inanimate; as animal, vegetable, or mineral; as human or nonhuman. There are trees, grasses, and flowers; residential and commercial buildings. Such categories enable us to cognitively control the world, to keep it neat and orderly. When our categories break down, difficulties and psychological distress, even extreme anxiety, can occur because generally we do not like our conception of what is real to be called into question. Some anthropologists have even suggested that it is precisely in areas where categories may seem to overlap that taboos (restrictions on behavior often involving total or near-total avoidance of something) operate because areas where categories break down are seen as dangerous.

However, we also realize that categories *do* overlap or are often far from perfectly conceived, and we probably realize that we cannot limit ourselves by tying ourselves up in unbending mental constructs as to what is what. We know that we must be able to transcend categories in order to adapt, to learn and to innovate, however threatening that effort may sometimes be. The riddle provides a folkloric method for showing, on an abstract level, that such transcendence is possible. Through a riddle we can call reality into question. What can have a head, yet not think? How can something be both that thing and simultaneously not that thing? ("When is a door not a door?" "When it's ajar [a jar].") We can show how things thought to be dissimilar in fact have common properties. But the riddle does this safely. Playful, a recognized "institution," its ultimately logical answer provides a relief to confusion. It shows, in a symbolic way, that categories and reality can be played with, questioned, and transcended. Perhaps all uses of metaphor do this to some extent, but the riddle provides a way of doing so which is a direct challenge to our sense of how things are supposed to be.

The riddle, then, provides a reassuring, folkloric "model" for a larger intellectual activity. That might explain why riddles are mostly a children's genre in modern industrial and postindustrial societies like the United States. It may be that in our society we have come to an easier accommodation with shifting conceptual categories than have more tradition-oriented cultures, and only our children still need to learn the thought patterns that riddles teach. This also suggests something about the appearance of riddles in narratives. It is doubtful that anyone ever really preserved his or her life though riddling ability, but the very idea that riddling could relate to a life and death context, even in a story, may indicate that riddles deal with a fundamental intellectual process; hence they can be used to symbolize the power to escape life-threatening situations or the intellectual ability to deal with the most dangerous problems.[10]

This may not be the only cognitive function which the riddle has, of course. One study has suggested that a correspondence exists between a culture's riddling ability and the tendency for that culture to have systems in which rote learning is important, and in which authority figures commonly pose questions orally to subordinates. Hence, the riddle may serve as a model or teaching device for coping with such intellectual methods.[11] However, it does seem that riddles involve not merely the playful, artful use of language; they involve basic human thought processes and patterns as well.

The riddle is certainly not the only folklore genre which relies upon metaphor. Metaphorical language is regularly found in tales and folksongs, for example. However, the proverb is the other genre which has metaphor at its core and which has often been seen as closely related to the riddle. The relationship perceived between the two genres is in part posited on the key position metaphor plays in each. In the past the relationship has often been perceived somewhat vaguely and intuitively rather than analytically; and folklorists have often lumped the two together, partly because they are both "minor genres." This did not mean riddles and proverbs were thought unimportant, but they both are much more concise than verbal genres like the epic, folktale, or ballad. Recently, some folklorists have begun to look at other aspects of the relationship.

Whereas a riddle requires a question and an answer, a proverb is a statement, a traditional statement passed on in fixed form by oral transmission and assumed to convey some ethical or philosophical truth (or some other wise observation about life, the world, or human nature). "A watched pot never boils," "A stitch in time saves nine," "The early bird catches the worm," "Great oaks from little acorns grow," and "People who live in glass houses shouldn't throw stones" are all well-known English language proverbs. Other cultures have their proverbs also, such as "Honor the tree which gives one shade" (Dutch), "One should turn his coat according to the weather" (German), and "A leopard conceals his spots" (Nigerian). Proverbs commonly employ poetic devices such as rhyme ("A friend in need is a friend indeed") and alliteration ("The more, the merrier"). A proverb in English is usually a single sentence, often dipodic in structure, that is, clearly broken in the middle, so that it consists of two balanced parts — as in "The early bird/catches the worm." Proverbs catch our attention partly because they are familiar, but also because of their rhythm and use of poetic devices. (Riddles, of course, can be found in poetic form, though the length of riddles tends to be more variable than the length of proverbs.)

Folklorists sometimes give the name *proverbial phrases* or *proverbial comparisons* to shorter traditional phrases like "to pull the chestnuts out of the fire," "to blow hot and cold," "as dead as a doornail," and "slower than molasses." They also consider the Wellerism, a type of proverb in which a quotation, its "speaker," and some attribute or action of this "speaker" are fused for humorous effect ("'I see,' said the blind man as he picked up his hammer and saw"). Yet how closely related such kinds of folklore are to the proverb as just defined, in terms of functions and contexts for use, is debatable, though proverbial phrases certainly indulge in metaphor.

Before considering just how proverbs do use metaphor, we should note something about the contexts in which proverbs are used. Although occasional reports of proverb sessions in which people exchange proverbs to show their knowledge of them and to entertain each other have come from tradition-oriented societies, such as certain African groups, proverbs normally are part of ordinary conversation or play a role in argument of one kind or another. Proverbs may be said to have, generally, a rhetorical function, to be used to convince someone of some point (although they can also be used to agree with someone else's point or to reinforce an opinion even if no one present actually disagrees with it). For example, two people (A and B) might be discussing a third person's criticism (we'll call the third person X) of yet a fourth person (Y), and one suggests the the third person is really rather rash to be critical because, "People who live in glass houses shouldn't throw stones." What A means, of course, is that X is in no position to criticize Y because X himself suffers from the same faults for which Y is being criticized. But what do glass houses and stones have to do with it? It is very unlikely that Y actually lives in a house made of glass; glass houses are, after all, most uncommon. What has happened in our hypothetical conversation is that a point has been made through a proverb and through metaphor. A real social situation (X's criticism of Y and X's being open to criticism himself) has been compared, via the proverb, to another "fictional" situation, which is conveyed by the rather vivid image in the proverb — that a person who did live in a glass house ought to be wary of throwing stones at someone else because his own residence is so vulnerable to similar attack. Because B understands the conventions of proverb use, B recognizes that A is not really talking about glass houses, but is saying that X is like someone who lives in a glass house. It would be the same if B said to A, in talking about how Y kept waiting for some event to transpire and was becoming anxious when it did not, "Well, you know, watched pots never boil." Here, too, B and A would understand that no literal reference was being made to cookware and water being heated, but that the image referred metaphorically to Y's predicament.[12]

Proverbs can be seen as a sort of "shorthand" method of communication (though to speak of them thus is also to use an analogy). A ready-made statement, a proverb conveys a culturally agreed-upon idea

185

which can be used to make a point that may only be made less succinctly and perhaps less clearly and effectively in a speaker's own words. In the few words of the proverb about glass houses, A can concisely make the point about X and expect to be clearly understood (though the proverb's conciseness is by no means the only reason why A might use it). Indeed, the very fact that B easily understands the comments leads A to think that his analogy is apt.

· Of course, just as not all riddles rely on metaphor, not all proverbs are metaphorical (such as "Waste not, want not," and "Two wrongs don't make a right"). Nonmetaphorical proverbs communicate through a direct statement of a presumed truth that supposedly applies to a situation, rather than by invoking a poetic image to which a situation is compared metaphorically. Nevertheless, even these proverbs are ways of encapsulating an argument in easily understood, pre-formulated language.

And proverbs *are*, for the most part, easily understood. We may not be able to understand the proverbs of another culture, which in fact may seem baffling. How many Americans could understand, without explanation, the Rwandan proverb, "You lodge the Tuutsi in the ingle-nook and he forces you out of the upper room"? Even when we think a proverb from another culture is clear, we may be misunderstanding. But most Americans whose native language is English understand the meanings of common, current English-language proverbs and have done so from a fairly early age. That doesn't mean that we all use proverbs. Our involvement with proverbs may be limited to passive understanding, without becoming active in our daily speech. In fact, we may even have ambivalent or negative attitudes toward proverbs. Our culture emphasizes the value of originality and creativity and we may regard the traditional, passed-down proverbs as mere clichés or "old saws." Nevertheless, we continue to know and understand them. If we did not, proverbs would not be used in advertising (for decades the slogan of Morton's salt has been, "When it rains, it pours") or twisted around for purposes of humor. The term "perverted proverb" has sometimes been used to refer to parodies of well-known sayings. In fact, in England there was a whole series of "Potty Proverbs" postcards; one shows a parked couple, the young woman obviously annoyed at having had to fight off the advances of her date, with the caption "Familiarity breeds attempt." Some jokes contain a punch line which is a distorted proverb.

> Well, there were these two moose, two male moose, and they both were in love with the same lady moose; they were rivals for her hand, or hoof, as the case may be. Now she didn't have any preference, she liked them about the same, so she couldn't decide which one to marry. So she told them each to go out and gather up a bunch of stones and to bring them to her and whichever brought her the most stones at the end of the day, she would marry him. Well, they both went out and started gathering up stones, but after a while one of them got a little too wrapped up in it and didn't notice where he was going. He got too close to the edge of a really steep hill and he tripped and, carrying all these rocks, he was really off balance. So he just rolled and rolled down that hill, and he dropped all of his stones. So the moral of this story is, "A rolling moose gathers no stones."

The humor of the story, such as it is, relies on the hearer knowing the proverb, "A rolling stone gathers no moss."

Mock written tests sometimes circulate in offices and schools, which ask the "examinee" to reformulate verbose statements into other language. The "correct" answer turns out to be a well-known proverb. For example, "Individuals who perforce are constrained to be domiciled in vitreous structures of patent frangibility should on no account employ petrous formations as projectiles" becomes "People who live in glass houses shouldn't throw stones." Such "tests," of course, lampoon the bureaucracy's tendency to make the simple complex, especially in linguistic matters, but they also recognize that the proverb makes a point clearly and succinctly.

However, the proverb's powerful conciseness as a form of communication is not the only reason that we have recourse to it. In order to get at some of the other reasons, let us look briefly at one other case in which familiar proverbs were distorted, not for comic effect in this instance but rather for a quite serious one. The context for this particular use of proverbs was the liturgy (the ritual of public worship) of a Texas

187

religious group in the 1960s which used the illegal hallucinogenic drug LSD as the central part of a religious service.[13] During the 1960s the use of illegal hallucinogens was fairly widespread in the United States. This particular group professed to believe that the drug could be used to produce a powerful spiritual experience (not an idea unique to them at the time), although they may also have been trying to establish their right to use illegal substances by claiming that it was protected by a Constitutional right to freedom of religion. (American Indian groups had had some success in establishing their legal right to use otherwise illegal hallucinogenic mushrooms because this was part of traditional Native American religious practice.) Whatever their motives, the LSD was ingested at the ceremony open to members of the cult only, and we are concerned only with the liturgy that preceded the taking of the drug and which was open to nonmembers.

The liturgy involved recitation by a leader with a chorus repeating certain phrases. The recitation consisted mostly of quotations from English translations of sacred texts of Eastern mystical religions. However, interspersed with these quotations and generally coming at the end of a string of quotations were sentences clearly modeled on traditional proverbs, such as "Void will be void" ("Boys will be boys"), and "Any saved is a fortune spurned" ("A penny saved is a penny earned"). We can see how these sentences might refer to mystical concepts (some sort of spiritual void; the idea that an attachment to material reality results in losing a spiritual fortune), but the phrasing in distorted proverb form is interesting and perhaps even startling. This, however, suggests something more about why we use proverbs.

Most of the liturgy, drawn from exotic nonwestern religious tradition, might well seem foreign to someone hearing it; however, the proverbs, even in distorted form, have the ring of something familiar and hence are reassuring, even comforting. And proverbs do succeed because they are familiar. Furthermore, we tend to think of them, rightly or wrongly, as embodying not some mere insight of the moment but rather the wisdom of the ages (hence they are at home in what is meant as a serious religious rite, however odd it may seem to some of us). Proverbs are authoritative, and when we use one we are appealing to the authority of the ancients and the ancestors. We can more easily dismiss someone who mumbles "Well, you know, really, we ought to take a few precautions because that could, perhaps, save us some trouble in the long run," than someone who boldly states, "After all, a stitch in time saves nine," invoking ancient revealed truth. The proverb depersonalizes a situation by appealing to traditional precedents, a strategy which can be especially helpful in the context of an argument. The user of the proverb in effect is saying, "It is not I who tells you this; it is the wisdom of the ages telling you this."

We may sometimes dismiss proverbs as clichés and proverbial wisdom certainly may break down under analysis. (Does anyone really think that an apple eaten every day, however salubrious, will alone keep one healthy ["keep the doctor away"]?) Furthermore, in the proverb repertoire of any culture, proverbs may contradict each other, such as "Nothing ventured, nothing gained," and "Nothing ventured, nothing lost." Nevertheless, the authority and power of proverbs is certainly felt even in our society. In other cultures proverbs may be an even more potent force. African societies use them in many communication contexts, and the ability to use them effectively is thought an important social and intellectual skill. In one study, an anthropologist noted the role of proverbs in African courts. In one court case that he observed, proverbs were freely used by both sides and the outcome of the case depended, at least in part, on how skillfully they were used to sway opinion in the case. They functioned rather like legal precedents in American courts: they involved matters already decided (not by another court but by past wisdom) and which could be referred to in making the decision at hand.[14]

As with all forms of folklore, we ultimately must ask of the proverb what it tells us about culture and society. Of course, an examination of proverbs and proverb usage tells us about one way in which human beings communicate in certain contexts. Beyond that, however, people interested in the proverb as a form are apt to be intrigued with the question of what proverbs reveal about a society's morals, values, and attitudes. We think of proverbs as having something to do with morality.

Value-laden statements, they can be used to call somebody to account for misbehavior. Could an analysis of a culture's proverbs provide a picture of that culture's moral system? Unfortunately, asking such a question creates a very tricky problem, though also a fascinating one.

In addition to the fact that the members of a culture may use contradictory proverbs, the users of a proverb may sometimes disagree over its meaning. For example, in the metaphorical proverb "A rolling stone gathers no moss," is it good or bad to be the rolling stone or to gather moss? Some may think that to be a rolling stone indicates a free spirit not covered by the fungus of stale, humdrum life. But others may see the rolling stone as one who foolishly does not put down the settled roots which can give life comfort and special meaning. Finally, a proverb's meaning changes, at least to some extent, depending on the situation in which it is used. The proverb "Money talks" can be used to express awe at the power of wealth, to neutrally state what is perceived as a social fact, or to express bitter disapproval at what is seen as corruption. The proverb may have a "base meaning," the general point upon which many or most could agree, but also "performance meanings," which shift situationally.[15]

Given these facts, it is difficult and perhaps impossible to conclude what a culture's whole system of morality is from proverbs. Nevertheless, proverbs do have meaningful content and it may still be possible to draw conclusions about values and attitudes by analyzing that content.

Certainly the sayings of a culture may be entirely consistent with the overall world view of the culture. (World view means the way in which the members of a group characteristically envision their lives, their society, and even "reality" itself.) For example, Tamil proverbs (Tamil is one of the major languages of South India) frequently contain images of the parts of the human body; such imagery is twice as common there as it is in English proverbs. Furthermore, there is an extreme emphasis on the head and the neck (over 51 percent of the proverbs in question mention these parts) and a decreasing emphasis on those body parts encountered as one proceeds down the body to the feet (16.5 percent mention the trunk, 15.4 percent the arms and hands, 9.4 percent legs and feet, and the rest mention skin and bones or the body as a whole). This emphasis is consistent with other aspects of Tamil Hindu culture. The four Hindu castes are said to have sprung from the body parts of the creator god and in social status they also descend from head to foot. In Hindu meditation a person may be told to start by concentrating on the feet and to move upward to the more important head; in Indian dance the greatest number of movements are those made with the head. Also, the majority of the body images in Tamil proverbs are negative, the parts of the body depicted as defective or problematic. This fits with the Hindu view of the body as merely a transient shell in which the soul temporarily resides and which must be transcended for spiritual enlightenment.

It is also possible to work cross-culturally and examine how the proverbs of several cultures depict the same limited area of concern. One such area might be human speech, which could be of particular interest to folklorists, who are, after all, largely concerned with the study of certain elements of *oral* culture. Can proverbs give us insight into how various cultures regard the faculty of speech itself, and could we then relate these attitudes to other conditions prevailing in the society in question?

Japanese proverbs seem to depict speech in a negative light. Some Japanese sayings go so far as to counsel against saying anything at all, such as "One should keep both jars and mouth tightly shut" and "Mouths are to eat with, not to speak with." Speaking too much is seen as a sign of vulgarity ("Many words, little refinement"), and speech can even be harmful to a person who is the subject of the conversation ("The mouth is an axe which wounds a man"). Antagonistic speech can rebound and harm the speaker as well as the person spoken to ("When you curse a man [you dig] two graves"). Speech is thought to conceal the truth ("Speech is half") and to be a cloak for deception ("Honey in his mouth, a sword in his belly"; "People who praise things don't buy them"). Or talking produces only empty dreams, as in "In words even Osaka Castle can be built."

In spite of their proverbs, the Japanese are probably no more silent than any other nation, but the proverbs do suggest a basic distrust of speech and perhaps strongly emphasize the need to speak carefully.

Japanese society stresses the importance of decorous, formal behavior, especially in terms of socially fixed relationships. The careless use of spoken words could be particularly disruptive in such a context. Also, Japan is, and has been for a long time, a densely settled country. People live in crowded conditions, in highly cohesive local communities. In such a setting human aggression must be tightly controlled and even verbal aggression is perhaps too much to tolerate. That human speech has to be carefully controlled would seem to be a postulate of Japanese world view.

If this last hypothesis is correct, we might be able to find a less densely populated society with proverbs more tolerant of speech acts. India is another Asian country which, though populous, has a lesser population density than Japan. It is also vastly more diverse ethnically, a factor that affects personal interrelationships. Indeed, we find in Indian proverbs a much less restrictive attitude toward speech. "It is stupid to suppress what comes into the mind" and "Eat what you get and speak what you think" both advise that one should not refrain from speaking. And it is silence rather than talking that engenders the fear of deceit ("Beware of silent dogs and still waters"; "An open talker is not generally deceitful"). There are people, such as gossips, who abuse speech ("The telltale causes the downfall of a kingdom") and there must be a balance ("Too much speaking, too much silence, too much rain, too much sun are not good"), but the general attitude seems to be that speech, used wisely, is good, not something to be deeply suspicious of. The Indian case may support the idea that population density is a key factor in proverbial attitudes toward speech.

When one turns to American proverbs, however, one finds a predominantly negative attitude toward speech, despite the fact that American population density is considerably less than that of India, and that American culture does not particularly stress formally polite, highly decorous behavior (as was suggested might be a factor in negative Japanese attitudes). Americans are told that "Men of few words are the best men" and "Talk much, err much." Another saying has it that "A great talker may be no fool, but he is one that relies on him." "From words to blows" suggests that speech can lead to violence, and even "A word to the wise is sufficient" suggests the less said the better. Though some American proverbs view speech benignly, such as "Talk don't hurt," the great majority view speech skeptically at best: "Talk's cheap but it takes money to buy whiskey"; "Talking will never build a stone wall or pay our taxes"; "Big talk won't boil the pot"; "Speech is silver; silence is golden."

Indeed, there may be culturally induced reasons for such American proverbial attitudes toward speech. Several proverbs already quoted and others, such as "Many words will not fill a bushel" and "Talk does not cook rice," draw a connection between talking and doing or accomplishing, making the point that speech does not accomplish anything, and that talk can be an empty substitute for deeds. The doer and the builder are character types much admired in American society, and we like to think of ourselves as men and women of action. We know "how to get things done" through Yankee ingenuity, and we want to be achievers and go-getters. If mere talk impedes achievement or substitutes something insubstantial for solid accomplishment, then it is not surprising to find a negative attitude toward speech in American sayings, for on some level speech would be seen as undermining important values of the culture. Such an explanation is admittedly speculative, but hypotheses which appeal to factors of population density or types of social relationships would not seem to make sense for the American case. This is not to say that these other explanations do not hold for the Japanese or Indian proverb repertoires; it only means that they are not universally applicable. It also reaffirms the need for folklore to be examined and analyzed in regard to particular cultural contexts.[16]

From whatever perspective, the examination and analysis of proverbs and riddles can certainly be rewarding. Both genres are indeed much shorter than many other verbal genres. Proverbs may be thought of as worn out cliches and riddles considered fit entertainment only for children. Yet each form survives in tradition and continues to have some sort of appeal to new generations, and on that account alone they cannot be dismissed as insignificant or insubstantial. Indeed, careful analysis can reveal that these genres are connected to basic patterns of thought and effectively communicate basic ideas and cultural values. Thus the study of proverbs and riddles can show us how thought is conditioned by and expressed through those cultural forms we call folklore.

Notes

1. J. R. R. Tolkien, *The Hobbit; or, There and Back Again* (Boston: Houghton Mifflin Co., 1964), 80-101.

2. F. J. Norton, "Prisoner Who Saved His Neck with a Riddle," *Folk-Lore* 53(1942): 35-36.

3. Robert A. Georges and Alan Dundes, "Toward a Structural Definition of the Riddle," *Journal of American Folklore* 76(1963): 113.

4. It has been criticized by Charles T. Scott, "On Defining the Riddle: The Problem of a Structural Unit," in Dan Ben-Amos, ed., *Folklore Genres* (Austin, Tex.: University of Texas Press, 1976), 80-88, and others.

5. Ilhan Basgöz, "Functions of Turkish Riddles," *Journal of the Folklore Institute* 2(1965): 132-47.

6. Thomas Rhys Williams, "The Form and Function of Tambunan Dusun Riddles," *Journal of American Folklore* 76(1963): 102-3.

7. John Blacking, "The Social Value of Venda Riddles," *African Studies* 20(1961): 5-7.

8. Thomas A. Burns, "Riddling: Occasion to Act," *Journal of American Folklore* 89(1976): 102-3.

9. Roger D. Abrahams, "Introductory Remarks to a Rhetorical Theory of Folklore," *Journal of American Folklore* 81(1968): 156. Alan Dundes, "Texture, Text, and Context," *Southern Folklore Quarterly* 28(1964): 256-59, is also relevant on this point.

10. The cognitive function of riddles has been discussed in several places. Ian Hamnett, "Ambiguity, Classification and Change: The Function of Riddles," *Man* 2(1967): 379-92 is the most cogent discussion. For another important statement of the idea, see Elli Köngäs Maranda, "Theory and Practice of Riddle Analysis," *Journal of American Folklore* 84(1971): 53-55.

11. J. M. Roberts and M. L. Forman, "Riddles: Expressive Models of Interrogation," *Ethnology* 10(1971): 509-33.

12.   Peter Seitel, "Proverbs: A Social Use of Metaphor," *Genre* 2(1969): 143-61, is a useful basic discussion of proverbs and metaphor.

13.   Richard Bauman and Neil McCabe, "Proverbs in an LSD Cult," *Journal of American Folklore* 83(1970): 318-24.

14.   John C. Messenger, "The Role of Proverbs in a Nigerian Judicial System," *Southwestern Journal of Anthropology* 15(1959): 64-73.

15.   Barbara Kirshenblatt-Gimblett, "Toward a Theory of Proverb Meaning," *Proverbium* 22(1973): 821-27, is the origin of the terms "base meaning" and "performance meaning" and is an important discussion of how proverb meaning shifts.

16.   Discussion of Tamil proverbs is drawn from Brenda E. F. Beck, "Body Imagery in the Tamil Proverbs of South India," *Western Folklore* 38(1979): 21-41; of Japanese proverbs from J. L. Fischer and Teigo Yoshida, "The Nature of Speech According to Japanese Proverbs," *Journal of American Folklore* 81(1968): 34-43; and of Indian proverbs from W. K. McNeil, "The Nature of Speech According to Indian Proverbs," *Folklore Forum* 4(1971): 2-14. Discussion of American proverbs is based on a consideration of the proverbs under selected headings in Archer Taylor and Bartlett Jere Whiting, eds., *A Dictionary of American Proverbs and Proverbial Phrases, 1820-1880* (Cambridge, Mass.: Belknap Press of Harvard University Press, 1958); David Kin, ed., *Dictionary of American Proverbs* (New York: Philosophical Library, 1955); and Frances M. Barbour, *Proverbs and Proverbial Phrases of Illinois* (Carbondale, Ill.: Southern Illinois University Press, 1965), and should be seen as especially tentative.

Further Readings

Archer Taylor was the preeminent scholar of both the proverb and the riddle and several of his works remain the basic descriptive studies of these forms: *The Proverb and Index to "The Proverb"* (Hatboro, Penn.: Folklore Associates; Copenhagen: Rosenkilde and Bagger, 1962) covers the origins, content, and style of proverbs, but not the social contexts of proverb use. His "Proverb" entry in *The Standard Dictionary of Folklore, Mythology and Legend*, 2 vols., edited by Maria Leach (New York: Funk &

Wagnalls, Inc. 1950), is an excellent short introduction to the genre.
Taylor's "The Riddle," *California Folklore Quarterly* 2(1943): 129-47, is a
valuable general discussion of various formal aspects of the riddle, and his
English Riddles from Oral Tradition (Berkeley, Cal.: University of California
Press, 1951) is the best collection of riddle texts in English, in fact, one
of the best in any language. With B. J. Whiting, Taylor edited *A Dictionary
of American Proverbs and Proverbial Phrases, 1820-1880* (Cambridge, Mass.:
Belknap Press of Harvard University Press, 1958), a major reference
source for individual American proverbs despite the limitations of its time
frame.

    Wolfgang Mieder and Alan Dundes, eds., *The Wisdom of Many: Essays
on the Proverb* (New York and London: Garland Publishing, Inc., 1981) is
a collection of twenty previously published articles on proverbs. It
includes many of the most important and perceptive short studies of
proverbs, including Seitel's "Proverbs: A Social Use of Metaphor," and
Kirshenblatt-Gimblett's "Toward a Theory of Proverb Meaning," both
cited in this chapter and both central to an understanding of how proverbs
"work" in context; the book is thus an excellent introduction to various
aspects of the study of proverbs. Wolfgang Mieder, *International Proverb
Scholarship: An Annotated Bibliography* (New York: Garland Publishing, Inc.,
1983) is a most comprehensive, annotated guide to publications on
proverbs, and F. A. de Caro and W. K. McNeil, *American Proverb
Literature: A Bibliography*, Bibliographic and Special Series No. 6
(Bloomington, Ind.: Folklore Forum, 1970) provides information on
publications dealing with American proverbs. John C. Messenger, "The
Role of Proverbs in a Nigerian Judicial System," *Southwestern Journal of
Anthropology* 15(1959): 64-73 gives an excellent illustration of the use of
proverbs in a nonwestern culture.

    Roger D. Abrahams, "Introductory Remarks to a Rhetorical Theory
of Folklore," *Journal of American Folklore* 81(1968): 143-58, presents an
insightful approach to riddles in the larger context of human interaction,
and Abrahams's "The Literary Study of the Riddle," *Texas Studies in
Literature and Language* 14(1972): 177-97, though it focuses upon
approaches to the study of the riddle as found in narratives, has much of

interest to say about the nature of the riddle and of riddling generally. Volume 89, number 352 of the *Journal of American Folklore* (1976) is a special issue devoted to "Riddles and Riddling," edited by Elli Köngäs Maranda; it contains six essays which could be said to represent some of the latest thinking on riddles up to that time. Bibliographies of riddle scholarship are not as up-to-date as those for the proverb, but there is a brief but useful discussion of publications on the riddle in Barbara Kirshenblatt-Gimblett, ed., *Speech Play* (Philadelphia: University of Pennsylvania Press, 1976), 214-18. Donn V. Hart, *Riddles in Filipino Folklore: An Anthropological Analysis* (Syracuse, N.Y.: Syracuse University Press, 1964), one of the few book-length studies of riddles from a particular culture, also contains an extensive survey of published information on riddles and riddling.

Chapter 9
Folk Objects

Simon J. Bronner

In Utah, two-story houses display their symmetrical faces of stone against a mountainous backdrop. In Indiana, woodcarvers show chains and caged balls amazingly made out of one piece of wood with the aid of only a pocketknife. In Pennsylvania, New Year's Day is greeted with the making of sauerkraut and pork. These things are folk objects, or more accurately, the material products of folkways.

Folk objects materialize tradition. Typically learned by imitating the work of community or family members and by participating in local customs, folk objects exhibit the repetition and variation common to other forms of folklore such as tales, songs, proverbs, and riddles. Of course, folk objects show the interconnections common to all forms of folklore. A house, a carving, or a food dish reflects shared experience, community ideas and values connecting individuals and groups to one another and to the environment. To stress these interconnections, the term "material culture" is often used to point to the weave of objects in the everyday lives of individuals and communities.

Things so woven give us texts to read. Indeed, "text" is a term so characteristic of narrative and other verbal forms, that we forget that it comes from the Latin for "woven thing," and therefore should be applicable to the characterization of objects as well. But because folk objects exist in material, rather than verbal or gestural form, differences arise in the way they are studied. Because an object takes up space, because it endures, and because it can be seen, smelled, and touched, the study of folk objects takes on additional dimensions. These additional dimensions will be addressed in this chapter.

The study of objects tends to emphasize aspects of form. An object is visible and three dimensional; indeed, the word "form" is taken from the Greek for "visible shape." An object is described primarily by its stable, visible features — its contour, size, and structure. To be sure, the object has other components to record — its material, construction, use, and design. But while the color and material may vary in one type of object, its form remains fairly constant and readily lends itself to comparison. Aluminum siding can be tacked onto a log building; the carving of a wooden chain can become a pastime in retirement while it was once plied by active young men. Yet the forms of these buildings and chains do not change. With a form that is easily discernible and stable, measurements can be made.

An object's ability to be measured allows for the expression of repetition and variation in exact and comparable units. Measurement helps us to describe standards of form within a culture. Words may change radically from one tale version to the next, and the other versions are irretrievable. To change an object, the maker must create a new object or significantly alter an existing one. The older versions remain for us to see and to conceptualize as some kind of series; e.g., the versions can be arranged by when or where they were made. Measurement permits a discussion of pattern and symmetry through time and space. It reveals that the middle-Virginia folk house is based upon transformations of a basic square, and that a type of stone house in Utah is typically two rooms wide and has a two-to-one ratio of length to width.[1]

The forms of folk objects are usually slow to change. Consequently, form becomes an especially good indicator of a historical region and its culture. Stone houses with the symmetrical form of one room on either side of a hallway and an elevation of one or two stories are so pervasive in Utah and surrounding areas that they place a distinctive mark upon the landscape (Figure 1). The distribution of this central-hall house and similar forms parallel the distribution of Mormon settlement in the West.

Figure 1.   Stone house; near Brigham City, Utah (Simon Bronner)

Geographers see in the houses a visible and enduring imprint of a unique region of Mormon culture with sources in the Midwest and New England.[2]

If the similarities of forms within a region indicate a shared culture, then the differences of basic forms may suggest differences of culture and world view. The bilateral symmetry of Utah's stone houses came into prominence as western society was increasingly transformed by science and technology in the late eighteenth century. To underscore human control over nature, the design of objects became less tied to natural forms. Surfaces were smoothed; their designs stressed frontal appearance; they relied more on the rectangle as a fundamental shape; they stood more erect. For the Navajo, who share the landscape with the Mormons in the Southwest, the more natural shape of the circle is the basic form in their houses, religious rituals, and art. Cultures that emphasize circles typically believe in a cycle of life rather than a linear span of years as western

201

society does. Even the abstract notion of progress is given form in western society. Progress is often imagined as a line, moving upward or from left to right.[3]

Unlike tales and songs, objects persist beyond the moment of their creation; they have an "objective existence." Indeed, the term "object" comes from the Latin for "throw." Objects are created by humans but once created, they stand apart. This difference between folk objects and other folklore genres has several consequences. One consequence is that objects have an obvious historical significance. Objects claim a historical character because they endure. They are intrusions from the past. Since folk objects commonly have to do with everyday life — the needs of shelter, work, prayer, and play — objects may help us to re-experience something of that everyday past.

One telling reminder of a life past is the gravemarker. In the cemeteries of eastern Massachusetts in the seventeenth and eighteenth centuries, three gravemarker designs predominate. Early stones, carved roughly between 1670 and 1760, show a winged death's head. By the mid-eighteenth century, winged cherubs replaced the grim visages of the skulls on the stones. By the end of the eighteenth century, the image of a willow tree overhanging a pedestaled urn appears, and in the early nineteenth century it quickly overtakes the cherub in popularity (Figure 2).

The life of late-seventeenth-century Puritanism is inscribed into the image of the death's head. Death's heads emphasize the mortality of man; accompanying symbols such as an hourglass or crossed bones underscore the brevity of life and quick decay in death. The imposing visage of the death's head reminded the Puritans of the severe judgement of a distant God who stood beyond the control or appeal of the individual. At the time when the winged cherubs appear, revivalist preachers such as Jonathan Edwards preached the individual's relationship with the deity; individuals felt they had more of a hand in the determination of their ultimate fate. The winged cherubs materialized the promise of heavenly reward and reflected the growing confidence in personal salvation. Accompanying the change to the willow and urn is a shift in form, for in this phase square shoulders replace the rounded shoulders of the stones

202

Figure 2. Gravestone designs from eastern Massachusetts: top, death's head (1678); middle, winged cherub (1759); bottom, urn and willow (1822) (Drawing by Shirley Marquet)

carrying death's heads and winged cherubs. The squaring of the shoulders reflects a shifting attitude toward the significance of death and religious devotion. The new stones were markers of mourning, rather than doctrines of orthodoxy. Puritanism in Massachusetts at the time was giving way to new religions stressing individual intellect and volition, such as Unitarianism and Methodism, rather than community emotion and supernatural control. Death appeared less immediate; it had become an interruption of a full life. Emphasis changed from the supernatural status of the deceased to the secular mourning of the survivors.[4]

Although objects stand apart, their relations with their human creators and owners are still recognizable. Human characteristics are attributed to object forms, so that chairs are described as having legs, lamps as having necks, and clocks as having faces. Some individuals interact with objects as though they were people. They give them names, talk to them, and decorate or "dress" them. In American culture, for example, cars are regularly named or personalized with special license plates or paint jobs. They may be praised for good performance or cursed for bad. Some individuals conceptualize the purchase of new mats, covers, or ornaments as buying "gifts" for their cars. So, despite the "otherness" of objects, humans nevertheless project their own ideas and emotions onto them and see them as reflections of themselves.

Because objects both stand apart from and stand for their creators and owners, they can be used for display purposes. They may serve as emblems of class, occupation, or ethnicity. The "star barn" (as it is known locally) stands near Middletown, Pennsylvania (Figure 3). Through time, its distinctive appearance has displayed different values. Built around 1868, its overhanging forebay, banked entrance on the nongable end, three levels, and three bays represent German-American folk tradition prevalent in southcentral Pennsylvania. The builder added "Carpenter Gothic" decorations such as high-arched louvers, a large cupola, and an octogonal spire to give the building a modern appearance. Following the heightened symmetry brought over by English design, especially after the eighteenth century, the doors, window, and louvers are geometrically placed and laterally paired. Two matching silos once

Figure 3. "Star Barn," a bank barn; Middletown, Pennsylvania (Simon
Bronner)

flanked the banked entrance. The barn's colonial bannerette weathervane
capped an eclectic American approach to the built environment — a
combination of local and national, ethnic and American, old and new, folk
and popular. The barn announced the social status and values of its
builder, John Motter. Motter traded horses, farmed, and prospered
enough to become head of a local bank. Upon his death in 1901, an
obituary described Motter as "a most worthy and highly respected
citizen, a man who through an active business career accumulated a
handsome competence through the exercise of perseverance, thrift,
economy and integrity. His family . . . represents several homes within the
county." Reaching 106 feet across, 66 feet deep, and 80 feet high, and
lying next to a major highway, the imposing (and still working) barn
today is a celebrated symbol of the region's ethnic and agricultural past.

A contemporary example of object display can be found in front of houses. In Utah, one can find driveways lined with wheels, and gates welded from commercial objects. Mailboxes must conform to official standards of measurement, but owners personalize them nevertheless. With front porches gone, the mailboxes are, in a sense, symbols of the relation of the individual family to community. In a society wary of the conformity which commercialization can foster, the mailboxes are converted into symbols of personal, occupational, or regional identity. Cowboys and horses made from horseshoes and bolts straddle the tops. Cream separators, plows, milkcans, and wheels support the bottom (Figure 4). Iron chains have appeal as well as wooden ones, and many mailboxes have chains welded into supports, bent to form initials or abstract shapes. In Pennsylvania, many men who weld these chains commonly work in the nearby steel industries; indeed, the welded chains are often made, unofficially, at work. The chains make a manly statement in iron of their skill, strength, and occupation.[5] They visibly display their distinctiveness

Figure 4.   Converted mailboxes; near Malad, Idaho (Simon Bronner)

within what they perceive to be a more uniform culture. Like the chains of wood, the iron chains attract attention because they appear an improbable construction. The chain stands straight and still when one expects it to fall (Figure 5).

Beliefs can also be communicated through objects. Material things can objectify ideas and feelings of fear, luck, or religious experience. Haunted houses are, in a sense, the objective correlatives of the fear and wonder of the supernatural. For Pennsylvania Germans, the New Year's Day meal of pork and sauerkraut engenders good luck for the coming year. Among Jews, some mothers decorate a prayer shawl for their son's bar mitzvah. The shawl remains a visible and tangible reminder of the youth's status in the adult ritual community.

Because they stand apart from capricious humans, because their form seems fixed, because they can be seen and touched, and because they endure, objects appear reliable — indeed truthful. Seeing the object alone doesn't satisfy completely; reality comes from touching the object, feeling its three dimensionality. Rather than being accused of "seeing things," we want to be "in touch with reality." The truthfulness attached to objects is evinced by the biblical parable of "doubting Thomas." Thomas doubted Jesus Christ's resurrection until he had tactile proof. Until he could put his finger into the print of the nails and thrust his hand into Jesus's side, he would not be convinced. More recently, Apollo 10's close sighting of the moon failed to satisfy the American public; Neil Armstrong in Apollo 11 captured the imagination of the American public with his walk on the moon. The media glorified his grasp of a terrain at which we could formerly only look. The rocks Armstrong brought back held a special fascination for the public because they could be touched, literally apprehended firsthand.

Thus, objects can be used to confirm belief. Even if they are not folk objects, they contribute to a system of folk belief. According to southern Indiana legend, Floyd E. Pruett was suspected of killing his wife with a logging chain. After Floyd died in 1920, people discovered the image of a chain on his tombstone which confirmed their suspicions. Said one informant:

Figure 5.   Welded chain mailbox; Harrisburg, Pennsylvania (Simon Bronner)

Everybody goes out there and looks at it. If it's got thirteen links on it, you know, they stand back. But if you touch it during the time of a full moon, you're supposed to go insane or lose your mind. And there's been several incidents of people touching it, you know, during full moon; and, well they get chased by a big bright light all the way back to Orleans. I know we were chased one night; but we didn't believe it, you know. We touched it during full moon and got out into the car and started to leave, and the driver looked in the rear-view mirror, and that was all, you know. "Look there's a white light!"[6]

If folk objects are historical because they survive from the past, their existence in the present is defined by their use. With objects, use may change even if form remains stable. The use of wooden chains changed during the life span of the carvers. In childhood, these midwestern carvers lived in farming communities. As children, learning to carve the chains was a playful way to learn the properties of woods, to use tools, and to solve technical problems. As adults, they commonly dropped their carving when they moved into cities and took up work in industries. In retirement, the carvers revived their craft, but they found new uses for it. They used the chains to give as friendship tokens; they used them to show off skills that seemed unappreciated by a younger generation. These older carvers also felt that the chains would remain after they were gone — small memorials to their creators' existence.

Another difference between folk objects and other forms of folklore is that folk objects are commonly crafted from the materials of nature. Tales or dances rely upon speech and gesture. Many objects, especially larger objects like houses, tend to have a direct relationship to the place where they are found. They become a "built landscape." The construction and materials of the built landscape show the character of the human relationship to the environment. Austin Fife observed of Utah's stone houses:

Their earth origins are still visible in the finished products, and dwelling houses built thereof bespeak man at one with his environment rather than in arrogant conflict. With steel, concrete, macadam, plastics, fiberboard,

209

and a host of other industrial concoctions, man's marriage with the earth is leached out, and his architectural creations stand out upon the landscape like tumors, despite titillations wrought by form, line, pattern, or simply mass.[7]

Western European stone masons, converted to Mormonism, constructed the stone houses of Utah from stones quarried from the nearby mountains. Granite and limestone commonly compose houses in northern Utah; limestone and sandstone are frequently used in southern Utah. A material culture emerged from an adaptation to the natural environment and the creation of a human environment.

The relation of environment to folk objects can also be seen in the example of carved chains and sauerkraut and pork. Carved chains are common in southern Indiana where woods and a furniture industry provide abundant materials for carving. In Pennsylvania, a strong corn crop encouraged the raising of hogs. Corn-fattened hogs gave a quick return, especially important in America's early years. Hogs increased their weight one hundred and fifty fold in the first eight months of life. Counties in southeastern Pennsylvania, where corn was produced in the greatest amount in the early nineteenth century, led the nation in swine production. Cheaper prices from the western states cut into the late-nineteenth-century production of both corn and hogs in Pennsylvania, but the favor for pork products, now attached to a regional German identity common to southeastern Pennsylvania, is perpetuated in its folk cookery.

The conversion from natural object to artifact is accomplished with skill and time. Unlike other folklore forms, we can study the process of creation in distinctive stages because the process is deliberate and takes time. With objects made in folkways, the maker commonly controls the steps of production from start to finish. Many of the chain carvers I studied were also furniture-factory workers. They contrasted the folk and factory means of production. In the factory, they worked on only one small step of the conversion of natural material to human-made product. In making the chains, they picked out the wood, they roughed out the shape, they carved the details, they smoothed the finish, and they distributed the final product. The cooking of food has preserved many folkways, even when the building of folk houses and the doing of crafts is no longer common. Folk production means the control of tools and procedures. This control is commonly exercised in traditional home cooking but surrendered with the purchase of fast foods. With fast foods, the means of production are unseen; an order is taken and a product appears. As a result, legends have arisen that question the preparation. In the widely circulated story of the batter-fried rat, a customer unknowingly eats a rodent instead of a piece of chicken. The story, in part, would seem to be a warning against surrender of control over food preparation. In many versions, the person stuck with the rodent is the woman who tried to pass off the chicken to her family as home cooking.[8]

The processes involved in constructing objects are extended in time. With narratives and other forms of verbal folklore, the steps in construction are compressed and less visible. Furthermore, in narration, construction and embellishment appear as one and the same process. With objects, embellishments can be added long after construction has been completed. Layers of modification may be apparent. The plain, mid-nineteenth-century stone houses of Utah were made contemporary in the latter parts of the century by the addition of Greek Revival pediments, Victorian gingerbread carving, and porches. In the early twentieth century, some took on a Colonial Revival style as Williamsburg shutters were added.

It may be difficult to trace a folk narrative to a single tale teller, but objects often seem typical of a single maker or group of makers. The study of folk objects frequently leads to encounters with the individual folk artisans who create them. Because of the tactile involvement a maker has with his creation, the object becomes personal. In many traditional communities, folk objects lack signatures, but they still bear the stamp of the maker. Identification may be difficult for the outsider. Within the community, however, a signature is unnecessary; persons recognize the style, the personal "touch" of the maker.

Because the maker of objects is often a specialist, a gulf can exist between the maker and the viewer, who may not share or understand the skills of the craftsman. Chain carvers often would enact a little ritual to help bridge this gulf between themselves and their audiences. Wandley

211

Burch would walk down the street and if you stopped to visit, he would pull a carved chain from his pocket. "Bet you don't know how I made this," he would challenge. You would instinctively reach for the chain and try to figure out the puzzle in your hands. At that moment, Wandley has converted you to his way of thinking, for you were using your hands and mind to conceptualize his technique. The chain became a visual riddle. Riddling presents apparent contradictions and asks the listener or, in the case of chains, the viewer, to resolve them. The riddler has a special knowledge that puts him above the viewer. The viewer must accept that all is not what it appears to be, that looks are deceiving, and that old and traditional skills and techniques still have power and exert control. The "trick" of chain carving involves fooling the viewer's assumption that the links of the chain must have been cut out and then connected by glue or screws. The process of making the chain, however, involves cutting into the wood to release the links. The carver has to patiently stick the knife in between the carved links to release them. So also do caged balls, pliers, and fans involve cutting away from a single piece of wood (Figure 6).

Understanding folk carving involves more than documenting the techniques of the carver. Knowing the carver's life history helps us to fathom the appeal and meaning of carving for such men. "Part of you is in a carving," Floyd Bennington would tell me, and he would describe how in old age, chain carving helped objectify some of the values he held dear: reliance on handwork, closeness to nature, and his connection to community. He recalled his fascination as a child with the iron chains made in the blacksmith shop where adult males commonly gathered in his home town. As a youth, chains symbolized the adult community. At retirement, chains helped him adjust to his senior status when he found himself, as in his youth, with time on his hands and outside the mainstream. For someone like Floyd Bennington, who had been proud of his productivity during his work life, the carving of chains attracted notice; people could continue to recognize his productivity and creativity. George Blume also displayed his chains to the young workers at the furniture factory. They responded, "I didn't know you could do that! If I had known, I would have come around." They acknowledged his worth by

Figure 6.   Earnest Bennett cutting into his chain; Indianapolis, Indiana (Simon
Bronner)

admitting that the objects intrigued them. At the time he brought his
chains to the factory, he was readying himself for a change in status in the
workplace — his impending retirement.

Beyond the display of their virtuosity and worth to the younger
workers, chains carry other messages. Making the chains from fragile
wood, when one would expect them to be of iron; releasing them from a
single plank, rather than forging together individual links; and reducing
their size and altering their function all serve as a commentary on contemporary industrial society. The chains speak for handwrought, personal, and
rural values as against the machine-wrought uniformities of factory production. Chain carvers are fond of accompanying their carved chains with
an assortment of replicas of old-time tools. They will carve a pocketknife
or wheat cradle from a single piece of wood. For many, these miniatures of

213

old tools are portable reminders of a past that they shared. They are objectifications of personal history.

Objects, especially folk objects, remind us of who we are and where we have been. Commenting on the stone houses of Willard, Utah, for example, Teddy Griffith commented that the stone houses signaled that the Mormons intended to stay. "This was their land of Zion," Griffith said, "and by their faith and toil this desert would bloom!" Griffith went on to comment on the display of stone houses today: "The demand for historic buildings in Willard seems to exceed the supply. When the William Jacksons wanted to move into a stone home in Willard and found none available, they built one themselves with the thick walls characteristic of the old stone homes."[9] In Pennsylvania, few people butcher hogs or grow their cabbages to get their pork and sauerkraut these days. But New Year's Day provides the chance to feel connected to the past. In cutting the cabbage and preparing the purchased pork, people celebrate what others before them had done more laboriously. The holiday is not just another day, but a time to re-establish bonds. Tradition is miniaturized in time and space, but at the same time it is given more intensity and focus.

The notion of folk objects tends to emphasize the handmade over machine manufactured. Folk objects imply a mode of production common to preindustrial communal society where knowledge and skills were personal and traditional. Yet some industrial skills are passed on by tradition as well, and shop settings can resemble the informal social settings associated with past handicrafts. Sheet metal work is an example of a trade in the construction industry which has retained much of its craft character. Many small shops of ten to twenty workers contract out to various job sites and custom fabricate their own products. They design, cut, shape, assemble, and install items such as air-conditioning ducts, gutters, and downspouts. The sheet metal trade has historical precedents in nineteenth-century tinsmiths and tinkerers who would make pans and implements out of sheet metal and even patch roofs. Max Shuldiner comments on the sheet metal trade in the small shops where he has worked:

In fabricating things out of metal, I get the satisfaction of laying it out and forming it together. They're designed and fabricated for the particular installation which is in a sense an interesting aspect of the trade. It's non-repetitive . . . . There is solving certain particular problems, and there's a satisfaction in that . . . . I see directly the result of my work; I mean, I'm right there. It isn't something that's shipped a thousand miles away, and someone installs it, and I have no idea where it goes or where it's put. If the boss hasn't designed a particular item, I go into the field and take the field measurements and design something which is going to solve this particular problem.

Although formal schooling has become a standard part of the training of sheet metal workers, workers rely on oral tradition and regularly exchange skills and techniques that meet those problems not solved by mass-produced items.

Industrial workers who do not share this craft shop setting, who find themselves at a repetitive task which is a small part of a larger industrial process, can still express their folk craftsmanship by making objects that use the skills and materials of their trade. Ron Thiesse, a titanium welder for a large aircraft manufacturer, forms small animals out of titanium at work. He shares them with friends and fellow workers. Making them was Thiesse's way to show his mastery of the techniques of welding and his control of the material. The animals, like the welded chains made by steel workers mentioned earlier, allow the makers to express themselves in ways not possible during the normal job routine; they offer some of the personal involvement, social connection, and traditional creativity associated with the making of folk objects.[10]

Today, many of our social and cultural institutions govern our exposure to, and our perception of, folk objects. In Pennsylvania, the traditional preparation of pork and sauerkraut dinner is encouraged by churches. They sponsor communal suppers where people come to share traditional foods. In so doing, the church stresses its communal character by offering a special food which has the binding force of tradition. Pork and sauerkraut stand apart from ordinary menus. Their linkage with the past gives them a ritual value. In southern Indiana, Catholic churches

215

similarly offer picnics featuring homemade turtle soup, a folk food identified with that region.[11]

Institutions such as art galleries, museums, and schools also influence our experience of folk material culture. New markets are created for folk goods that affect items once made for private consumption and personal exchange. For instance, the exhibit and sale of carvings like chains are becoming more common. In 1983 a carved wooden chain lay starkly in a case in the Seton Hall Art Gallery marked with the caption, "Wooden Chain, 20th century. Artist unidentified. Wood. Length 78½ inches. Private collection, New Jersey." The museum display only could tolerate communications concerning form, dimension, and texture. The display obscured the object's social significance and silenced its maker. Museum settings make objects speak to different groups of people in different terms.[12] Calling it "art" creates a distance in time and space between the object and viewer, often implying that the object lacked use and was never embedded in a web of human relationships.

The designation "folk object" is not restricted to objects only from the past. New folk objects are continually emerging. Working with wood may not be the training for future skills as it once had been for the chain carvers, but handling, manipulating, and arranging paper may be. Just look in children's schoolroom desks. Children make paper airplanes, footballs, frogs, stars, cubes, poppers, and fortune-telling devices (Figure 7). The appeal of the chain form reappears in the chains that girls fashion from gum wrappers. The chains can be a demonstration of skill and patience, and they can also be used to verify belief. A girl may make the chain as tall as her boyfriend, or the boyfriend she desires. She may even ignite the bottom of the chain with a match. If the paper burns, then, according to belief, the boyfriend is true; if it doesn't, then he isn't.

As reliance on craft processes in the twentieth century diminishes, forms increasingly arise that stress arrangement. As the economy comes to stress consumption of ready-made items, the folk response is to alter and arrange such items into new, unofficial forms. For example, "yard art," is usually the arrangement of discarded items into an aesthetically pleasing pattern. The arranger is exerting control and emulating the making of

216

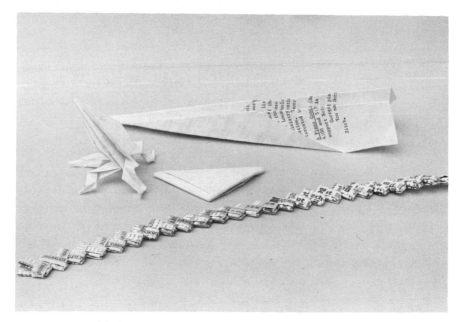

Figure 7. Folded paper objects: frog, football, airplane, and chain; Harrisburg,
Pennsylvania (Simon Bronner)

objects by creating a new appearance and use from prefabricated materials.
The emphasis here is less the conversion of natural materials to built
landscape than the organizing of commercially manufactured materials to
create folk environments which make personal and collective statements.

In 1985, Helen Griebel conducted a material culture study to
delineate the characteristics of that statement. She inventoried every
house in two counties along the Pennsylvania-Maryland border. She found
"yard art" most frequently attached to tract houses built after World
War II. Discarded tires and aluminum gutters would be used for planters,
rocks would be painted to line a drive or make a design, and wagon
wheels and milkcans along with commercial concrete figures would dot
the lawns. After inventorying the forms, she talked to the residents. Most
talked about making their property personal by arranging the items. They

217

did not participate in the construction of the house, but they could still organize their environment. Although this environment was personal, their ideas were taken from observing the designs of other residents. Some arrangements stood out, and Griebel asked their makers about their motivations for making them. Nellie Plitt, for example, created a yard ornament she referred to as her "monument." It is a concrete structure covered with glass, mirrors, and crockery. It has three rounded tiers that angle up like a pyramid.

> "Somewhere I saw one," Plitt reflected, "and I said I'm gonna make one. I like it. I told him [Mr. Plitt] when I die just plow it under with me. It took about six to eight weeks to make, scrounging in dumps for bottles to break and tiles. Even found things in ditches. I wanted to put in more mirrors, but I couldn't find enough. First layer I built up cinder blocks and kept putting in mud. The top is a keg. I filled it with cement, then tore off the keg."

It was an innovative object in the area, Griebel observed, but Plitt's recycling of commercial objects to create a folk environment springs from a common technique of ornamentation found in other yards in the region.[13]

The modern workplace also fosters new kinds of material culture. There are photocopied cartoons, memos, and announcements satirizing the official culture of the workplace. They are not crafted but mechanically reproduced. Their forms repeat and vary; their images often deal with feelings hidden beneath the surface of bureaucracy and dispassionate service work. One example depicts a portly figure beside himself with laughter, and the caption reads, "You Want It When?" The illustration has no official sanction. But it can be readily found in shops and offices throughout the country. These objects are copied, hung on walls, or circulated privately in the workplace. In a setting where looking busy is defined by working at one's desk or providing service to the public, the objects provide a chance for co-workers to silently communicate. Using the very material and technology of the official culture, they express an unofficial social commentary. The frustrations, hopes, and tensions of the office are read into the illustrations. "The job isn't finished until the

218

paperwork is done," one cartoon reads, and the picture shows a character sitting on the toilet. The cartoon is a commentary on bureaucracy and its preoccupation with paperwork. It humorously suggests that, in the privacy of the restroom, where official culture should not operate, bureaucratic principles and objectives still apply. The cartoon can function to represent the many service workers who feel that paperwork has supplanted the very tasks which it was designed to facilitate.

Folk objects, then, give added dimensions to cultural study. In today's world, older folk objects endure on the landscape to comment on history and change; meanwhile, new folk objects arise in modern cultural settings. Folk objects provide the tangible evidence of the everyday past; they supply visible proof of the changing beliefs and customs people hold today. Patterns discovered in the objects and technical processes of everyday life can help to reveal the hidden attitudes underlying our world, and perhaps predict the direction of our society in the future. Joining the study of objects to that of words and behaviors paints a broad and vivid picture of human endeavor.

Notes

1.   See Henry Glassie, *Folk Housing in Middle Virginia* (Knoxville, Tenn.: University of Tennessee Press, 1975); Austin Fife, "Stone Houses of Northern Utah," *Utah Historical Quarterly* 40(1972): 6-23.

2.   J. E. Spencer, "House Types of Southern Utah," *Geographical Review* 35(1945): 444-57; Richard V. Francaviglia, "The Mormon Landscape: Definition of an Image in the American West," *Proceedings of the Association of American Geographers* 2(1970): 59-61; Allen G. Noble, "Building Mormon Houses: A Preliminary Typology," *Pioneer America* 15(1983): 55-66.

3.   See Alan Dundes, "Thinking Ahead: A Folkloristic Reflection of the Future Orientation in American Worldview," in *Interpreting Folklore* (Bloomington, Ind.: Indiana University Press, 1980), 69-85; Michael Owen Jones, "The Study of Folk Art Study: Reflections on Images," in *Folklore Today* ed. Linda Dégh, Henry Glassie, and Felix J. Oinas (Bloomington, Ind.: Research Center for Language and Semiotic Studies, Indiana

University, 1976), 291-303; Lewis Henry Morgan, *Ancient Society: Or Researches in the Lines of Human Progress from Savagery through Barbarism to Civilization* (Gloucester, Mass.: Peter Smith, 1974 [1877]).

4. See Allan I. Ludwig, *Graven Images* (Middletown, Conn.: Wesleyan University Press, 1966); Peter Benes, *The Masks of Orthodoxy* (Amherst, Mass.: University of Massachusetts Press, 1977); James Deetz, *In Small Things Forgotten* (Garden City, N.Y.: Anchor Press, Doubleday, 1977), 64-90; James Deetz and Edwin S. Dethlefsen, "Death's Head, Cherub, Urn and Willow," in *Material Culture Studies in America*, ed. Thomas Schlereth (Nashville, Tenn.: American Association for State and Local History, 1982), 195-205; James Higiya, "American Gravestones and Attitudes Toward Death: A Brief History," *Proceedings of the American Philosophical Society* 127(1983): 339-63.

5. Alan E. Mays, "The Welded Chain Mailbox Support: A Study in Material Culture" (Typescript, Pennsylvania State University, Harrisburg, Folklore Archives, 1985).

6. William Clements, "The Chain on the Tombstone," in *Indiana Folklore: A Reader*, ed. Linda Dégh, (Bloomington, Ind.: Indiana University Press, 1980), 258-64.

7. Fife, 6.

8. Gary Alan Fine, "The Kentucky Fried Rat: Legends and Modern Society," *Journal of the Folklore Institute* 17(1980): 222-43.

9. Teddy Griffith, "A Heritage of Stone in Willard," *Utah Historical Quarterly* 43(1975): 286-300.

10. David Shuldiner, "The Art of Sheet Metal Work: Traditional Craft in a Modern Industrial Setting," *Southwest Folklore* 4(1980): 37-41; Bruce Nickerson, "Ron Thiesse, Industrial Folk Sculptor," *Western Folklore* 37(1978): 128-33; Yvonne R. Lockwood, "The Joy of Labor," *Western Folklore* 43(1984): 202-11. See also, Robert S. McCarl, "The Production Welder: Product, Process and the Industrial Craftsman," *New York Folklore Quarterly* 30(1974): 243-53; C. Kurt Dewhurst, "The Arts of Working: Manipulating the Urban Work Environment," *Western Folklore* 43(1984): 192-202.

11. See Don Yoder, "Sauerkraut in the Pennsylvania Folk Culture," *Pennsylvania Folklife* 12(1961), 56-69; idem, "Historical

Sources for American Traditional Cookery: Examples from the Pennsylvania German Culture," 20(1971): 16-29. Turtle soup consumption is documented in Simon J. Bronner, *Grasping Things: Folk Material Culture and Mass Society in America* (Lexington, Ky.: University Press of Kentucky 1986), 160-78.

12. See Thomas Schlereth, "It Wasn't That Simple," *Museum News* 56(1978): 36-44; Ormond Loomis, "Folk Artisans Under Glass: Practical and Ethical Considerations. for the Museum," in *American Material Culture and Folklife*, ed. Simon J. Bronner (Ann Arbor, Mich.: UMI Research Press, 1985), 193-99; J. Geraint Jenkins, "The Use of Artifacts and Folk Art in the Folk Museum," in *Folklore and Folklife: An Introduction*, ed. Richard M. Dorson (Chicago: The University of Chicago Press, 1972), 497-516; Howard Wight Marshall, "Folklife and the Rise of American Folk Museums," *Journal of American Folklore* 90(1977): 391-413; Jay Anderson, *Time Machines* (Nashville, Tenn.: American Association for State and Local History, 1984).

13. Helen Bradley Griebel, "Worldview on the Landscape: A Regional Yard Art Study," *Pennsylvania Folklife* 36 (Autumn 1986): 39-48.

Further Readings

Several collections of essays offer investigations of folk objects. The most recent is *American Material Culture and Folklife*, edited by Simon J. Bronner (Ann Arbor, Mich.: UMI Research Press, 1985). Exploratory essays are provided in two earlier anthologies: *American Folklife* by Don Yoder (Austin, Tex.: University of Texas Press, 1976) and *Forms Upon the Frontier: Folklife and Folk Arts in the United States*, edited by Austin Fife, Alta Fife, and Henry Glassie (Logan, Utah: Utah State University Press, 1969). *Folklore and Folklife: An Introduction*, edited by Richard M. Dorson (Chicago: The University of Chicago Press, 1972) includes essays on folk craft, architecture, art, cookery, and costume. An overview of material culture study is found in *Material Culture: A Research Guide* (Lawrence, Kan.: University Press of Kansas, 1985) and *Material Culture Studies in America* (Nashville, Tenn.: American Association for State and Local History, 1982), both edited by Thomas Schlereth.

Simon J. Bronner

The bookshelf of folk material culture study has emphasized case studies more than syntheses. An important synthetic book which combines geographic and folklife approaches is *Pattern in the Material Folk Culture of the Eastern United States* by Henry Glassie (Philadelphia: University of Pennsylvania Press, 1968). Concern for a social structural approach is found in another synthetic book, *Grasping Things: Folk Material Culture and Mass Society in America*, by Simon J. Bronner (Lexington, Ky.: University Press of Kentucky, 1986).

The case studies of material folk culture show the breadth of approaches and subjects in the field. A case study that uses life history and psychology to analyze the work of a single craftsman is *The Hand Made Object and Its Maker* by Michael Owen Jones (Berkeley, Cal.: University of California Press, 1975). *Folk Housing in Middle Virginia: A Structural Analysis of Historic Artifacts* by Henry Glassie (Knoxville, Tenn.: University of Tennessee Press, 1975) identifies the artifactual "grammar" used by eighteenth-century builders in a single region. Expanding on the subject of chain carving covered in this chapter is *Chain Carvers: Old Men Crafting Meaning* by Simon J. Bronner (Lexington, Ky.: University Press of Kentucky, 1985). Stone carving is given extensive treatment in *Graven Images: New England Stonecarving and Its Symbols, 1650-1815* by Allan I. Ludwig (Middletown, Conn.: Wesleyan University Press, 1966) and *The Masks of Orthodoxy: Folk Gravestone Carving in Plymouth County, Massachusetts, 1689-1805* by Peter Benes (Amherst, Mass.: University of Massachusetts Press, 1977).

The emergent folk material culture in contemporary life has a growing bookshelf. Yard art and folk recycling is studied in *Making Do or Making Art: A Study of American Recycling* by Verni Greenfield (Ann Arbor, Mich.: UMI Research Press, 1985) and *Personal Places: Perspectives on Informal Art Environments*, edited by Daniel Franklin Ward (Bowling Green, Oh.: Popular Press, 1984). Photocopied folklore is documented in *Work Hard and You Shall Be Rewarded: Urban Folklore from the Paperwork Empire* by Alan Dundes and Carl Pagter (Bloomington, Ind.: Indiana University Press, 1978).

Separate anthologies of essays exist for the categories of food, craft, art, and architecture. Various perspectives on foodways research can be found in two collections of essays: *Foodways and Eating Habits: Directions for Research*, edited by Michael Owen Jones, Bruce Giuliano, and Roberta Krell (Los Angeles: California Folklore Society, 1983) and *Ethnic and Regional Foodways in the United States*, edited by Linda Keller Brown and Kay Mussell (Knoxville, Tenn.: University of Tennessee Press, 1984). Portraits of craftsworkers and field reports by folklorists are included in *Traditional Craftsmanship in America*, edited by Charles Camp (Washington, D.C.: National Council for the Traditional Arts, 1983). Folk art research by art historians, anthropologists, and folklorists can be found in *Perspectives on American Folk Art*, edited by Ian M. G. Quimby and Scott T. Swank (New York: W. W. Norton & Co., Inc., 1980) and *Folk Art and Art Worlds*, edited by John Michael Vlach and Simon J. Bronner (Ann Arbor, Mich.: UMI Research Press, 1986). Folk architecture is covered in *Common Places: Readings in American Vernacular Architecture*, edited by Dell Upton and John Michael Vlach (Athens, Ga.: University of Georgia Press, 1985).

Chapter 10
Documenting Folklore

William A. Wilson

Not long ago I attended an informal dinner party with a number of faculty members and spouses. Midway through dinner the associate dean of my college said, "Bert, tell us some folklore." I replied that I would rather experience folklore than tell it. He looked at me blankly for a moment and then turned his attention to the obviously more intelligent faculty member seated across the table. They were soon engaged in an animated discussion of Southeast Asians who kill and eat their own dogs as well as those of their unwary neighbors. A few minutes later, as we complimented our hostess on the excellent fish she had just served, her husband, a fine poet and an even better storyteller, told us of another serving of fish at another dinner party in his native Wales. An up-and-coming young businessman and his wife, friends of a relative of our host, had thrown an elaborate party which they were sure would guarantee the husband's entry into the elite business circles in their community. A few minutes before the guests arrived, the family cat jumped on the table and ate a hole in the beautifully prepared and garnished salmon which was to serve as the dinner's main course. Horrified, the wife threw the cat outside and camouflaged the hole with parsley and other condiments. The party was a success — no one discovered the damage. Convinced that a good reputation among his colleagues was now assured, the husband bade farewell to the last guest and then walked outside, where he discovered the cat dead by the driveway. Mortified, he called everyone who had attended the party, confessed that they, with the cat, had evidently eaten spoiled fish, and urged them to rush to the hospital to have their stomachs pumped. The next morning, as the husband was contemplating his ruined career, his neighbor came by and apologized for having run over and killed the cat the night before. So as not to bother the dinner guests, he explained, he had quietly placed the cat by the driveway and waited until morning to tell what he had done. The story both shocked and amused the people at our dinner party. Most of these aspiring professionals felt genuine sympathy over the tragedy which had befallen the aspiring businessman. I smiled at my wife but said nothing.

The next day I xeroxed a story called "The Poisoned Pussy Cat at the Party" from Jan Brunvand's *The Vanishing Hitchhiker: American Urban Legends and Their Meanings*,[1] and copied an entire article from *Western Folklore*,[2] which discussed widely told stories about Southeast Asians stealing and eating dogs. On a piece of paper, I scribbled, "See what I mean!" and sent the note and the xeroxed pieces to the associate dean. He replied that he did now see and that in the future he would be careful what he said around me.

More than almost any other subject, folklore must be experienced directly in actual life, as I experienced these narratives, to be properly understood. In twenty years of teaching, I have discovered that my students can listen to my lectures, can read assigned books and essays on the subject, and can still leave the course not understanding folklore unless they have encountered it in the actual settings in which it is performed. I encourage students to achieve this end by keeping their eyes and ears open to what is going on around them — even to pay close attention to dinner-party talk; and I make sure they do this by requiring them to submit, first to me and then to the university archive, folklore they have collected themselves. Writing up these collections carefully enough to help potential archive users understand the substance and significance of the material submitted requires students to look more analytically at the folklore which surrounds them than they might have otherwise. The byproduct of this collecting, of course, is the development of folklore archives to support folklore research. But the main benefit is the increased understanding that comes to the students themselves.

If you are a beginning collector in search of this understanding, you will want to work closely with your teacher or with the archivist to whom you will submit your work. What follows is designed to supplement, not supplant, what they tell you. As you face for the first time the somewhat bewildering task of actually collecting and documenting some of the subject matter you will study, you must develop fairly clear notions about where to collect, what to collect, how to collect, and how to write up your data.

The Tradition-Bearers

The essays in this book should have taught you that the study of folklore seldom leads to the strange and exotic, but rather to much of what you have already known and experienced but not recognized as folklore. The essays should also have shown you that folklore is transmitted through time and space, not just by old, rural, uneducated, and ethnically different people, as is often believed to be the case, but by the doctor next door, by the fellow computer programmer at work, by the members of your religious congregation, by your younger brothers and sisters, by friends at a dinner party, and often by yourself. To collect folklore, then, you needn't pack your bags and head for some exotic place (as exciting as that might be); the lore you are after may be no further away than your workplace, your church, your mother's kitchen, your sister's playground, a casual gathering of friends, or your own memory.

As you try to decide where and from whom to collect, think of the different social identities (shaped by the social groups to which you belong) which make up your own personality. You are probably a student. You may belong to a religious group and live in a constant swirl of religious traditions and religious legends. You may have learned to view the world through ethnic or immigrant eyes. You probably have hobbies. You may already belong to an occupational group and may have learned much of what you must know to succeed not from job manuals but from traditional knowledge passed from person to person at work. You may live in a small, homogeneous community. You belong to a family. You have been a child and may still have close ties with children. Think for a moment of the rhymes, the chants, the songs, the games, the riddles, the superstitions, the traditional rules of conduct, and the taboos which you could collect from these youngsters with little difficulty. Other groups you are familiar with share equally rich lore. Though it is possible, and often rewarding, to collect from members of social groups different from your own, the price you will have to pay to establish rapport, win trust, and avoid violation of cultural taboos may be too high for the beginner. You will probably be more successful if you will do your first collecting among people you know. Once you have mastered collecting techniques and gained a better understanding of folklore in general, then you can turn your attention to people whose lifestyles and world views differ from your own.

Folklorists customarily refer to the people from whom they collect, whether from their own groups or not, as "informants"; some prefer a more deferential word like "consultants." What you should remember, whatever term you use, is that the people sharing their knowledge with you are the tradition-bearers and should be treated with respect. That means you must never collect from them in secret and without their permission. (Sources in the bibliography discuss means of securing permissions.)

The Traditional World

As you think about the particular social group from which you wish to collect, try to determine what is traditional within that group. What are the behavioral consistencies and continuities? Ask yourselves as many questions as you can: Are there rites to initiate new members? Are there superstitions and taboos connected with the group? Are there stories of group heroes or anti-heroes? Are there jokes and anecdotes that ridicule outsiders with whom group members must carry on social exchange (doctors versus patients, for example)? Are there jokes about members of subgroups within the same larger social organization (doctors versus nurses)? Do group members wear distinctive clothing, eat distinctive food, use a distinctive, and often highly specialized vocabulary? Is there a traditional code of conduct? Are there ways of punishing violators of the code? And so on.

You may find it useful to divide the folklore these questions will call forth into three broad categories: things people make with words (verbal lore), things they make with their hands (material lore), and things they make with their actions (customary lore). Such a division is, of course, highly arbitrary, but it does help order the materials of folklore and get you thinking about what you could most profitably collect. The following lists drawn from these categories suggest some, but certainly not all, the folklore awaiting the collector's hand:

•*Things people make with words (verbal lore)*: Ballads, lyrical songs, legends, folktales, jokes, proverbs, riddles, chants, curses, insults, retorts, teases, toasts, tongue twisters, greetings, leave-takings, autograph-book verses, limericks, graffiti, epitaphs.

•*Things people make with their hands (material lore)*: Houses, barns, fences, gardens, tools, toys, tombstones, foods, costumes, and things stitched, woven, whittled, quilted, braided, and sculpted.

•*Things people make with their actions (customary lore)*: Dances, instrumental music, gestures, pranks, games, work processes, rituals, community and family celebrations such as weddings, birthdays, anniversaries, funerals, holidays, and religious ceremonies.

Many forms of folklore, of course, overlap these categories. For example, a song is an item of verbal lore and a quilt material lore, but the singing of the song and the making of the quilt are customary practices. In many folklore events, all three media merge. At a birthday celebration, the making and decorating of the cake are customary practices, and the cake itself is an item of material lore; the singing of the birthday song is a customary practice, and the song is an item of verbal lore. What this means, as we shall see, is that you really can't, or shouldn't, collect individual forms of folklore isolated from the other forms that surround them. You can, obviously, record only the words and music of a birthday song, but if you do not describe the setting in which the song is performed, including at least a brief description of the other forms of folklore also present, your recording really will not help you or a potential archive user properly understand the significance of the song in the lives of its performers.

Collecting Folklore

This brings us to the issue of how actually to collect the folklore, how to record it so that archive users will recognize the importance of the lore to those who express it.

You will probably do a better job of collecting if you are fortunate enough to be present when folklore is performed naturally, without any prompting from you. Sometimes this happens by accident, as it did with me at the dinner party. More often you can arrange to be present where you know the kind of folklore you are interested in is likely to occur — at a bridal party, for example, where you will collect wedding or shower games. At times you may be able to bring a number of people together who will probably generate the lore you are after. If you arrange a skiing party, you will surely hear a lot of skiers' lore before the evening is over.

The value of this kind of "participant observation" is that you have the opportunity to observe firsthand what sparked the performance of a particular item of folklore, how successful the performance was, and what impact it had on the audience (including the impact it had on you). When you write up the event for submission to the archive, you may first want to interview other members of the audience for their responses to the performance, but, if you have observed carefully, most of what you need to describe of the social setting will already be in your own head.

The difficulty with this kind of collecting is that in many instances you will not be able to record the actual performance as it occurs. You can, of course, set up a tape recorder in advance at a bridal shower or a skiing party and record what takes place there. But if you hear a good story at a dinner party, you will have to go back to the narrator later and ask him to tell you the story again. When you do this, you may want to bring along a couple of people who have not heard the story before so the narrator's retelling will be as spontaneous as possible.

Much of the collecting you do will be by "direct interviewing" from the beginning. Once you have decided what kind of lore you wish to collect, then you must determine which people are most likely to possess the information you are after. As you collect using this method, you will be collecting folklore not from firsthand observation but from other people who were firsthand observers — from somebody else who has been at a bridal shower, skiing party, or dinner party. In this instance, you will have little trouble recording the folklore but will have to work much harder to get the necessary contextual background. You will have to elicit from the person who was present at the folklore performance what you would have observed had you been there yourself.

Don't hesitate at times to interview yourself. Without reaching far into memory, you should remember all kinds of folklore events in which you have taken part. You may never be able to discover completely how a folklore performance affected somone else, but you do know how participation in folklore events affected you. If you were once initiated into a fraternal order, you can not only describe the initiation, but tell how it made you feel. Some of our best contextual data come this way.

As you begin to gather material, you should understand at the outset that you can't record all the information every potential archive user may one day need to interpret a body of lore. This is why serious folklorists, while using archive data, will collect much of their material in the field — it's the only way to get exactly what they want. But you can record enough data to make your document useful. No matter what kind of lore you collect, you should always ask yourself a number of important questions. First, what is there about this lore that is pleasing? What makes it artistically powerful, or persuasive? Second, how does the lore function in the lives of the people who possess it? What needs does it meet in their lives? Third, what does the lore tell us about the values and attitudes of individuals and the groups to which they belong?

The Art of Folklore

In many ways the performance of folklore could be called an exercise in behavior modification. Through the things people make with their words, hands, and actions, they attempt to create a social world more to their own liking. When they tell a story, or make a quilt, or perform an initiation ceremony, they are usually attempting, through the power of artistically successful forms, to influence the way people act, including at times themselves. We cannot hope to understand the artistic impact of these forms unless they are recorded as precisely as possible as they live in actual performance.

Verbal lore: To capture the art of verbal lore you should, where possible, record your material with a tape recorder, especially free narrative forms in which the wording and presentational style may change strikingly from telling to telling. It is possible to take down material with pen or pencil, but this usually impedes the performance and brings you a truncated bit of reality. The following tape-recorded "scary story," told by an exuberant fourteen-year-old girl at summer camp, captures the essence of the real narrative with an exactness seldom matched in hand-written recordings:

> There was these couples that ran away from home to get married, and they were driving out on the desert, and all of a sudden he ranned out of gas, and she says, "Well, I told you to get some gas at that last town, but you just wouldn't listen."
>
> And he goes, "Well, I'll walk back and get some." And he goes, "Now lock all the doors and windows, because they've heard about this hook man who goes around the desert trying to kill people." And he goes, "Now lock all the doors and windows and don't let it open for anyone or anything that you hear."
>
> And so she locked them all and started listening to the radio. And she heard more about that hooked man that went around killing people. And so she got really scared. So she turned it off and she fell asleep. And during the

night she woke up and she heard a scratching sound. And, and she got kind of worked up about that and so, so she just went back to sleep. And all of a sudden she woke up and she was wondering what woke her up. And there was that hook man outside, and he was sitting there trying to get in the car. And she just kind of got really scared and everything, but she didn't dare try to get out of the car or move. And so she fell asleep just sitting there.

And so, when she woke up again he was gone, but there was still that swishing and thumping sound kind of on the roof of the car, but she didn't dare open it.

Pretty soon she was getting worried about her boyfriend because he hadn't come back all night. And so she fell asleep again because she was really tired.

And pretty soon a cop came — it was in the morning — and he sat there knocking on the windows. And she woke up and she saw the cop and, and he goes, "Open the door."

And so she opened the door.

And he goes, "What do you know about this?"

And she goes, "Know about what?"

And he pointed in this tree above their car — they parked by a tree. And there was the guy, there was her boyfriend hooked to the tree, and he'd been all clawed up by that hooked man.[3]

One of the values of the tape recorder is that it frees you to write down information which *should* be recorded on a note pad, information about the circumstances of the storytelling situation: the setting in which the story was told; the nature of the audience; movements and hand gestures made during the telling; responses and promptings of the audience; everything, in short, to help the reader of your document not only hear the story but also visualize the setting in which it was related.

While the collector of the above item claimed to have recorded it word-for-word as it was told, I suspect that a few false starts and an occasional "uh" were edited out. Many collectors of oral documents, in fact, encourage editing. Folklorists do not, at least not for the archive document. It should be recorded just as it was spoken. If one later wishes to edit the piece for publication, at least the original remains available for scrutiny in the archive. Above all, when you prepare a document for archive submission, be sure to tell whether the item recorded is a verbatim transcription, an edited transcription (tell the extent of the editing), a close (but not totally accurate) shorthand recording, or a paraphrase of the original.

Good transcriptions are hard to make from unclear tape recordings. The bibliographical section following this essay will guide you to sources which will instruct you in the proper use of recording devices — tape recorders, cameras, video machines. But you should understand that you needn't be an expert or own expensive equipment to get a satisfactory recording. You must, however, use a machine with a separable microphone (in-machine microphones record mostly the whirring of the drive belts), keep the microphone within a foot of the speaker's mouth, and avoid touching or moving the microphone wire during the recording (each stroke of the wire will be transmitted to the tape).

Material lore: Beginning folklore collectors seldom focus on material lore — not because the things people make with their hands are any less worthy of study, but because accurately documenting them is a difficult task not easily achieved by the novice. This is not to say that if you are interested in ranch fences, quilts, barn styles, or sculpted gravestone motifs, you should not set out to document them. But you should realize that the task will not be particularly easy.

To help archive users understand what is artistically pleasing about the artifacts you document, you must begin with accurate pictures of the objects. Occasionally, you can record these pictures with line drawings just as you can occasionally record verbal lore with a pencil. I have seen excellent sketches of folk toys — rubber guns, sling shots, clothespin pistols, handkerchief dolls, cootie catchers — which vividly depict these objects. But in most instances, you will need to record material culture with a camera, and a good one at that, preferably a 35-mm, single-lens reflex camera which can be set for varying light intensities and distances.

You may take either color slides or black-and-white prints. Just as your sound recordings will reveal narrative texture, so too must these pictures display the stylistic and textural features of the artifacts being

234

photographed. That means you will need to take a number of shots of the same object. If you were documenting a quilt, you would want a photograph of the entire quilt so that the overall design would be clear; you would take a close-up of individual blocks in the quilt; and you would want a still closer shot of the needlework in the block. If possible, you would also take pictures of different stages in the quilt making, from assembling the quilting frames to removing the quilt at its completion; and, because material objects are made to be used, you ought to get a picture of the quilt on the bed for which it was made.

Through your photographs, you should give an accurate view of material artifacts as they exist in actual life. To do this, you will have to do more than take pictures. You will need also to submit written texts that explain in considerable detail what appears in the pictures. A photograph of a well-crafted saddle, for example, without an explanation of its different parts and their functions, will be of limited value.

Customary lore: If the pleasure derived from verbal and material folklore comes principally from hearing and seeing, the artistic satisfaction derived from customary lore results primarily from participating in action. Customary practices range broadly across the full spectrum of human activity, but they tend to focus on ceremonies and festive events which tie people more closely to their family, ethnic, religious, occupational, and regional groups; on rites of passage which move people through transitional stages of life such as birth, puberty, marriage, incorporation into new social groups, and death; and on work processes which make easier and more enjoyable the hours people spend earning their bread.

Customary lore is a good place to begin collecting because you will often have to go no further than your own memory and because attempting to understand the significance of the traditional activities which make up your life will help you discover significance in the practices you collect from others. The following excerpt from a Swiss-American student describing Swiss Independence Day (August 1) in her Minnesota community should stir memories of important ceremonial events you could record from your own life:

235

William A. Wilson

Between one and two hundred Swiss-Americans will gather at one of the homes (lately, my family's) and sing traditional songs, play traditional music, dance, eat bratwurst, good Swiss bread and cheese, and drink wine. As the sun sets, the highlight of the evening is reached. A huge bonfire is lit, and everyone gathers around it to soak up its warmth and glow and to sing late into the night — until the fire has died down to a pile of glowing coals.

The creation of this bonfire is a task undertaken with care and great enthusiasm. The men build it, using scrap lumber and carefully balancing and arranging them teepee style till the structure is about 10-15 feet high. The lighting of it is made to be spectacular (with the help of gasoline) and worthy of the long "oohs" and "ahhs" it inevitably gets.

The bonfire is a very old tradition in Switzerland for celebrating Independence Day. Neighborhoods and towns will get together to create one. It is important for the Swiss in America to continue to celebrate the day in this way, for the very reason of being so far from their homeland. The closeness, the oneness, the nostalgic comfort that building and standing 'round the fire fosters is an important binding force among the Swiss-American group.

When you collect customary practices, the camera will once again serve as a useful tool to record steps in processes like branding cattle, felling trees, preserving food, playing games, and celebrating Christmas. But you must, above all, observe keenly and describe accurately the action itself and the interplay of people involved in the event described. The following description of a fraternity birthday celebration, witnessed for the first time by a new pledge, catches in exemplary fashion both the actions and the joyful spirit of the occasion:

After everyone had finished dinner, one of the brothers started to sneak away from the table, at which time another brother yelled out that it was that guy's birthday. Everybody grabbed him and dragged him into the living room (he didn't fight too hard). Everyone was having a fun time of it. They put the guy face down on a table and then carried out the following rite, which I have recorded as I witnessed it:

Every brother got the chance to paddle the birthday brother. The

236

paddles were the ones given by the pledges to their Big Brothers. [This point needs further explanation.] Every brother had a favorite paddle and talked about how each one was most effective at inflicting pain (much to the dismay of the birthday brother). The brothers got their chances alphabetically. They were allowed one swat apiece, but the swing was only allowed from the wrist (so as not to do much damage). A painful swat could still be achieved by most. Most of the swatters would put up the act that they were about to wail on the birthday brother. Some of them would, but others would take it easy and just let the paddle flop down. When hit hard, the swattee would cry out pledges for vengeance. When hit softly, he usually called the swatter a gentleman and gave him sincere thanks. After everyone got their chance, somebody gave the birthday brother a beer. Then they all started singing the following song while they shook his hand:

> Happy birthday to you; happy birthday to you.
> Happy birthday dear_____; happy birthday to you.
> May you live a thousand years.
> May you drink a thousand beers.
> Get plastered, you bastard; happy birthday to you.

After the song, everyone joined in the following cheer:

> Rah, rah, rah, Phi Kappa Tau!
> Live or die for Phi Kappa Tau! Rah!

Meaning and aesthetic judgments: As you record data to help the archive user better understand the meaning or artistic significance of the material collected, try to give the tradition-bearer's own point of view, not yours, of why something is meaningful or aesthetically pleasing. People who sing working songs, braid hackamores, and ritually celebrate the birth of a child know what pleases them and what does not. And if you ask the right questions, they will tell you.

This is not a particularly easy task. If someone tells you a moving family story about her grandparents keeping the bodies of children dead from the flu in the woodshed until the weather finally warmed enough in the spring to dig the frozen ground, and you respond by asking, "What does that story mean to you?" you will probably be considered both stupid and bad-mannered. But if you can get her talking about the occasion on which she heard the story, those on which she tells it, and her reasons for telling it, you should gain a fair notion of what the story *means* to her. Similarly, if you can get a quilter to tell you why she chooses certain colors for her patterns, a housewife to explain why she arranges food on the table in a given way, a rancher to explain why he prefers to rope calves for branding instead of using a cattle chute, you will have recorded at least some aesthetic judgments. These judgments, to be sure, are usually shaped by the tradition-bearer's larger community or social group, but the group aesthetic can be generalized only after the responses of numerous individuals have been documented and archived.

You will discover that while the people you interview, like everyone else, make artistic judgments on formal criteria (the pleasing inter-relationship of parts), they also judge folklore creations on functional and associational grounds. A rawhide rocking chair that does not "set well," or does not rock (function) properly, will not be judged artistically successful by the craftsman and his community, no matter how handsome it might appear to the outsider. Similarly, folklore which does not call forth the proper associations will probably not be valued as much as that which does. Children insist on celebrating Christmas the same way each year because doing so brings forth pleasant memories of Christmases past. A housewife continues to use the same decorative pattern in her pie crusts, not because the pattern itself particularly pleases her but because she learned it from her mother as a child and almost feels her mother's presence as she now decorates her own pies.

When I asked a quilter one day which of all the wonderful quilts she had shown me she liked best, she picked out one which to me seemed no more distinctive than the rest. She then explained that she had made the quilt while recovering from an arthritis attack and had hurt more during the quilting than she ever had before. The quilt reminded her of her triumph over pain — and was therefore beautiful. A young woman in my folklore class, expecting her second child and experiencing considerable discomfort, collected and submitted a joke which she found especially funny. It was a joke about a pain machine that supposedly transferred the pains from a woman in labor to the father of the child. The night the baby was due, the doctor hooked husband and wife up to the machine and, as the labor intensified, gradually turned the machine up to its limit. The wife's pains disappeared, but for some reason the husband felt no dis-comfort himself. The baby safely delivered, the husband returned home, opened the door, and found the milkman dead on the kitchen floor. I thought the joke passingly funny because of the cuckolding of the husband and because of the surprise ending. My student commented, "I found this joke to be very funny. It is funny because it demonstrates to women that men cannot stand as much pain as a woman even though they think they can." As you collect and document folklore, you must discover, through careful questioning, the *tradition-bearer's view* of why the quilt is beautiful or the joke is funny.

The Social Function of Folklore

Folklore persists through time and space because the things people traditionally make with their words, hands, and actions continue to give pleasure and satisfy artistic impulses common to the species. Folklore persists also because it continues to meet basic human needs. This means that to properly document folklore you will have to record not just a proverb, or a recipe, or a game, or a story about a poisoned cat at a dinner party, but also the social settings in which these items were performed — not just what was said or made or done, but also the circumstances that generated the performances and the participants' responses to them. The following description of a recitation of traditional rhyme points the direction you should take:

> Sara [age 62, the collector's maternal aunt, a Swedish immigrant] currently babysits small children in her home for a living. She enjoys her work because she is always around children and always says that she's just a kid herself.
>
> Sara is one of the funniest ladies I've ever known. She's always joking

239

about how she's going on a diet and that we won't even recognize her when we see her next. She has a lot of funny rhymes and a poem for every occasion.

One Thanksgiving Day (last year) she came to Idaho for dinner in Pocatello. We were all just finished with dinner and everyone was letting out their moans and groans from eating too much. Nobody was saying too much at the time because of the agony of bloating ourselves. We were all family members, my mom and dad, some of my sisters, and about three cousins. The little incident that happened wouldn't have been nearly as funny if a couple of our friends (non-family members who are considered "high class") had not been there.

What happended was that Sara let go with a *loud* burp. I quickly looked over to see the expressions on the faces of the "high class" friends. It was a little embarrassing for us all, but Sara really smoothed things out well when she said this little rhyme immediately afterwards:

It's better to burp and bear the shame,
Than not to burp and bear the pain!

After she said it, we *all* had a good laugh, even the two friends who normally wouldn't laugh at such a thing.

Note what the collector has told us in this description. We know a little about Sara's personality; we know what the occasion for the gathering was; we know who was present and something about the way they related to each other; we are aware of the embarrassment caused by the burp; we learn how Sara dealt with the embarrassment through reciting a traditional rhyme; and we learn what impact the recitation had on the others.

Because of what the collector has told us about the social setting in which the rhyme was used, we can now move beyond the rhyme, which by itself could be dismissed as an interesting bit of trivia, toward a better understanding of the way folklore, skillfully used, can help people affect the social environment to their own advantage. One description of one rhyme will not bring us to this end, but enough good descriptions of enough folklore performances will. Again, this is the function of an archive, to keep on file the folklore you collect until enough of it is available to move from descriptions of individual folklore performances to generalizations about folklore's larger social uses.

Just as you should let those from whom you collect interpret their folklore, so, too, should you allow them to comment on their reasons for performing it. I once listened to a tape-recorded story of a family supernatural legend in which the narrator became so emotionally involved in the story that she broke into tears. When the narration ended, the collector, evidently remembering that she was supposed to record information about her informant's attitude toward her narratives, asked, "Now, do you believe the story?" The woman was highly offended, and rightly so. Of course, you will want to know what the tradition-bearers believe about their material, but if you will listen to and observe their performances carefully enough, and if you will get them to describe the social settings in which they have performed, or might perform, their lore, then you won't have to ask boorish questions to get your information. Certainly in the following illustration there can be little doubt about the attitude of the tradition-bearer, a rodeo cowboy, toward the tradition he describes:

> Many competing cowboys like myself believe and practice this rule whenever competing in a rodeo. The belief is that if you have ever been injured in a certain piece of clothing, whether it be a pair of stockings, Levis, or a shirt, then this article of clothing has been cleansed of bad luck and now every time you wear it, it shall bring you luck.
>
> I got in a fight on a Friday night several years ago, and I was beat rather badly by my opponent. But I was to compete in a jackpot rodeo on the following morning, even though I hurt everywhere. So I took the opportunity to wear a pair of "Wrangler Jeans" that I had been beat up in the night before, feeling that it would be a good omen. And I won the jackpot with one of the classiest hareback rides I have ever made.

The Cultural Background of Folklore

Perhaps the most difficult data to collect is that which places folklore in its larger cultural context. And in this instance, collecting from your peers may be a disadvantage, primarily because the tradition-bearers from whom you collect will probably speak a cultural language you already understand; and further, trapped by your mutual understanding, you may feel little need to explain the language for the cultural outsiders who may one day study your collection. For example, the following supernatural legend from Mormon tradition will be rich in meaning for most Mormons but may make little sense to non-Mormons:

This man and woman was going through the temple doing work for the dead, and they got out to Salt Lake, and they had kids. And at the last minute the babysitter didn't come, and so they had to take their kids to the temple with them. And they were standing outside the temple waiting to get in, and they didn't know what they were going to do with their kids. There was no one around there they could leave them with, and they didn't know what they were going to do with them. While they were standing there, this strange man and woman came up to them and introduced themselves and said they would tend their kids while they went through the temple. The man and woman tended their kids, and the couple went in and did work for the dead, and that couple tending their kids turned out to be the couple they did the work for. When they came out of the temple, the man and woman were no longer there.

The individual who collected this narrative submitted it to the archive with the name of the teller attached plus a brief description of the storytelling setting, but with no information to help the non-Mormon user of the archive understand what is really happening in the story and happening in the minds of those who tell and listen to it. He should have included a statement something like this:

Mormons believe they have an obligation to save not only themselves and, through missionary work, their neighbors, but also all their kinsmen who have died without benefit of gospel law. Thus, they seek the names of their ancestors through genealogical research and then in their sacred temples vicariously perform for these ancestors all the saving ordinances of their gospel. In this particular narrative, the couple evidently came "out to

Salt Lake" to participate in temple activity because one of the church's limited number of temples is located there. The man and woman who tend the baby are spirits of the dead who have probably long been waiting for saving ordinance work to be performed on their behalf. In a neat turn, the deceased husband and wife take care of the physical needs of the baby while the baby's parents attend to their spiritual needs. A story like this will be considered very sacred to many Mormons and should be treated with respect.

As any Mormon readers of these lines will know, we could still say a good deal more about this story, but the above information should place it in a cultural context making it at least partially intelligible to non-Mormons.

As you record cultural data for your folklore documentation, you should always ask what behaviors, ideas, and concepts people bring to the social setting in which a folklore performance takes place. And then you should include your answers to these questions in your document. What attitudes about Southeast Asians, for example, did the member of the dinner party bring to the discussion of Southeast Asians eating dogs? What feelings about the importance of national heritage did Swiss-Americans in Minnesota bring to their celebration of Swiss Independence Day? What concept of salvation did the teller of the temple story bring to his narration?

If you are collecting from members of your own group, you may already know the answers to these questions and can pull from your own head the information necessary to make the folklore clear to an outsider. If you are not a part of the group, you will have to get this information by learning as much about the group as possible before you begin collecting and then by asking the tradition-bearers themselves to explain what you do not understand in the folklore they give you. In the illustration above, asking no more than "What's the difference between a temple and a regular house of worship?" and "What is 'work for the dead'?" would probably produce enough information to make the story understandable.

Because the controlling concepts and the value center of any group are, in the final analysis, the composite concepts and values of individuals in the group, you will need to record as much information as possible about the tradition-bearers themselves. You should elicit information that relates directly to the lore being collected — ethnic attitudes from people who tell ethnic jokes — but you should also gather general information: sex, age, ethnic ancestry, education, religion, occupation, hobbies, and so on. And it's probably better to record too much than too little, since you can't know the uses to which your collections might be put in the future. Writing down the occupation of a teller of sexist jokes may seem unnecessary at the moment of collecting, but to the researcher who will one day use your material to study sex role attitudes of different male occupational groups, such information will prove crucial.

The Folklore Document

Once you have brought together the kinds of data discussed in the sections above, your final task will be to write up your material for submission to the folklore archive. You should visit the archive to see where your collections will finally be located, to glimpse the range of materials filed there, to gain a better understanding of the contribution you can really make through careful work, and especially, to review the documentary forms used by the archive. In the absence of specific requirements from the archive or from your instructor, you may want to use the format below (a format used, in varying degrees, by a number of university archives). Remember that your ultimate goal is to capture on paper what took place in a particular folklore performance. Let the format be your servant, not your master. Follow it as closely as possible, but alter it if necessary to meet the demands of the material collected.

1.   In the upper right-hand corner, in three lines, put the name of the informant, the place the lore was collected, and the date it was collected. If you submit lore culled from your own memory, write "Myself" for the informant's name and then record where and when you learned the lore.

2.   In the upper left-hand corner put the form of folklore collected and, when possible, a title for the lore which suggests its content.

244

3.　Three spaces below the title, at the left-hand margin, write "Informant Data:" and then give general biographical information about the informant and any details, including personal comments, which would give a clearer picture of the informant's relationship to and understanding of the folklore recorded. If you are your own informant, give the same kinds of details about yourself as you would for someone else.

4.　Three spaces further down, at the left-hand margin, write "Contextual Data:" and then give both the social and cultural context for the folklore.

Under social context describe the circumstances under which you collected the folklore and under which your informant originally learned it, focusing, as already noted, on such things as the people present when the folklore performance occurred, the circumstances that generated the performance, the way people present participated in or influenced the performance, and the impact of the performance on them. Be sure to indicate if the folklore is normally performed at specific times and before certain people (at family reunions, for instance, or before women only). Other methods failing, you can often get good information about the social uses of folklore by asking for a description of a hypothetical context in which the informant might tell a particular story or take part in a particular ritual. Under cultural context, give information about the informant's culture which would make the folklore understandable to outsiders.

5.　Three spaces further down, at the left-hand margin, write "Item:" and then present the folklore collected. Be sure to tell how the lore was recorded and to what extent the words on paper faithfully follow or depart from those of the informant.

If you collect folksongs, try to record both words and music. Put at least one verse directly under the music.

If you submit line drawings or diagrams of steps in an action (finger games, for example), test the accuracy of these drawings before you submit them; see if a friend can perform the actions you have illustrated in the drawing.

If you collect folk speech, or jargon, explain the words and expressions submitted and use them in sentences which communicate the meaning.

If you submit photographs or slides, clearly identify each one and key it to the accompanying written document.

6. In the bottom right-hand corner, give your name and age, your home address (including street number), your school address if you wish, your university (if applicable), the course for which you are submitting the folklore (if applicable), and the semester or quarter and year (if applicable).

Each folklore document submitted to the archive, then, should contain the following:

Genre
Title

Name of the informant
Place the folklore was collected
Date the folklore was collected

Informant Data:

Contextual Data:
    Social Context:
    Cultural Context:

Text:

Your name and age
Your home address
Your school address
Your school
Course number
Semester/quarter and year

The three examples given below (drawn from Utah State University and Brigham Young University Folklore Archives) follow the format quite closely: each does a reasonably credible job of describing the folklore submitted, although each could be improved.

The collector/informant of Sample #1 describes well enough the hunting practice he witnessed, but does not comment on its impact on him personally, something he could easily have told us since he serves as his own informant. How does he feel about hunting in general? Does he share the attitude of his companions about the manliness of the sport? What kind of verbal teasing accompanies the shooting of the clothing? Did others (insiders) in the party who failed to bag a deer shoot up their clothing? How did they seem to respond to the ritual? Was he, an outsider, treated differently from them? Did he actually shoot his own hat or coat? How did this make him feel? Did he wear the wounded article of clothing during the year? When and where? How did this make him feel? Did he go hunting again?

(Sample #1)

Hunting Custom   Myself
"Shooting Hunting Clothing"   Spanish Fork, Utah
October 1979

Informant Data:
Walter M. Jones was born in Richland, Washington, on July 8, 1960. His father was in the military and moved around the country a lot. Walter's background is basically western. His family origins are northern European. He is a member of the LDS (Mormon) church. Walter is married and is a junior at Brigham Young University.

Contextual Data:
Walter attended BYU back in 1978 and 1979, before entering the armed forces. He lived with a family in Spanish Fork, Utah, and became very close to them. During the month of October, Utah holds its annual deer hunt. The family in Spanish Fork participated in the

William A. Wilson

(Sample #1 continued)

hunt the same way as most residents of the state, with much enthusiasm. The family invited Walter to participate, and he went along. He had never been on a deer hunt and was ignorant of the great fervor that surrounds it. He and a few others in the hunting party did not shoot a deer and had to go through the punishment described below. The members of the group are a hardy bunch who pride themselves on being very manly. Not bagging a deer is considered not manly, and the person committing the sin is humiliated as a means of punishment. The evidence of humiliation is worn throughout the year to prompt the individual to do a better job in hunting next year.

Item:
If, at the end of the deer hunt, a person hasn't killed a deer, he must take off his hat or coat and lay it on the ground. He is then ordered to shoot the article of clothing and put it back on. When you wear the hat or coat, then everyone will know that you didn't get a deer. The only way to earn the right to wear a good hat or coat is to shoot a deer the next hunt.

Walter G. Jones
373 N. 400 W.
Provo, Utah
Brigham Young University
English 391   Fall 1985

The collector of Sample #2 records not only a belief (superstition), but also a story (in the informant's own words) about the belief. Whether the informant has actually "gotten over" the experience related we may never know, but at least we know, through her excellent little narrative, how it once affected her behavior. Beyond the narrative itself, we do not learn much about the informant and the role of folk belief in her life and in the rural Mormon community where she lived. For people who may have never seen anything but a gas or electric clothes dryer, the collector probably should have explained "leaving clothes out on the line."

248

(Sample #2)

Belief   Chris Sorenson
"Diapers on Clothesline"   Logan, Utah
                                                          Feb. 5, 1983

Informant Data:

Chris Sorenson, 51, was born (1932) and raised in Roosevelt, Utah. She is an active member of the Mormon church. She has two children and four grandchildren. She presently owns and manages a dress shop. She has a heart of gold and would give anything to her family if she thought it would make them happy.

Contextual Data:

Chris said she heard this a long time ago, when she was about seven. What happened made a big impression on her. She says she knows the event could not really have happened, but it took her a long time to get over it. This is what she said, taken down in shorthand as she spoke.:

"When I was little, people told me that if anyone left their clothes out on the line over New Year's Eve, someone in their family would die during the year. One year me and a few of my friends were talking and one of them said, 'I don't believe it, and just to prove it, I'm gonna leave ours out.' In those days we used to have to leave the clothes on the line for quite a few days before they were dry, especially during the winter. Anyway, this girl left their clothes out over New Year's, and a few months later her brother died. This made a really big impression on me. For many years I'd call around to everyone in the family on New Year's Eve and remind them to get their clothes in."

Item:

If you leave your clothes on the line on New Year's Eve, someone in the family will die the coming year.

                                                          Mary Sorenson
                                                          234 Maple
                                                          Logan, Utah
                                                          Utah State University
                                                          Hist 423   Winter 1983

The collector of Sample #3 gives fairly good information about the social setting but very weak information about the cultural background. He describes the informant's religious feelings and activity, though he does not explain how someone of Jewish ancestry happens to be a Mormon. He describes the natural setting in which the informant told his story, elicits a good statement of the contexts in which the informant would recount the story, and gets at the intensity of the informant's feeling about the story, partly through an ill-advised question which brought informative results. He should also have asked the informant to describe the circumstances under which he originally learned the story. Further, since the collector is Mormon himself, and was a participant observer during the narration, he should have said something about his own response to the event.

The collector tells us almost nothing about the culture which shapes and gives meaning to the narrative. What are a mission (a two-year proselytizing endeavor), an elder (an office in the lay priesthood), a ward (a local congregation), a sacrament meeting (the weekly ward meeting in which the sacrament ordinance is administered and certain members are assigned in advance to give inspirational talks), and the Nephites (ancient American followers of Christ who, according to Mormon tradition, wander the earth helping the faithful in time of need)? Why does the collector call this account a Nephite story when the word "Nephite" is not mentioned in the narrative itself?

Finally, the collector has not just relied on his memory of the story told in the church meeting but has correctly gone to the teller later and had him tell the story again. Unfortunately, he has not recorded the story on tape, and we are therefore denied a verbatim transcription.

(Sample #3)

Legend
"Nephite Story: Missionaries Rescued"

Chad Newman
Pasadena, California
September 1970

Informant Data:
Chad Newman is my brother-in-law. He was born in Pasadena, California, in 1948 and

---

(Sample #3 continued)

has lived there all his life. He is currently in electrical engineering at Utah State University in Logan, Utah. He is of Jewish ancestry, but no one in his family practices Judaism, and all but his father are active members of the Mormon church. Chad has not served as a missionary, but he is an elder and at USU lives in the Delta Phi house, built by the church and run by the "returned missionary" fraternity. His home address is 5473 Cheery Pl., Pasadena, California.

Contextual Data:
Chad told this story as part of a talk he gave in sacrament meeting in the Pasadena Ward, as an illustration of the ability of the Lord to protect those who place their faith in Him and live good lives. As nearly as I could tell, everyone present took the story in the way he intended it. Of course, I can not be sure if they all believed it to be a true story, but Chad himself was completely sure of its veracity. I later asked him (somewhat ill-advisedly, as it turned out) if he really believed it, to his immediate indignation. He said he knew it was true because it had happened to a companion of someone a friend of his had known in the mission field. He said he didn't know very many Nephite stories, so he couldn't be sure if they were all true, but that he very definitely does believe the Nephites are somewhere here on the earth and have a mission to perform such as told in this story. When asked when and where else he would tell this story, Chad said only to people who were members of the church and who would probably believe in the Nephites and understand what their purpose was.

Item:
[I have recorded the story here not exactly as Chad told it in that particular sacrament meeting, but as he told it to me again in September 1970. I took notes as he told it, and it is close to his version, but mainly in my own words.]
Two missionaries in the Canadian Mission were driving home from a discussion meeting one day and there was quite a bad storm going. They were clear out in the middle of nowhere when their car broke down, and they were unable to repair it. They decided that they would just freeze to death if they stayed there, so they got out of the car and started walking down the road. After a couple of hours they were pretty badly frozen anyway and could tell they weren't going to be able to go much farther. Just then they heard a car coming behind them. It stopped and the man opened the door, and they got into the back seat. They were so cold they just laid down on the floor and didn't even look at the man. Finally they came to a service station, and the man stopped the car at the

---

(Sample #3 continued)

side of the road to let them out. They got out and stumbled over to the station, but they still hadn't really got a look at the man in the car. When they got up to the station, the attendant looked surprised, and asked where they had come from. They said, "From the car that had just stopped out in front." He said, "There hasn't been any car come along here for a couple of hours." They went out to the road and looked, but there weren't even any tire tracks.

Bill Henry
Route 1, Box 212
Moses Lake, Washington

364 E. 8974 S. #7
Provo, Utah
Brigham Young University
English 391   Spring 1971

Conclusion

I have not yet documented the story of the poisoned cat that I heard at the dinner party, but I intend to. I have arranged a gathering at my house, have invited my poet friend, and will ask him to tell the story again, this time with a tape recorder turning. If I am then able to follow the instructions I have given above, I will soon turn into the archive a document which may one day prove valuable to a researcher interested in contemporary legends. And I will in the process have increased my own understanding of folklore and its significance in people's lives. Through collecting and documenting folklore, you too can make an important contribution to folklore research and, in the process, increase your understanding of what it means to be human.

Notes

1.   Jan Harold Brunvand, *The Vanishing Hitchhiker: American Urban Legends and their Meanings* (New York: W. W. Norton & Company, Inc., 1981), 112.

2.   Florence E. Baer, "'Give me . . . your huddled masses': Anti-Vietnamese Refugee Lore and the 'Image of Limited Good,'" *Western Folklore* 61(1982): 275-91.

3.   All examples quoted in this paper are from student collections on file at the Brigham Young University Folklore Archives, Provo, Utah 84602.

Further Readings

An early but valuable guide to collecting folklore is Kenneth S. Goldstein, *A Guide for Field Workers in Folklore* (Hatboro, Penn.: Folklore Associates, 1964); its discussion of mechanical recording equipment is badly outdated, but its treatment of different interview methods is still instructive. The most complete and up-to-date work on collecting is Bruce Jackson, *Fieldwork* (Urbana, Ill.: University of Illinois Press, scheduled for release in the spring of 1987); this book, which I have seen in manuscript, covers in great detail major steps in collecting: planning, finding informants, interviewing, using mechanical equipment, and keeping records; it also discusses the ethics of collecting and gives good advice on obtaining releases. For the collector of verbal lore, one of the most useful works is Edward D. Ives, *The Tape-Recorded Interview: A Manual for Field Workers in Folklore and Oral History* (Knoxville, Tenn.: The University of Tennessee Press, 1974); particularly helpful are Ives's careful instructions on using tape recorders and his discussions of transcribing, processing, and preparing manuscripts for archive submission. For the collector of visual materials, a good work is John Collier, Jr., *Visual Anthropology: Photography as a Research Method* (New York: Holt, Rinehart, & Winston, Inc., 1967). To move beyond technique and to gain better understanding of the ways collectors and informants interrelate and together shape the document collected, every beginning fieldworker should read Robert A. Georges and Michael O. Jones, *People Studying People: The Human Element in Fieldwork* (Berkeley, Cal.: University of California Press, 1980).

Introductory folklore textbooks and manuals often contain sections on collecting and documenting folklore which are helpful to the beginner.

One of the best of these, "The Methods of Folklore Study," in Richard M. Dorson, ed., *Folklore and Folklife: An Introduction* (Chicago: The University of Chicago Press, 1972), 405-533, contains good essays on archiving and on the techniques of collecting different forms of folklore —music, narrative, material culture — and provides bibliographies for further reading. Two fine chapters, "Being a Folklorist" and "Folklore Research," in Barre Toelken, *The Dynamics of Folklore* (Boston: Houghton Mifflin Co., 1979), 263-329, briefly survey major steps in collecting and documenting folklore and, once again, include valuable bibliographical notes.

Journal articles are too numerous and varied to list here. (See the bibliographical references in the works cited above.) But two articles every first-time collector ought to read are Alan Dundes, "Texture, Text, and Context," *Southern Folklore Quarterly* 28(1964): 251-65, which, though dated, was one of the first pieces to plead for the recording of both the folklore text and its social setting; and James E. Myers, "Unleashing the Untrained: Some Observations on Student Ethnographers," *Human Organization* 28(1969): 155-59, which describes in humorous detail the pitfalls awaiting the student collector, but nevertheless argues in favor of student collecting.

Contributors

SIMON J. BRONNER is Associate Professor of Folklore and American Studies and Coordinator of the undergraduate program in American Studies at the Pennsylvania State University, Harrisburg, Pennsylvania. He is the author of *Grasping Things: Folk Material Culture and Mass Society in America* (Lexington, Ky.: University Press of Kentucky, 1986), *American Folklore Studies: An Intellectual History* (Lawrence, Kan.: University Press of Kansas, 1986), and *Chain Carvers: Old Men Crafting Meaning* (Lexington, Ky.: University Press of Kentucky, 1985). He is the editor of *American Material Culture and Folklife* (Ann Arbor, Mich.: UMI Research Press, 1985) and *American Folk Art: A Guide to Sources* (New York: Garland Publishing, 1984), and co-editor of *Folk Art and Art Worlds* (Ann Arbor, Mich.: UMI Research Press, 1986). In addition to serving as president of the Pennsylvania Folklore Society, he has been editor of *Material Culture: Journal of the Pioneer America Society* and is now editor of *The Folklore Historian*. He has held fellowships from the Rockefeller Foundation, the New York Council on the Arts, and the National Endowment for the Humanities.

LARRY DANIELSON is Associate Professor of English at the University of Illinois, Urbana-Champaign, where he teaches courses in folklore and literature. He is editor of the monograph series, *Publications of the American Folklore Society*, and has edited a collection of original essays, *Studies in Folklore and Ethnicity* (Los Angeles: California Folklore Society, 1978). He has published articles on Swedish-American folk tradition, supernatural narrative, and oral history. He has also directed workshops on folklore and local history research and on the uses of folklore studies in the public school curriculum. Danielson's present research interests concern the paranormal personal experience narrative, ethnic folk tradition in the United States, and family ritual.

F.A. DE CARO received his Ph.D in folklore from Indiana University and is presently Professor of English at Louisiana State

University in Baton Rouge; he has also taught at the University of Indore in central India and the University of Texas at Austin. His principal areas of interest are the proverb, folk narrative, folklore and literature, the history of folklore studies, the lore of elite groups, and Louisiana folk culture, and he is currently at work on a book about the photographers who have documented folklife in Louisiana. He has published *Women and Folklore: A Bibliographical Survey* (Westport, Conn.: Greenwood Press, 1983), and with W.K. McNeil co-compiled *American Proverb Literature: A Bibliography*, Bibliographic and Special Series No. 6 (Bloomington, Ind.: Folklore Forum, 1970). He has also published articles and reviews in *Western Folklore, Journal of American Folklore, Revue de Louisiane*, and *Signs*. He was the first Chairman of the Louisiana Governor's Commission on Folklife.

ROBERT MCCARL is an Assistant Professor of Folklore and Anthropology at the University of South Carolina. His interest in occupational culture grew out of his experiences as a fire fighter and smokejumper in the Pacific Northwest. He has published articles in major folklore journals based upon his research with welders and textile workers as well as fire fighters and smokejumpers. His monograph, *The District of Columbia Fire Fighters' Project*, was published by the Smithsonian Institution Press in 1985. He has also worked extensively in the presentation of occupational folklore to the public through folk festivals and popular publication. He is currently working on a book dealing with the documentation and presentation of occupational folklore and folklife.

JAY MECHLING is Professor and Director of the American Studies Program at the University of California, Davis. His advanced degrees are in American Civilization from the University of Pennsylvania and he was a 1975-76 Fellow at the Yale National Humanities Institute. For five years (1974-79) he edited the annual bibliographic issue of the *American Quarterly* and he is currently editor of *Western Folklore*, the quarterly journal of the California Folklore Society. He was an at-large member of the National Council of the American Studies Association and is a past president of the Northern California American Studies Association. His essays have appeared in the *American Quarterly, Prospects, Journal of Popular Culture, Journal of American Folklore, Journal of Social History, Soundings, Central States Journal of Speech, Sociological Inquiry, Journal of Psychoanalytic Anthropology,* and *Human Organization,* as well as in anthologies devoted to play and to children's organizations. Much of his published work is on the Boy Scouts of America. He has been a consultant for the National American Studies Faculty, for the National Humanities Insititute, for the National Endowment for the Humanities, for the National Humanities Faculty, and for the United States Information Agency.

ELLIOTT ORING is a Professor of Anthropology at California State University, Los Angeles, and a Research Associate in the Center for the Study of Comparative Folklore and Mythology at UCLA. He was a founder of *Folklore Forum* and edited *Western Folklore* from 1976 through 1978. He currently serves on the advisory boards of the Wayne State University Press Folklore Archive Series and the Publications of the American Folklore Society. He has published essays on humor, narrative, folksong, custom, and folklore theory in a variety of books and journals. His books include *Israeli Humor: The Content and Structure of the Chizbat of the Palmah* (Albany, N.Y.: State University of New York Press, 1981), *The Jokes of Sigmund Freud: A Study in Humor and Jewish Identity* (Philadelphia: University of Pennsylvania Press, 1984), and *Humor and the Individual* (Los Angeles: California Folklore Society, 1984).

BARRE TOELKEN was Professor of English and Director of the Folklore and Ethnic Studies Program at the University of Oregon until 1985. He currently directs the Folklore Program at Utah State University and administers the graduate program in American Studies. He also participates in the university's Mountain West Center for Regional

257

Studies. He was an editor of the *Journal of American Folklore*, and served as the President of the American Folklore Society. A member of the Fellows of the American Folklore Society, he is currently serving a five-year term on the Board of Trustees of the American Folklife Center in the Library of Congress. Over the past twenty-five years he has published articles on ballads and folksongs, as well as studies of Native American narrative and occupational folklore. His book, *The Dynamics of Folklore* (Boston: Houghton Mifflin Co., 1979), is widely used as a text.

WILLIAM A. WILSON is Chairman of the English Department and Director of the Folklore Archives at Brigham Young University. He is former Director of the Folklore Program at Utah State University, where he helped establish the Fife Folklore Archive and developed the annual Fife Folklore Conference. Wilson has served as Editor of *Western Folklore*, as President of the Utah Folklore Society, as Chairman of the Board of Directors of the Utah Folklife Center, and as Chairman of the Folk Arts Panel of the National Endowment of the Arts. He currently serves on the Board of Directors of the Western Folklife Center, on the Board of Directors of the Utah Arts Council, and on the Executive Board of the American Folklore Society. He has done fieldwork for the American Folklife Center, documenting contemporary folklore and ranching customs in Paradise Valley, Nevada, and consults regularly on public folklore projects. Wilson has published widely on religious folklore, on folk narrative, and on the history of folklore scholarship. He is author of the award-winning *Folklore and Nationalism in Modern Finland* (Bloomington, Ind.: Indiana University Press, 1976).